M000084220

Flavius Philostratus: *On Heroes*

Society of Biblical Literature

Writings from the Greco-Roman World

John T. Fitzgerald, General Editor

Editorial Board

David Armstrong
Elizabeth Asmis
Brian E. Daley, S.J.
David G. Hunter
David Konstan
Michael J. Roberts
Johan C. Thom
Yun Lee Too
James C. VanderKam

Number 3

Flavius Philostratus: *On Heroes*

Flavius Philostratus:
On Heroes

Translated with an Introduction
and Notes by

Jennifer K. Berenson Maclean

and

Ellen Bradshaw Aitken

With a Preliminary Essay by

Casey Dué and Gregory Nagy

Society of Biblical Literature
Atlanta

FLAVIUS PHILOSTRATUS: ON HEROES

Original Title: Flavius Philostratus: Heroicus, edited by Ludo de Lannoy,
copyright © 1977 by K. G. Saur Verlag GmbH, Munich and Leipzig
(first published in 1977 by B. G. Teubner, Leipzig).
English translation from the original Greek edition arranged with the
approval of the publisher, K. G. Saur Verlag GmbH, Munich and Leipzig.

English translation and notes, preliminary essay, introduction, maps, and
glossary copyright © 2001, 2002, by the Society of Biblical Literature.

All rights reserved.

No part of this work may be reproduced or transmitted in any form or by any
means, electronic or mechanical, including photocopying and recording, or by
means of any information storage or retrieval system, except as may be ex-
pressly permitted by the 1976 Copyright Act or in writing from the publisher.
Requests for permission should be addressed in writing to the Rights and Per-
missions Department, Society of Biblical Literature, 825 Houston Mill Road,
Suite 350, Atlanta, GA 30329, USA.

Library of Congress Cataloging-in-Publication Data

Philostratus, the Athenian, 2nd/3rd cent.
   [Heroicus. English]
   On heroes / Flavius Philostratus; translated with an introduction and
notes by Jennifer K. Berenson Maclean and Ellen Bradshaw Aitken ; with
a preliminary essay by Casey Dué and Gregory Nagy.
          p. cm. — (Writings from the Greco-Roman world; v. 3)
   Includes bibliographical references and index.
   ISBN: 1-58983-037-7 (paper binding : alk. paper)
   1. Dialogues, Greek—Translations into English. 2. Trojan War—Early
works to 1800. 3. Heroes—Early works to 1800. I. Maclean, Jennifer K.
Berenson, 1963- II. Aitken, Ellen Bradshaw, 1961- III. Title. IV. Series.

PA4272.A45 2002b
882'.01–dc21   2002012599

The photograph on page v of the statue of a warrior thought to represent the Greek
hero Protesilaos is reproduced with the permission of The Metropolitan Museum
of Art (Hewitt Fund, 1925; 25.116).

The photograph on page vi of the coin from Elaious depicting Protesilaos appears through the generous permission and assistance of the Staatliche Museen zu
Berlin—Preußischer Kulturbesitz, Münzkabinett (1873 Fox).

02 03 04 05 06 07 08 09 — 5 4 3 2 1

The book is printed in the United States of America
on recycled, acid-free paper.

Roman-era marble statue of a Greek hero, probably Protesilaos. This image is reproduced with the permission of The Metropolitan Museum of Art (Hewitt Fund, 1925; 25.116).

Bronze coin (28 mm) from Elaious (180–192 C.E.)—obverse: Portrait of the emperor Commodus; reverse: Protesilaos armed and at the prow of a ship. This image is reproduced with the permission of the Staatliche Museen zu Berlin—Preußischer Kulturbesitz, Münzkabinett (1873 Fox).

Table of Contents

Acknowledgments

A multitude of heroes, gods, and mortals populate *On Heroes* and its world; likewise our work with this text over the course of several years has been assisted by many friends and scholars. Our acquaintance with *On Heroes* began at Harvard Divinity School, when from 1991 to 1993 a group of doctoral students from the Department of New Testament and Early Christian Studies gathered weekly, under the direction of Professor Helmut Koester, to read *On Heroes* together in Greek. This group included, in addition to us, Marianne Bonz, Denise Buell, Liza Burr, Cynthia Kittredge, Iain Maclean, Shelly Matthews, Barbara Rossing, James Skedros, and Christine Thomas. We are grateful to these colleagues for the hours spent together in congenial and dedicated work. Fascinated by the text and its vivid depiction of Greek heroes, we decided at that time that *On Heroes* needed to be made accessible in English translation so as to be useful to students and scholars alike.

Interdisciplinary conversation has proved invaluable in understanding this text. Our special thanks go to Helmut Koester for his conviction about the importance of this text for Early Christian studies and for his continual encouragement. We are also grateful for the ways he nurtured the climate of inquiry in which this volume took shape. Gregory Nagy, whose work on Homer and Greek heroes undergirds our work, has been our constant mentor, critic, and fan during the preparation of this volume. His undying enthusiasm for Philostratus's *On Heroes* strengthened us when our spirits flagged.

We are delighted that Casey Dué and Gregory Nagy have graced this volume with their "Preliminaries." This essay grows out of their use of *On Heroes* in the course "The Concept of the Hero in Hellenic Civilization" in Harvard's Core Curriculum. Their sensitivity to the educational potential of this text thoroughly informs their essay and initiates the reader into the world of heroes.

We deeply appreciate the assistance of Jackson P. Hershbell, professor emeritus of Classics at the University of Minnesota, who read earlier drafts of our translation with care. Jack's keen eyes have caught many errors and infelicities, his thorough knowledge of the literature of the Second Sophistic has greatly stimulated our thinking about Philostratus, and his questions have enriched the notes and Glossary. Jack also sent us early ideas for the Introduction, which have formed a core of some portions of it. We thank him for his unstinting help.

Our research assistants, Laura Nasrallah, Sarah Stewart, Douglas Young, Anna Miller, and Jenna Zamesnik have provided timely and accurate help along the way, often when they had only a partial view of the entire project. Christopher P. Jones, Kimberley Patton, Jeffrey Rusten, and Timothy Whitmarsh have generously advised us on particular points or shared drafts of their own work with us. Jennifer Phillips read an earlier version of the translation. We are grateful to Catherine Playoust, Christina Salowey, and Florinda Ruiz; their careful reading of our work has saved us from many errors. Thomas J. Wells of Invisible Productions expertly created the maps in this volume. Our thanks go to all of them, as well as to the staffs of Fintel Library at Roanoke College and of the Andover-Harvard Theological Library. Research funds from Roanoke College and Harvard Divinity School have helped in making our collaboration possible on a practical level. We also thank John Herrmann from the Museum of Fine Arts, Boston; Jody Maxmin of the Department of Art and Art History, Stanford University; Elizabeth Milleker from The Metropolitan Museum of Art, New York; and Bernhard Weisser, conservator of the Münzkabinett in the Bodesmuseum, Berlin, for their assistance with the appearances of Protesilaos on coins, gems, reliefs, and statuary and for providing the plates included in this volume.

This Student Edition was preceded by the publication of our translation accompanied by the Greek text on facing pages as the first volume in the Society of Biblical Literature's new series Writings from the Greco-Roman World. We have taken this opportunity to make a few minor corrections to the Translation and Glossary. We offer our profound appreciation to the editor of this series, John Fitzgerald, for his continual support and encouragement through the process of preparing this volume and for his availability for counsel from the time we first approached him. We are also grateful to Rex Matthews, Editorial Director of the Society of Biblical Literature, for his enthusiasm for this project and

his many contributions to the preparation of this volume. Yan-
nis Haralambous, of Atelier Fluxus Virus, is responsible for the
design, typesetting, and layout of the volume; we express our admiration for the care he has devoted to it.

To those who introduced us to the Greeks and instilled in us
a love of things Greek—in particular the faculties of the Classics
Departments at Stanford University and Harvard University—
we are greatly indebted. Now we in turn take great pleasure
in introducing students to this world through Philostratus's *On
Heroes*. It is to our students, whose enthusiasm for this text has
matched our own, that this volume is dedicated. And to our
"friend" Protesilaos, who loves things Greek even more vigorously, a libation is no doubt in order as we participate in his
literary resurrection.

Jennifer K. Berenson Maclean   Ellen Bradshaw Aitken
Salem, Virginia   Cambridge, Massachusetts

Abbreviations

ABD	*Anchor Bible Dictionary*
ANRW	*Aufstieg und Niedergang der römischen Welt*
B.C.E.	Before the Common Era
C.E.	Common Era
CP	*Classical Philology*
CQ	*Classical Quarterly*
GRBS	*Greek, Roman, and Byzantine Studies*
Her.	*On Heroes*
Hist.	*Histories*
HTR	*Harvard Theological Review*
IG	*Inscriptiones Graecae*
Il.	*Iliad*
JHS	*Journal of Hellenic Studies*
JRA	*Journal of Roman Archaeology*
JRS	*Journal of Roman Studies*
LCL	Loeb Classical Library
LIMC	*Lexicon iconographicum mythologiae classicae*
LSJ	Liddell, H. G., R. Scott, H. S. Jones, *A Greek-English Lexicon*
LXX	Septuagint
MT	Masoretic Text
Od.	*Odyssey*
PMG	Denys Lionel Page, ed., *Poetae Melici Graeci*. Oxford: Clarendon, 1962.
PW	Pauly, A. F. *Paulys Realencyclopädie der classischen Altertumswissenschaft*
SBLWGRW	Society of Biblical Literature Writings from the Greco-Roman World
TAPA	*Transactions of the American Philological Association*

NOTE ON NUMBERING SYSTEM

The numbering system used for references to *On Heroes* in the present volume reflects the chapter and paragraph divisions assigned by Ludo de Lannoy in his critical edition of the Greek text (*Flavii Philostrati Heroicus* [Leipzig: Teubner, 1977]). Advanced students should note that citations of *On Heroes* in LSJ refer to the chapter and paragraph numbers of Carl Ludwig Kayser's 1870 edition of the Greek text (*Flavii Philostrati opera auctiora edidit C. L. Kayser; accedunt Apollonii Epistolae, Eusebius Adversus Hieroclem, Philostrati junioris Imagines, Callistrati Descriptiones* [2 vols.; Leipzig: Teubner, 1870–1871; repr., Hildesheim: Olms, 1964]). Kayser's numbering system, along with de Lannoy's, appears in the margins of the Greek text reproduced in our full version of Philostratus's *Heroikos* (SBLWGRW 1; Atlanta: Society of Biblical Literature, 2001).

Preliminaries to
Philostratus's *On Heroes*

by

Casey Dué and Gregory Nagy

THE HEROES OF PHILOSTRATUS'S *ON HEROES*: FICTION, EPIC, AND HERO-CULT

In the literature of the so-called Second Sophistic era (around 60 to 230 C.E.), as best exemplified by Philostratus's *On Heroes* (written toward the end of this era), ancient readers were treated to claims of a truer and more accurate account of the Trojan War—truer even than the version they were used to reading in the epic poetry of the Homeric *Iliad* and *Odyssey*.* In the polished prose of *On Heroes*, such a claim was made not by the author himself, Philostratus, but by a creation of the author. This creation is a fictional character known simply as the *ampelourgos*, "vinedresser," who is telling another character—a mysterious Phoenician—all about an ancient hero who fought and died at Troy. This hero, Protesilaos by name, now communicates mysteriously from beyond the grave his eyewitness accounts about what really happened in the Trojan War and beyond. Similar claims were made by shady "authors" like Dictys of Crete and Dares the Phrygian, offering what were described as eyewitness accounts.

What was the cause for such intense interest in trying to validate the stories of the Trojan War? For an answer, it is essential to understand the agenda underlying the stories themselves. The Trojan War was viewed by the ancients as the primary testing ground for the ancient concept of the hero. The heroes who populated the stories about the Trojan War were the primary focus of interest. These heroes were the real agenda.

---

* In this essay, all translations of Philostratus's *On Heroes* are by Jennifer K. Berenson Maclean and Ellen Bradshaw Aitken. All other translations are our own, except where indicated.

In ancient Greek myth, heroes were humans, male or female, of the remote past, endowed with superhuman abilities and
descended from the immortal gods themselves. The prime example is Akhilleus, more commonly known as Achilles in the English
tradition. This, the greatest hero of the Homeric *Iliad*, was the
son of Thetis, a sea-goddess known for her far-reaching cosmic
powers.

There was a major problem, however, with the actual stories
that told about such heroes. The classical versions of these stories
had been crystallized in the epic poetry of Homer and, later on, in
the dramas of Aeschylus, Sophocles, and Euripides. As literature,
the media of epic and drama could be seen as perfect expressions
of classical ideals. By the time of the Second Sophistic, however, these same media were far less than perfect in expressing the
essence of the ancient heroes. What seemed to be missing in the
classical media? It was the older concept of the *cult* hero, which
continued to be a vital part of the overall concept of the hero in the
era of the Second Sophistic. In this era, even new fiction seemed
superior to classical epic and drama in giving full expression to
that older concept.

The cult hero, the object of hero cult, was a basic historical
fact of Greek civilization. Hero cult was the traditional practice
of worshipping heroes, and the evidence for it goes back at least
as far as the "Geometric" period of the first millennium B.C.E.[1]
There is broad cultural evidence indicating that hero cult in ancient Greece was not created out of epic stories like those of the
Iliad and *Odyssey* but was in fact independent of them. The epic
stories, on the other hand, were actually based on the religious
practices, though not always directly.

Paradoxically, references to the practice of worshipping
heroes are not obvious—at first sight—in the prime media of archaic and classical Greek literature that deal most directly with

---

[1] On the history and archaeology of hero cults, see Anthony M. Snod-
grass, *An Archaeology of Greece: The Present State and Future Scope of a Discipline* (Berkeley: University of California Press, 1987), 159–65. Two pathfinding
general works on hero cults are Angelo Brelich, *Gli eroi greci: Un problema
storico-religioso* (Rome: Edizioni dell'Ateneo, 1958) and Friedrich Pfister, *Der
Reliquienkult im Altertum* (2 vols.; Giessen: A. Topelmann, 1909–1912). Spe-
cialized works include Corinne Pache, "Baby and Child Heroes in Ancient
Greece" (Ph.D. diss., Harvard University, 1999).

heroes. Current research on the traditions underlying the Homeric *Iliad* and *Odyssey* as well as the dramas of Aeschylus, Sophocles, and Euripides has demonstrated the pervasive influence of hero cults in shaping the media of epic and drama, but the fact remains that most references to the actual cults of heroes are only implicit in these forms of archaic and classical Greek literature.² It is the historians of the classical period who give us the earliest explicit references to hero cults, and the most prominent example is the narrative of Herodotus about the cult of Protesilaos at Elaious (*Hist.* 7.33; 9.116–120).³ Yet, even in the medium of classical Greek historiography, the actual meaning of such a hero cult remains something of a mystery. That mystery, as we shall see later, is intentional.

As Ellen Bradshaw Aitken and Jennifer Berenson Maclean show clearly in their detailed Introduction to Philostratus's *On Heroes*, the numerous references in this work to the hero cults of Protesilaos, Achilles, Ajax, and other heroes of the epic tradition reflect accurately the historical realities of hero cults as they persisted into the third century C.E. They show further that the traditionalism of Philostratus's *On Heroes* in its treatment of hero cults is not necessarily at odds with the literary and philosophical modernities that pervade this masterpiece of the Second Sophistic era of Hellenic civilization.

---

² For epic, see Gregory Nagy, *The Best of the Achaeans: Concepts of the Hero in Archaic Greek Poetry* (Baltimore: Johns Hopkins University Press, 1979; 2d ed., with new introduction, 1999), 9–11 (also p. vii in the new introduction). For drama, see Albert Henrichs, "The Tomb of Aias and the Prospect of Hero Cult in Sophokles," *Classical Antiquity* 12 (1993): 165–80. In Homeric usage, a key word for implicitly referring to the cult of a hero is *sêma*, meaning "sign, signal" *and* "tomb [of a hero]": see Nagy, *Best of the Achaeans*, 340–43; cf. Henrichs, "The Tomb of Aias," 171–72.

³ See Gregory Nagy, "The Sign of Protesilaos," *MHTIΣ: Revue d'anthropologie du monde grec ancien* 2/2 (1987): 207–13; and Gregory Nagy, *Pindar's Homer: The Lyric Possession of an Epic Past* (Baltimore: Johns Hopkins University Press, 1990), 268–73, as well as Deborah Boedeker, "Protesilaos and the End of Herodotus' *Histories*," *Classical Antiquity* 7/1 (1988): 30–48.

A key aspect of these modernities is the use of fiction.[4] The framing devices used by authors of the Second Sophistic to claim authenticity are patently fictional. Yet, at the same time, the authors of works like *On Heroes* of Philostratus and the *Journal of the Trojan War* attributed to Dictys of Crete strive to emphasize the truth and credibility of their accounts. As Stefan Merkle points out, Dictys of Crete presents himself as a reliable historian. Dictys is represented as referring to his own credibility as an eyewitness and claims to have questioned other eyewitnesses. He uses the rhetoric and methods of historiography to distinguish between versions and provide the most reliable account.[5] Merkle also notes that, unlike the literary game of Lucian's *The Dream, or The Cock*, there are no parodic features in Dictys. The unadorned style of the military diary is adopted in order to give the account the greatest weight.[6]

Philostratus's *On Heroes* is similar in that there are no parodic features that undermine the authority of the framing narrative. The vinedresser who tends the sacred grove of the cult hero Protesilaos engages in a dialogue with a Phoenician who seems to know nothing about Greek hero cult.[7] The vinedresser communes frequently with the hero and has heard from him a more accurate account of the Trojan War.[8] This account (as mediated

---

[4] See for example Ewen L. Bowie, "Philostratus: Writer of Fiction," in J. R. Morgan and Richard Stoneman, eds., *Greek Fiction: The Greek Novel in Context* (New York: Routledge, 1994). Bowie notes that "the fictional dialogue had a long and respectable ancestry in Greek prose" (p. 184) and goes on to highlight a "second level of fiction," that is, the content of the given dialogues. This content includes narratives about the Trojan War not found in Homer, information about the afterlife and cult of Achilles, as well as an account of the powers and habits of the hero Protesilaos. Very many of these framing narratives involve discovery of ancient writing in tombs. For examples of other truth-claiming framing devices see Nathaniel Edward Griffin, *Dares and Dictys: An Introduction to the Study of Medieval Versions of the Story of Troy* (Baltimore: J. H. Furst, 1907), 14 n. 1; Stefan Merkle, "Telling the Truth of the Trojan War: The Eyewitness Account of Dictys of Crete," in Joseph Tatum, ed., *The Search for the Ancient Novel* (Baltimore: Johns Hopkins University Press, 1994), 195 n. 8, and discussion below.

[5] Merkle, "Telling the Truth," 185.

[6] Merkle, "Telling the Truth,"193.

[7] Note the Phoenician's questions in *Her.* 2.7–11.

[8] In *Her.* 23.1 the vinedresser says that Protesilaos has told him a story that is unknown to Homer and all other poets. In *Her.* 25.1–18 the vinedresser

through the vinedresser) not only directly contradicts Homer in many places, but it also includes narratives that are not featured in the Homeric tradition:

> Phoenician: And, vinedresser, what would be the contest over the shield?[9] No poet has mentioned it, nor does it appear in any story of the Trojan War.

> Vinedresser: That, my guest, you will say about many matters, because the hero tells many things about warriors as well as deeds of battles that are not yet known to most people. This is the reason. He says that, in their passion for the poems of Homer, most people, looking only at Achilles and Odysseus, neglect good and brave men, so that some are not remembered at all, and for others Homer dedicates a trireme of four verses. (*Her.* 14.1–2)

Philostratus, through the experiences of a worshipper of Protesilaos, claims to bring to light narratives about heroes that are not featured prominently in the panhellenic *Iliad* and *Odyssey*.

Philostratus uses the authority of a warrior hero who was reportedly present at Troy, seeking thus to authenticate narratives about the various other heroes who fought there. According to epic, Protesilaos was the first warrior to die at Troy (*Il.* 2.701–702). He was thus an eyewitness—as a warrior—only to the beginning of the war. Nevertheless, according to the vinedresser, once freed from the body after death, Protesilaos could "observe the affairs of mortals" (*Her.* 7.3). Thus both the Dictys narrative and *On Heroes* make use of an authoritative heroic source who, in communication with the participants in the Trojan War, corrects and supplements the Homer-centric understanding that most people of the day would have had about the Trojan War, particularly with respect to the heroes who fought there.

The vinedresser particularly calls attention to heroes who are not mentioned in the *Iliad* or *Odyssey* or who have only a few verses devoted to them in these epics. Protesilaos himself belongs to the latter group. The cult of this particular hero in the Chersonesus is featured prominently at the end of Herodotus's

---

relates the faults that Protesilaos finds in Homer's account (as well as the things for which he praises Homer).

[9] That is, the contest that takes place in the course of the war against the Mysians in *Her.* 23.2–30.

Histories, and it stems from an old tradition.[10] Narratives about
Protesilaos associated with that cult must have existed in classical
times and possibly even earlier. It could be argued that *On Heroes,*
far from being a playful fiction or a literary game, is a revival of
those narratives, an assertion of the "truth" about that hero. It
is possible that the other heroes and narratives that are featured
prominently in *On Heroes,* such as those about Achilles on the so-
called White Island, are also connected with a renewed interest in
the cult of various heroes.[11]

The question must then be asked: To what extent did such
writers of the Second Sophistic as Philostratus and the author behind Dictys of Crete conceive of their works as fictional? As Ewen
Bowie has pointed out, a fictional frame does not suffice to make
the overall work a fiction: the fictional dialogue, after all, is a common feature of Greek philosophical writings.[12] In the case of *On
Heroes,* the presence of polemic should perhaps be our first indication that something important is at stake when Philostratus the
author asserts his version of the Trojan War. In *On Heroes,* Philostratus indirectly attacks the credibility of Dictys's account of the
Trojan War in at least two places.[13] The *Journal of the Trojan
War,* attributed to Dictys of Crete, purports to be a journal kept
by a companion of the Cretan hero Idomeneus during the Trojan
War. This work is contradicted in Philostratus's *On Heroes* when
Protesilaos is cited as saying that Idomeneus never participated
in the Trojan War, thereby implicitly denying the authenticity of
Dictys's eyewitness report (*Her.* 30.1). It is also asserted in *On
Heroes* that the use of writing was first invented by Palamedes,
a prominent figure associated with the Trojan War (*Her.* 33.1).
This assertion, implying that writing was not yet in use at the
time of the Trojan War, seems once again to challenge the framing narrative of Dictys. The narrative of Philostratus undermines

---

[10] Herodotus *Hist.* 9.116. See Nagy, "The Sign of Protesilaos."

[11] For the White Island and the cult of Achilles in the area of the Black
Sea, see Guy Hedreen, "The Cult of Achilles in the Euxine," *Hesperia* 60/3
(1991): 313–30. For the renewed interest in hero cults in the Second Sophistic, with particular reference to *On Heroes* and the cult of Protesilaos, see
Christopher P. Jones, "Time and Place in Philostratus' *Heroikos,*" *JHS* 121
(2001): 141–48.

[12] Bowie, "Philostratus," 184.

[13] See Merkle, "Telling the Truth," 193–94.

the narrative of Dictys in the process of asserting the accuracy of Philostratus's own account.

Framing narratives of authentication can be found in the literature of many cultures. A less extraordinary but nevertheless comparable attempt to authenticate a new narrative of the past may be found in the Roman historian Sallust's *Jugurtha* (17):

> But what people first inhabited Africa and what people came later or in what way they became mixed together, although my account is different from the report that most people have heard, nevertheless how I have interpreted it using Punic books which are attributed to King Hiempsal, and how the cultivators of the land themselves think that it happened, I will relate as briefly as possible.

Sallust here claims to provide a more accurate history of Africa on the basis of his access to a special source: books, written in another language, attributed to an important historical figure from Numidia.

Another notable example comes from early medieval Irish evidence. It is an anecdote, dated to the ninth century C.E.,[14] concerning the rediscovery of a supposedly lost book, the *Táin Bó Cuailnge* ("The Cattle Raid of Cooley"), which is a collection of "epic" narratives about Ireland's greatest heroes.[15] This anecdote is in effect a "charter myth,"[16] explaining the essence of the *Táin*.[17] In terms of the myth, this book of narratives, the *Táin*, is equivalent to an integral epic performance. The myth narrates how this book had once been lost and how the assembled poets of Ireland "could not recall it in its entirety," since they knew only

[14] The anecdote is entitled *Dofallsigud Tána Bó Cuailnge* and was published at pp. 433–34 of Heinrich Zimmer, "Keltische Studien," *Zeitschrift für vergleichende Sprachforschung* 28 (1887): 417–689. It is taken from the *Book of Leinster* (twelfth century C.E.), on which see the next note.

[15] There are two main surviving recensions of the *Táin*, as attested in two manuscript families: (1) the *Book of the Dun Cow* (*Lebor na hUidre*, twelfth century C.E.) and the *Yellow Book of Lecan* (fourteenth century C.E.) and (2) the *Book of Leinster* (twelfth century C.E.). For a translation, see Thomas Kinsella, *The Táin: From the Irish Epic Táin Bó Cuailnge* (Oxford: Oxford University Press, 1969).

[16] On the concept of "charter myth," see especially p. 5 of Edmund R. Leach, "Critical Introduction" to Mikhail I. Steblin-Kamenskij, *Myth* (trans. Mary P. Coote; Ann Arbor: Karoma, 1982), 1–20.

[17] There is a translation provided by Kinsella, *The Táin*, 1–2.

"fragments" [*bloga*].[18] In a quest to find the lost integral book, the poet Muirgen happens to travel past the tomb of Fergus mac Roich, one of the chief heroes featured in the narrative of the *Táin*. It is nighttime. Muirgen sits down at the gravestone of the tomb, and he sings an incantation to this gravestone "as though it were Fergus himself."[19] Responding to the incantation, Fergus himself appears in all his heroic glory, and he "recited to him [= to Muirgen] the whole *Táin*, how everything had happened, from start to finish."[20] As in Philostratus's *On Heroes*, we see that the superhuman consciousness of the hero can take over or even possess the narration of epic.

Confronted with the idea that an oracular cult hero possesses total mastery of epic narrative, our first impression is that this idea cannot be reconciled with what we find in Homeric poetry. According to the poetics of the Homeric *Iliad* and *Odyssey*, it is of course the Muses who "inspire" epic narrative. At first glance then these goddesses of memory seem to be the sole source for the superhuman consciousness that informs the content of Homeric poetry and gives it the authority to tell about the gods and heroes of heroic times. This authority, however, is actually shared with the heroes who are "quoted" by Homeric performance, as a closer look at the *Iliad* and *Odyssey* reveals clearly.

In his book about the "quotations" of heroes in Homeric poetry, Richard Martin has demonstrated that the "voice" of the poet becomes traditionally identified with the "voices" of the heroes quoted by the poetic performance:

---

[18] Kinsella, *The Táin*, 1. The concept of a *blog* ("fragment") of a corpus that has disintegrated is a traditional theme found in the charter myths of many cultures; for a brief survey, see Gregory Nagy, *Homeric Questions* (Austin: University of Texas Press, 1996), 70–74.

[19] Kinsella, *The Táin*, 1.

[20] Kinsella, *The Táin*, 1–2. The point of this charter myth, then, is that the corpus of the *Táin* is reintegrated in performance, and thus the "lost book" is finally recovered, even resurrected. See Nagy, *Homeric Questions*, 70, following especially pp. 284 and 289 of the discussion in Joseph F. Nagy, "Orality in Medieval Irish Narrative," *Oral Tradition* 1 (1986): 272–301. On traditional metaphors about a book (or a library of books) as a corpus destined for resurrection, see pp. 196–98 of Gregory Nagy, "The Library of Pergamon as a Classical Model," *Pergamon: Citadel of the Gods* (ed. Helmut Koester; HTS 46; Harrisburg, Penn.: Trinity Press International, 1998), 185–232.

My central conclusion is that the *Iliad* takes shape as a poetic composition in precisely the same "speaking culture"
that we see foregrounded in the stylized words of the poem's heroic speakers, especially those speeches designated
as *muthos*, a word I redefine as "authoritative speech-act."
The poet and the hero are both "performers" in a traditional medium. The genre of muthos composing requires
that its practitioners improve on previous performances and
surpass them, by artfully manipulating traditional material
in new combinations. In other words, within the speeches
of the poem, we see that it is traditional to be spontaneous:
no hero ever merely repeats; each recomposes the traditional
text he performs, be it a boast, threat, command, or story, in
order to project his individual personality in the most convincing manner. I suggest that the "voice" of the poet is the
product of the same traditional performance technique.[21]

Recent ethnographic work on oral poetic performance traditions
has provided typological parallels in support of Martin's demon-
stration. In the *Sīrat Banī Hilāl* epic singing tradition of the poets
of al-Bakātūsh in contemporary Egypt, for example, Dwight
Reynolds has sought—and found—an analogy for Martin's model
of the interchangeable "voice" of poet and hero in epic performance:

> [T]he social reality of the al-Bakātūsh poets involves a
> distinctly negative position for the epic singer within the
> greater social hierarchy; in marked contrast to the poet's
> marginalized status in village society, however, are the mo-
> ments of centrality, power, and "voice" he achieves in epic
> performance. This disjunctive persona has produced not
> only a fascinating process of deep self-identification with the
> epic tradition on the part of the poets, but has clearly, over
> generations, shaped and indeed constituted many aspects of
> the content of the epic itself—an epic tradition, as I have
> termed it, of heroic poets and poetic heroes.[22]

[21] Richard P. Martin, *The Language of Heroes: Speech and Performance
in the Iliad* (Myth and Poetics; Ithaca: Cornell University Press, 1989), xiv.

[22] Dwight Fletcher Reynolds, *Heroic Poets, Poetic Heroes: The Ethnog-
raphy of Performance in an Arabic Oral Tradition* (Ithaca: Cornell University
Press, 1995), 208; at p. 207, Reynolds quotes the formulation of Martin, *The
Language of Heroes*, xiv, as a heuristic paradigm for his own ethnographic field-
work.

There is also a plethora of ethnographic work that documents the widespread mentality of heroic "possession," where the consciousness of the poet is "possessed" by the consciousness of the hero as soon as the poet, in performance, starts "quoting" the hero.[23] As one ethnographer puts it, there can be "a transition from a story *about* a spirit, to one told *to* a spirit, to one told *by* a spirit."[24]

We may infer, then, that Philostratus's *On Heroes* has preserved for us the memory of oral epic traditions where heroes are being "quoted" through the supernatural consciousness of the heroes themselves. This is not to say, however, that *On Heroes* itself represents a direct continuation of such oral traditions. We have little doubt that the oral traditions of composition-in-performance, as still reflected in the hexameter poetry of the *Iliad* and *Odyssey* and of the Epic Cycle in general, had been dead for well over half a millennium by the time Philostratus composed *On Heroes*. Still, it is essential to stress that the traditions of hero cults were evidently still alive in the era of Philostratus. Moreover, the archaic mentality of seeking communion with the consciousness of cult heroes was likewise still alive. Even though the Homeric

---

[23] For a particularly valuable collection of examples, see Stuart H. Blackburn, Peter J. Claus, Joyce B. Flueckiger, and Susan S. Wadley, eds., *Oral Epics in India* (Berkeley: University of California Press, 1989), especially Peter J. Claus, "Behind the Text: Performance and Ideology in a Tulu Oral Tradition," 55–74. At p. 60, Claus notes, "In his performance the possessed priest must not only recite Kordabbu's story, but also assume his character and dramatically portray his exploits for several hours on end."

[24] Claus, "Behind the Text," 74, who adds, "Accompanying these transitions are shifts in verbal style: from the third person pronominal referent, to the second, to the first. There are also changes in the behavior of the performers and the audience." In this comparative context, it is relevant to reconsider Philostratus *Her.* 12.3, where Protesilaos *epainei* ("confirms") the words spoken by Homer "to" (*es*) himself, not "about" himself. The implication of *epainei* is that Protesilaos "confirms" (*Il.* 2.695–709) the short narrative about his epic deeds at Troy, by way of *re-performing* these Homeric verses. On the poetics of authentication-by-reperformance, as implied by the verb *epaineô*, see the comments on the use of this word by Lycurgus *Against Leocrates* 102, at p. 129 n. 16 of Gregory Nagy, "Homer and Plato at the Panathenaia: Synchronic and Diachronic Perspectives," in *Contextualizing Classics: Ideology, Performance, Dialogue: Essays in Honor of John J. Peradotto* (ed. Thomas M. Falkner, Nancy Felson, and David Konstan; Lanham, Md.: Rowman & Littlefield, 1999), 123–50.

poems and the Epic Cycle were now literary rather than oral traditions, they still preserved, as traditions per se, a vital link with
the rituals of hero cult. *On Heroes* bridges the chasm between the
mythical world of epic heroes and the ritual world of cult heroes.
In this masterpiece of the Second Sophistic, a continuum is still
felt to exist between these two diverging worlds. The spirit of
this age is captured by the following formulation of the would-be
initiate Phoenician in *Her.* 6.3: "I dreamed I was reading aloud
(*anaginôskein*) the epic verses (*epos* plural) of Homer."

A telling feature of Philostratus's traditionalism is his consistent
use of mystical language in referring to the cult hero Protesilaos.
Throughout Philostratus's *On Heroes*, there is a sharp contrast
being made between the special understanding of the initiated—
in this case, he happens to be a local Greek "vinedresser" in
the hero's sacred space—and the everyday understanding of the
uninitiated—in this case, he happens to be a non-local non-Greek,
from Phoenicia. This special understanding is conveyed by words
that have a special meaning for the initiated but an everyday
meaning for the uninitiated. The process of initiation allows the
new initiate—hereafter we will refer to him as the "initiand"—to
transcend the everyday meaning of words and to achieve a special
understanding of their sacral meaning.

At the beginning of *On Heroes*, the reader learns that Protesilaos experienced not one but two resurrections in the heroic
past. The first time, the hero came back to life at Phthia in Thessaly after his death at Troy, all because of his love for his bride
Laodameia (*anabiôiê*; *Her.* 2.9). Then he died a second time—and
again it was because he loved his bride—only to come back to life
a second time thereafter (*anabiônai*; *Her.* 2.10). Just exactly how
he came back for the second time, however, is not revealed even to
the initiate, the vinedresser, who says to the initiand, the Phoenician, that Protesilaos chooses not to tell that particular "sacred
secret," that particular *aporrhêton* (*Her.* 2.11).[25]

---

[25] It is relevant to note the suggestive use of the word *pathos*
("experience") in an earlier context, "He himself [Protesilaos] does not

That was then, in the heroic past. Now, however, in the everyday present, the living hero continues to come back again and again, as a sacred epiphany or apparition, much like other heroes of the heroic past who likewise "appear in epiphanies" or "show up" (*phainontai*; *Her.* 2.11). So speaks the initiated vinedresser, and the Phoenician admits that he has a hard time believing all this: "I do not believe," he says (*apisteô*; *Her.* 3.1). In other words, the initiand is not yet an initiate. Still, he wants to be a "believer" (*pisteuôn*; *Her.* 3.1). The initiate responds by proceeding to tell the initiand all about the epiphanies of Protesilaos, describing the cult hero's interventions into the world of the everyday. Where is Protesilaos most likely to be sighted? The initiate reveals an array of places where the hero may "show up," as it were: sometimes he is in the Chersonesus, sometimes in Phthia, sometimes in Troy—a most notable of locations for frequent sightings of heroes who died in the Trojan War—and sometimes he is back in Hades (*Her.* 11.7). It is in Hades that he continues to have sex with his beloved bride Laodameia (*Her.* 11.8).

As the narrative of the hero's epiphanies proceeds, a gentle breeze carries the sweet aroma of flowers in bloom, and the initiand is feeling refreshed (*Her.* 3.2–5). He remarks that the plant life literally "breathes out" (*anapnei*) a sweetness of its own (*Her.* 3.3). It is the right season, the exact time, the perfect moment: it is the *hôra* (*Her.* 3.2, 5). One can begin to sense the hero's sacred presence. Through a sort of metonymy, the breath of the

speak about his own experiences [*pathê*]" (*Her.* 2.9). The speaker goes on to say that the *aporrhêton* ("sacred secret") belongs to the *Moirai* ("Fates"; *Her.* 2.11). In the formulaic language of epic diction, the name *Prôtesi-lâos* seems to be associated with the word *prôtos* ("first"), in the sense that this hero was the first Achaean to die at Troy (*Il.* 2.702: *prôtistos*). But the name seems also to be associated with the root of *pe-prô-tai* ("it is fated"; as in *Il.* 18.329), in that Protesilaos is linked with traditional epic narratives about the fate of the Achaean *lâos* or "people" (Nagy, *Best of the Achaeans*, 70). A turning point in the plot of the *Iliad* is the moment when the fire of Hektor reaches the ships of the Achaeans, and here the narrative focus centers on the ship of Protesilaos himself (*Il.* 15.704–705, 716–718; see also 16.286). This same precise moment is figured as a turning point for the very destiny of all Hellenes as descendants of the epic Achaeans, in that the *Iliad* equates the threat of destruction for the Achaeans' ships with the threat of extinction for the Hellenes that are yet to be (Nagy, *Best of the Achaeans*, 335–37).

hero himself animates the atmosphere, and Protesilaos is now revealing (*apophainôn*), the scent of the blossoms at their sweetest (*Her.* 11.3).[26] The hero's presence smells sweeter than myrtles in autumn (*Her.* 10.2).[27] The perfect moment or *hôra*, in all its natural beauty, becomes the ultimate epiphany of the cult hero.[28]

---

[26] Such a traditional metonymy depends on a preexisting traditional metaphor that pictures an interchangeability between breath and wind, on which see Gregory Nagy, "As the World Runs out of Breath: Metaphorical Perspectives on the Heavens and the Atmosphere in the Ancient World," in *Earth, Air, Fire, Water: Humanistic Studies of the Environment* (ed. Jill K. Conway, Kenneth Keniston, and Leo Marx; Amherst: University of Massachusetts Press, 1999), 37–50.

[27] In contexts of beautiful natural settings, the cult hero is conventionally eroticized, as here in *Her.* 10.2–4 and elsewhere; see especially *Her.* 11.2, describing the urge of the worshipper to embrace and kiss the hero. A sense of personal intimacy is conveyed by the worshipper of the hero when he says about Protesilaos (*Her.* 9.7): "I spend time with him [*autôi gar xuneimi*], and no cult statue [*agalma*] can be sweeter [*hêdion*] than he, that one [*ekeinos*]." The worshipper's experience of the hero as a real person, not as a cult statue (*agalma*), is here conveyed by the deictic pronoun *ekeinos* ("that one"), which is conventionally used to refer to a hero who appears in an epiphany (see Nagy, *Pindar's Homer*, 200–201, with special reference to Mimnermus and Sappho). The deixis of *ekeinos* conveys the remoteness ("that" not "this") of the hero, even in the immediacy of his epiphany. The gap between the superhuman and the human is so great that it sets the superhuman apart from the human even in the process of attempting to bridge that gap in an epiphany. The human response is a sense of longing and yearning as experienced even during the immediacy of an epiphany. We refer again to *Her.* 11.2, describing the urge of the worshipper to embrace and kiss the cult hero. The convention of eroticizing this sense of longing and yearning is implicit, we further suggest, in the epic usage of *potheô* ("long for, yearn for"), as at *Il.* 2.703, 709. On one level of meaning, the warriors native to Phthia long for the epic hero Protesilaos as their leader. On a deeper level, however, the reference implies the emotional response of native worshippers who are "yearning" for their local cult hero in all his immanent beauty; we may compare the application of *potheô* to Patroklos at his funeral, *Il.* 23.16. For other Homeric examples of similar two-level references to heroes of epic/cult, see Gregory Nagy, *Greek Mythology and Poetics* (Ithaca: Cornell University Press, 1990), 132–34 on the usage of the word *dêmos* (in the sense of "local district") as an index of localized cult practices.

[28] On the religious mentality of equating ritual perfection with beauty itself, see in general the work of Pache, "Baby and Child Heroes." The concept of *hôra* as the "right season" conveys the context of ritual perfection and correctness; in that sense, *hôra* is conceived as the perfect moment of beauty, as in Philostratus *Her.* 3.2, 5. The Modern Greek adjective *oréos* (*hôraios*), derived from *hôra*, means "beautiful." On the formal and semantic connections of *hôra*

The secrets of the cult hero Protesilaos are clearly visible to the initiate: since these are things that are *theia* ("divine") and *megala* ("larger than life"), they will not escape the notice of those who are "cultivated," (*kharientes*; *Her.* 3.2). For the uninitiated, however, these same secrets are veiled in language that expresses what seems quite ordinary and everyday on the surface. About the cult hero Protesilaos, the initiate starts by saying to the uninitiated: "He lives [*zêi*] here, and we work the land [*geôrgoumen*] together" (*Her.* 2.8). What image in life could be more straightforward, more everyday, than life itself? When the initiand follows up by asking whether Protesilaos "lives" in the sense that he is "resurrected" (*anabebiôkôs*), the initiate replies: "He himself does not speak about his own experiences [*pathos* plural]" (*Her.* 2.9). This absolutizing declaration is then followed by a series of qualifications: contradicting what he has just said, the initiate now goes on to say that the hero Protesilaos does indeed speak about his own death at Troy, about his first resurrection, and about his second death—though he does not speak about his second resurrection (*Her.* 2.9–11).

A vital question remains: How can a cult hero like Protesilaos actually communicate with those who are initiated into his mysteries? According to the traditional mentality of hero cults, the answer is simple: whenever they come back to life, cult heroes are endowed with a superhuman consciousness. This consciousness of the hero, activated by hero cult, performs the basic function of ensuring the seasonality of nature, and it manifests itself in such specific functions as the healing of humans or animals

and Hera and *hêrôs* ("hero"), see Nagy, *Homeric Questions*, 48 n. 79: heroes become "seasonal" after they die and achieve mystical immortalization, but they are "unseasonal" during their own lifetime in the heroic age (thus, for example, Achilles while he is alive in his own epic narrative is described as *pan-a-hôrios*, "the most unseasonal of them all," in *Il.* 24.540). The formal connections between *hôra* and hero cult are evident in *Her.* 18.2–3, a passage that describes in explicit terms the ritually correct times (*hôrai*) for slaughtering herd animals as sacrifices to cult heroes; in this particular context, diseases afflicting herd animals are said to be caused by an angry Ajax, *in his capacity as a cult hero*. In this context, such a belief is linked to the myth about the ritually incorrect slaughter of herd animals by Ajax (as dramatized, for example, in Sophocles' *Ajax*).

or plants: in *Her.* 4.10, for example, Protesilaos is described as the *iatros* ("healer") of sheep, beehives, trees.[29]

For this superhuman consciousness to be activated, the cult hero must be *consulted*. In the case of Philostratus's *On Heroes*, we see that a cult hero like Protesilaos has to be actively consulted by his worshippers: from the very beginning, in fact, the intent of the chief character, the worker in the vineyard of Protesilaos, is to make this cult hero his own personal "advisor," (*xumboulos*; *Her.* 4.7).[30] Whenever the ritual of consultation would fail, the worshipper says that he could know for sure, since the cult hero would be silent (*esiôpa*; *Her.* 4.7). By contrast, the success of the consultation is manifested whenever the cult hero speaks.

Such consulting of oracular cult heroes concerns not only the fundamentals of nature. It concerns also the fundamental nature of the heroes themselves. Their heroic essence has two aspects, one of which is defined by epic narrative traditions like the *Iliad* and *Odyssey*, while the other is defined by hero cult. In Philostratus's *On Heroes*, these two aspects of the hero are treated holistically as integral parts of a single concept. Thus the process of consulting oracular heroes leads to the initiate's knowledge about their epic aspects, as well as their ritual aspects. As the initiate declares, cult heroes have their own knowledge of epic narrative because they are endowed with *mantikê sophia* ("the skill of a seer [*mantis*]"), and there is an "oracular" principle (*khrêsmôdes*) operating within them (*Her.* 7.3). That is why a hero like Protesilaos "sees all the way through" (*di-horâi*) the poems of Homer (*Her.* 7.4), knowing things that go beyond his own experiences when he, Protesilaos, had lived in the past of heroes (*Her.* 7.5–6); the hero even knows things about which Homer himself did not sing (*Her.* 7.5).

[29] On the "iatric" function of cult heroes, see in general Brelich, *Gli eroi greci*, 113–18. Cult heroes, when they feel benign, will cure illnesses afflicting humans, animals, and plants—just as they will inflict these same illnesses when they feel malign (see the previous note). On the *phrikê* or sacred "frisson" induced by a cult hero's presence, see *Her.* 6.4; 8.11; 18.4; etc.

[30] See also *Her.* 14.4: Protesilaos is an "advisor" to athletes who cultivate him (cf. *Her.* 15.5, where Protesilaos is said to give oracular advice, *khrêsai*, to an athlete who consults him on how to win). Already in Homeric poetry, we see implicit references to consultations of cult heroes: in *Il.* 10.415, for example, Hektor *boulas bouleuei* ("plans his plans") at the *sêma* ("tomb") of Ilos, a stylized cult hero of Ilion.

In sum, *On Heroes* provides a model of poetic inspiration that centers on the superhuman consciousness of the oracular hero, which has a totalizing control of epic narrative. As we have seen, this model is not an innovation but an archaism, stemming from oral poetic traditions that predate even the Homeric traditions of the *Iliad* and *Odyssey*. Philostratus's *On Heroes* makes it clear that heroes cannot be defined exclusively in terms of their epic dimensions, though this aspect becomes vitally important in the history of ideas about heroism, especially in view of the ultimate cultural prestige surrounding the prime medium that conveys these ideas, Homeric poetry. For Philostratus, the prestige of Homer and the Homeric hero is a given. In *On Heroes*, however, he goes further, far further, by reconnecting that epic prestige with the sacred charisma possessed by the hero in cult.

CONTINUITY AND TRADITION IN PHILOSTRATUS'S *ON HEROES*

As noted above, references to the immortalization of heroes after death and their status as cult figures are almost never explicit in the *Iliad* and *Odyssey*.[31] Implicit references to hero cult, however, are pervasive. Indeed, much of epic diction resonates with religious undertones, resulting in a superficial meaning for certain key terms, as well as a deeper, sacred meaning for those "in the know"—the initiated worshippers. Philostratus's *On Heroes*, although composed many centuries after our *Iliad* and *Odyssey*, helps us to connect with the mentality of hero cults that lies beneath the surface of Homeric poetry. A closer examination of a few selected passages will illustrate the continuity of hero cult narratives about the immortality of heroes that can be traced in *On Heroes*. These same passages can in turn enhance our understanding of archaic and classical Greek poetry.

In *Iliad* 23, the *psukhê* of Patroklos visits Achilles in a dream and entreats Achilles to bury him in a golden amphora that Thetis gave to Achilles in anticipation of his death:

---

[31] For an exception to this formulation see Casey Dué, "Achilles' Golden Amphora and the Afterlife of Oral Tradition in Aeschines' *Against Timarchus*," *CP* 96 (2001): 33–47.

"Do not bury my bones apart from yours, Achilles,
but together, as we were raised in your house. . .
so may the same vessel contain both our bones,
the golden amphora, which your lady mother gave you."[32]

(*Il.* 23.83–84, 91–92)

This golden amphora is one of the only concrete symbols of Achilles' immortality after death in the *Iliad*.[33] The golden amphora signals the reassembly of Achilles' bones and his transformation into an immortalized hero after death. Elsewhere in the poem, however, only his short life and his grief while alive are emphasized. The anticipation of the finality of Achilles' death is so great that the mourning for Achilles begins while he is still alive. Similarly, Odysseus and Telemachus are lamented by Penelope repeatedly throughout the *Odyssey*.[34]

The religious dimension of Homeric poetry aids our interpretation of these lament-filled passages. As Nagy has argued, the funeral rituals and lamentation of the *Iliad* and *Odyssey* are a reflection of actual cult practice in the worship of heroes like Achilles and Odysseus as religious figures.[35] The songs of lament

[32] See *Od.* 24.73–77, "Your mother gave you a golden amphora and said that it was the gift of Dionysos, the work of most famous Hephaistos. In this amphora lie your white bones, radiant Achilles, and mixed with them are the bones of the dead Patroklos, son of Menoitios." In *Her.* 56.5 the vinedresser mentions a story about a golden pitcher (*kalpis*) that appeared, apparently mysteriously, on Chios, but declines to tell the tale because, he says, it is so well known. It is likely that this golden pitcher is also to be connected with the immortality of the cult hero.

[33] For the golden amphora as a symbol of immortality see Nagy, *Best of the Achaeans*, chs. 9–10. See also A. Stewart, "Stesichoros and the François Vase," in *Ancient Greek Art and Iconography* (ed. Warren G. Moon; Madison: University of Wisconsin Press, 1983), 53–74, who argues for a compositional unity to the so-called François Vase centered on the golden amphora depicted on it. The wedding of Peleus and Thetis is set amid narratives that explore the tensions between mortality and immortality, peerless heroism and savage wrath, and mighty prowess and terrible hubris in the figure of Achilles. Stewart notes (p. 66), "Appropriately, all these themes intersect in the motif of Dionysus' amphora and its twin promises of death and immortality."

[34] *Od.* 1.363–364; 4.716–741, 800–801, 810–823; 18.202–205, 603–605; 20.57–90; 21.54–57, 356–358.

[35] See Nagy, *Best of the Achaeans*, 94–117, especially 116–17, "As Rohde [1898] himself had noticed, the Funeral of Patroklos at *Iliad* XXIII has several features that connote the rituals of hero cults. For example, the wine libation

for Achilles and Odysseus within the epic are an important part of
ritual lamentation for the hero on the part of the communities for
whom the epics are performed.[36]

Similarly, Briseis' lament for Patroklos in *Iliad* 19 expresses
private grief that becomes transformed into a collective sorrow for
her audience both within the epic and beyond it:

> So she spoke lamenting, and the women wailed in response,
> with Patroklos as their pretext, but each woman for her own
> cares. (*Il.* 19.301–302)

Briseis' song extends not only to the collective experience of
the women around her who lament their fallen husbands, but

(XXIII 218–221) and the offering of honey with oil (XXIII 170; cf. xxiv 67–
68) 'can hardly be regarded as anything but sacrificial.' Such marginal details
of cult, as also the integral element of singing lamentations at XXIII 12 and 17,
give ritual *form* to the **ákhos** of Achilles for Patroklos at XXIII 47. Even the
central epic action of Book XXIII, the Funeral Games of Patroklos, has ritual form. In Homeric narrative, the funeral of a hero is the primary occasion
for athletic contests (XXIII 630–631: Amarynkeus; xxiv 85–86: Achilles himself). In classical times, local athletic contests were still motivated as funeral
games for the epichoric hero (cf., e.g., Pausanias 8.4.5). As a general principle,
the **agṓn** was connected with the cult of heroes, and even the Great Panhellenic
Games were originally conceived as funeral games for heroes. The custom of
mourning for Achilles at the beginning of the Olympics (Pausanias 6.23.3) is a
striking instance of this heritage. As a parallel, epic offers a corresponding single event in the mourning for Patroklos that inaugurates the Funeral Games in
Book XXIII. Even though there are hints within the *Iliad* that the Funeral of
Patroklos is presented as a grand beginning of cult (XXIV 592–595), the overt
singularity of the event forced Rohde to rule it out as a parallel to the cult of
heroes, which is recurrent. And yet, the *Iliad* itself is a singularity. What is recurrent in ritual is timeless in the epic tradition, just like the **kléos áphthiton**
of Achilles."

[36] On Greek laments in general see the seminal work of Margaret Alexiou, *Ritual Lament in the Greek Tradition* (2d ed.; Lanham, Md.: Rowman &
Littlefield, 2002).

to the audience of the epic as well.[37] Dué has argued that Briseis' lamentation for Patroklos is also a lament for Achilles.[38] Her lament becomes on the level of cult a communal expression of lamentation for Achilles as hero. It is not insignificant then that the final lament of the *Iliad*, sung by Helen (who is the cause of the war), ends not with the antiphonal wailing of the women (as at 6.499; 19.30; 22.515; and 24.746), but of the Trojan people: "So she spoke lamenting, and the people [*dêmos*] wailed in response" (*Il.* 24.776).

We may compare the lamentation for Achilles before his death in the *Iliad* to the very full description of his funeral in the *Odyssey*:

> "Happy [*olbios*] son of Peleus, Achilles like the gods," answered the ghost [*psukhê*] of Agamemnon, "for having died at Troy far from Argos, while the best of the Trojans and the Achaeans fell around you fighting for your body. There you lay in the whirling clouds of dust, all huge and hugely, heedless now of your horsemanship. We fought the whole of the livelong day, nor should we ever have left off if Zeus had not sent a storm to stay us. Then, when we had borne you to the ships out of the fray, we laid you on your bed and cleansed your fair skin with warm water and with ointments. The Danaans tore their hair and wept bitterly round about you. Your mother, when she heard, came with her immortal nymphs from out of the sea, and the sound of heavenly wailing went forth over the waters so that the Achaeans quaked for fear. They would have fled panic-stricken to

---

[37] For a similar transformation of the laments of women into a collective, civic sorrow, see Charles P. Segal's discussion of Euripides' *Hippolytus* 1462–1466 in *Euripides and the Poetics of Sorrow* (Durham: Duke University Press, 1993), 121; and Laura McClure, *Spoken Like a Woman: Speech and Gender in Athenian Drama* (Princeton: Princeton University Press, 1999), 41 and 156. Thomas M. Greene has noted that lamentation in epic collapses the boundaries between the audience and the heroic past, producing "a hallowed communion between the two" ("The Natural Tears of Epic," in *Epic Traditions in the Contemporary World: The Poetics of Community* [ed. Margaret Beissinger, Jane Tylus, and Susanne Wofford; Berkeley: University of California Press, 1999], 195). He argues that the *telos* of most of the European poetry known as epic is tears, and that through tears the communion between past and present is most accessible.

[38] See Casey Dué, *Homeric Variations on a Lament by Briseis* (Lanham, Md.: Rowman & Littlefield, 2002).

their ships had not wise old Nestor whose counsel was ever truest checked them saying, 'Hold, Argives, flee not, sons of the Achaeans, this is his mother coming from the sea with her immortal nymphs to view the body of her son.'

Thus he spoke, and the Achaeans feared no more. The daughters of the old man of the sea stood round you weeping bitterly, and clothed you in immortal raiment. The nine muses also came and lifted up their sweet voices in lament—calling and answering one another; there was not an Argive but wept for pity of the dirge they chanted. Days and nights seven and ten we mourned you, mortals and immortals, but on the eighteenth day we gave you to the flames, and many a fat sheep with many an ox did we slay in sacrifice around you. You were burnt in raiment of the gods, with rich resins and with honey, while Achaean heroes, horse and foot, clashed their armor round the pile as you were burning, with the tramp as of a great multitude. But when the flames of heaven had done their work, we gathered your white bones at daybreak and laid them in ointments and in pure wine. Your mother brought us a golden amphora to hold them—gift of Dionysos, and work of Hephaistos himself; in this we mingled your bleached bones with those of Patroklos who had gone before you, and separate we enclosed also those of Antilokhos, who had been closer to you than any other of your comrades now that Patroklos was no more.

Over their bodies we the sacred army of Argive spearmen piled up a huge and perfect tomb, on a jutting headland, by the wide Hellespont, so that it may be bright from afar for men coming from the sea, both those who are now and those who will be in the future. Your mother begged prizes from the gods, and offered them to be contended for [*agôn*] by the noblest of the Achaeans. You must have been present at the funeral of many a hero, when the young men gird themselves and make ready to contend for prizes on the death of some great chieftain, but you never saw such prizes as silver-footed Thetis offered in your honor; for the gods loved you well. Thus even in death your *kleos*, Achilles, has not been lost, and your name lives evermore among all humankind." (*Od.* 24.35–95)[39]

---

[39] Translation after Samuel Butler, trans. *The Odyssey* (London: Longmans, Green, & Co., 1900).

In the *Odyssey* tradition, the spectacular funeral, prominent tomb, and the lamentation of not only the Nereids but also the Muses themselves are a prelude to Achilles' immortality in song, his *kleos*.[40]

The lamentation for heroes within epic is a reflection of ritual lamentation on the part of the community outside of epic. There are clear traces we can find in the hero cults of Achilles in the classical and even postclassical periods. To cite just one example, let us consider a custom in Elis that Pausanias mentions in connection with various local athletic traditions. On an appointed day at the beginning of the Olympic Games, as the sun is sinking in the west, the women of Elis perform various rituals to worship Achilles (*tou Achilleôs drôsin es timên*), and the ritual that is singled out specifically is that of mourning (*koptesthai*; Pausanias *Description of Greece* 6.23.3).[41]

But whereas the mortality of the hero is emphasized in Homeric epic and in many rituals concerning heroes, it is likely that the immortalization of the hero after death played a role in the epic traditions that have come down to us as the Epic Cycle. These poems, attributed to various authors such as Arctinus of Miletus or Lesches of Mytilene, announce themselves as being more locally oriented than the *Iliad* or *Odyssey*.[42] Because they are more local in orientation, the poems of the Epic Cycle include relatively more romance, fantasy, folktale, and local color.[43] The poems of the Cycle survive only in fragments and

[40] *kleos* is fame or glory, especially the fame or glory that comes from being glorified by poetry or song; see Nagy, *Best of the Achaeans*, 16–18.

[41] For this and other examples of cult practices in honor of Achilles, see Martin P. Nilsson, *Griechische Feste* (Leipzig: Teubner, 1906), 457, as well as Hedreen, "Cult of Achilles."

[42] The *Iliad* and the *Odyssey*, by contrast with the Epic Cycle, were never explicitly said to belong to any one city. Many cities laid claim to being the birthplace of "Homer." See Thomas W. Allen, *Homer: The Origins and the Transmission* (Oxford: Clarendon, 1924), 11–41. On the local, that is, relatively less panhellenic nature of the poems of the Cycle, see Nagy, *Pindar's Homer*, 70–79, as well as Jonathan S. Burgess, "The Non-Homeric *Cypria*," *TAPA* 126 (1996): 77–99. For more on the Epic Cycle in general, see Malcolm Davies, *The Epic Cycle* (Bristol: Bristol Classical Press, 1989) and Jonathan S. Burgess, *The Tradition of the Trojan War in Homer and the Epic Cycle* (Baltimore: Johns Hopkins University Press, 2001).

[43] See J. Griffin, "The Epic Cycle and the Uniqueness of Homer," *JHS* 97 (1977): 39–53 and Davies, *The Epic Cycle*, 9–10, who view these

in the summaries written by an ancient scholar named Proclus;
our knowledge of their contents is therefore limited.[44] The summaries of Proclus, moreover, are not an entirely accurate reflection
of the poems in their earliest stages.[45] Nevertheless, the surviving
summaries and fragments give us an indication of the traditional
content of epic poetry that was composed and performed within
the same tradition as the *Iliad* and *Odyssey*.

In the *Aithiopis*, as it is summarized by Proclus, Thetis
snatches the corpse of Achilles from his funeral pyre and trans-
ports him to the island of Leukê:

> Then they hold funeral rites for Antilokhos and lay out
> Achilles' corpse; Thetis comes with the Muses and her sis-
> ters and makes a lament [*thrênos*] for her son. After that,
> Thetis snatches him off the pyre and carries him over to the
> island Leukê. But the Achaeans heap up his burial mound
> and hold funeral games.

Nagy has shown that the verb *anarpazô* ("snatch") used here has a
special meaning in connection with the death of heroes. *Anarpazô*
is the verb most commonly used in narratives of the abduction by
divinities of mortals who subsequently become immortalized.[46]
Such mortals include Phaethôn and Ganymede. In the *Aithiopis*
tradition, Achilles died and was buried, but was subsequently
imagined to come back to life as an immortalized hero on the so-
called White Island, the island of Leukê.

Philostratus's *On Heroes* represents a continuation of archaic
beliefs about the death (accompanied by intense lamentation and
elaborate funerals) and the subsequent immortalization of heroes.
The following is the vinedresser's account of the burial and tomb
of Achilles at Troy:

elements as signs of inferior poetry; contrast Nagy, *Pindar's Homer*, 60–61
and 70–71.

[44] It is not known whether this Proclus is the Neoplatonist of the fifth
century C.E. or another man from the second century C.E. See Burgess, *The
Tradition of the Trojan War*, 12.

[45] On the earliest recoverable scope and content of the poems of the Epic
Cycle, see especially Davies, *The Epic Cycle*; Ross Scaife, "The *Kypria* and its
Early Reception," *Classical Antiquity* 14 (1995): 164–92; Burgess, "The Non-
Homeric *Cypria*"; and Burgess, *The Tradition of the Trojan War*, 143–48.

[46] Nagy, *Best of the Achaeans*, 192–98.

This hill, my guest, which you see standing in line with the
headland, the Achaeans erected when they came together at
the time when Achilles was mingled with Patroklos in the
tomb and bequeathed to himself and that man the loveliest shroud. For this reason they who praise the marks of
friendship sing of him. He was buried most spectacularly
of mortals with all that Hellas offered to him. The Hellenes no longer considered it proper after Achilles' death to
wear their hair long, and they piled up in mass on a funeral
pyre their gold and whatever each of them had, whether he
had brought it to Troy or had taken it as booty, both right
then and when Neoptolemos came to Troy. For Achilles
obtained glorious gifts again from both his child and the
Achaeans, who were trying to show in return their gratitude
to him. (*Her.* 51.12–13)

The vinedresser believes that the Greeks of Achilles' day began to
confer a hero's honors upon Achilles immediately after his death.
These honors included a spectacular burial, precious gifts, and
perpetual mourning as expressed in the form of shorn hair.

The vinedresser goes on to describe in the course of the
dialogue many rituals performed at the tomb of Achilles by worshippers of the vinedresser's own day, a direct continuation of
those ancient rites.   According to the vinedresser, moreover,
Achilles continues to have an existence beyond death, much like
the primary hero of the dialogue, Protesilaos. As in the *Aithiopis*
tradition, Achilles lives on the island known as Leukê, the White
Island. His companion on this island is none other than Helen
of Troy. She is immortal, and so too has Achilles become immortal after death. Passing sailors can hear him singing songs,
and visitors to the island can sometimes experiences frightening
epiphanies by this hero.

In the preceding discussion we have already noted that
Protesilaos is a cult hero who, according to the vinedresser, has
died and been resurrected not once, but twice. Thus Achilles and
Protesilaos are both heroes who die an unseasonably early death
in epic, but live on as immortalized heroes in cult. The description of Protesilaos's tomb captures perfectly these two aspects of
the hero:

Listen to such stories now, my guest. Protesilaos does not
lie buried at Troy but here on the Chersonesus. This large
kolônos here on the left no doubt contains him. The nymphs

created these elms around the *kolônos*, and they made, I suppose, the following decree concerning these trees: "Those
branches turned toward Ilion will blossom early and will
then immediately shed their leaves and perish before their
season (this was indeed the misfortune of Protesilaos), but
a tree on the other side will live and prosper." All the trees
that were not set round the grave, such as these in the grove,
have strength in all their branches and flourish according to
their particular nature. (*Her.* 9.1–3)

Most noteworthy is the use here of the word *kolônos*, which we
propose to translate as "landmark" in this context. It marks the
mound, surrounded by elm trees, that "extends over" (*epekhei*)
the body of the cult hero Protesilaos at Elaious in the Chersonesus. At *Her.* 51.12, this same word *kolônos* designates the mound
that the Achaeans built (the verb here, *ageirô*, suggests a piling
of stones) over the bodies of Achilles and Patroklos, situated on
a headland overlooking the Hellespont, thus facing the mound of
Protesilaos on the other side of the strait.

At *Her.* 53.10–11, *kolônos* refers again to the tomb of Achilles, and here the word is used synonymously with *sêma* (the
"tomb" or "sign" of the hero; *Her.* 53.11). In Sophocles' *Oedipus at Colonus*, the place-name *Kolônos* refers to a sacred grove
(690, 889) where Oedipus's body is destined to receive an *oikos*,
that is, an "abode" befitting a cult hero (627).[47] There is a
metonymy implicit in the name: *kolônos* as a landmark becomes,
by extension, the name of the whole sacred grove—and, by further extension, the name of the whole deme of Attica in which
the grove is situated. Moreover, the landmark is associated with a
stone called the *Thorikios petros* (1595), sacred to Poseidon, which
marks the last place where Oedipus is to be seen before he is
mystically engulfed into the earth. As Nagy argues elsewhere,
the metonymy extends even further: the inherited imagery of the
Thorikios petros as a mystical "white rock" becomes coextensive
with the description of Colonus itself as a white rock shining from
afar (690; *argês*).[48]

Such connections between classical literature and the literary world of the Second Sophistic reveal strong undercurrents of
continuity in conceptualizing the cult hero. Still, the traditions

[47] On this context of *oikos*, see Nagy, *Pindar's Homer*, 269.
[48] See Nagy, *Greek Mythology and Poetics*, 231.

of hero cult were never fully spelled out in the classical period of Greek civilization. Only in the era of the Second Sophistic do these traditions—and the charismatic heroes who populate them—become manifest. Philostratus's *On Heroes*, this masterpiece of Second Sophistic, is not only the best literary source for understanding the ancient concept of the cult hero in Greek civilization. It is the only work of literature where the overall concept of the ancient Greek hero—in its religious as well as literary dimensions—is given a chance to reveal itself in all its wondrous splendor. Philostratus's *On Heroes* is the perfect literary initiation into a full understanding of what it really is to be a hero in the ancient Greek world.

THE EDUCATIONAL VALUE OF *ON HEROES*

Reading *On Heroes* is sure to enhance any undergraduate or graduate course centering on Greek civilization, literature, myth, or religion. This masterpiece of the Second Sophistic complements the older masterpieces of archaic and classical Greek poetry and prose. We have personal experience in team-teaching an undergraduate course that featured *On Heroes* in English (thanks to Jennifer Berenson Maclean and Ellen Bradshaw Aitken, who kindly gave us permission to use a preliminary version of their translation). We used *On Heroes* as a primary text to be read along with the Homeric *Iliad* and *Odyssey*, Herodotus, and nine tragedies selected from the works of Aeschylus, Sophocles, and Euripides. The course, "The Concept of the Hero in Greek Civilization," is a large Core Curriculum lecture course that has been offered yearly for over two decades to an average of around three hundred and fifty students, none of whom is assumed to have any prior background in Classics, let alone ancient Greek. In 1999, we required *On Heroes* to be read in its entirety. The students were assigned the work immediately after they had completed the *Iliad* and *Odyssey*, in the same week that they read selections from Herodotus and Pausanias concerning hero cult. In speaking with the students about Philostratus's *On Heroes*, we emphasized the sections on Protesilaos (*Her.* 9.1–23.30) and Achilles (*Her.* 44.5–57.17).

By including *On Heroes* in the assigned reading for the course, we were able to address directly both of the historical dimensions of ancient Greek heroic traditions, cult as well as literature. When readers are exposed to the *Iliad* and *Odyssey* for the first time, references to the immortalization of heroes after death and their status as religious beings are most difficult to grasp, since such references are almost never explicit. With Philostratus's *On Heroes* as a background, the reader begins to appreciate how much of epic and dramatic language resonates with religious undertones. The surface meaning of key heroic terms can be juxtaposed with a deeper, sacred meaning intended for those "in the know," the initiated worshippers. In the lectures on the *Iliad* and *Odyssey* as well as tragedy, the religious significance of such terms as *timê* and *sêma* were emphasized, and these key Greek terms were included in a glossary as part of the course sourcebook.[49] Reading *On Heroes* was the context for confronting these terms for the first time in their explicitly cultic contexts. Building on the background provided by Philostratus's *On Heroes*, students had the opportunity to juxtapose the implicit references to hero cult in the *Iliad*, *Odyssey*, and Greek tragedy with the explicit worship of heroes in cult. Moreover, by combining *On Heroes* with selections from Herodotus and Pausanias, we were able to give students a sense of the continuity of heroic traditions over the course of more than a thousand years.

Finally, the learning experience to be gained from reading *On Heroes* is practically unique in conveying the realities of how it must have felt for a worshipper to participate in hero cult. *On Heroes* conveys more than any other work of literature the emotional ties that bind hero and worshipper together. This deeply personal aspect of hero cult is perhaps the most difficult thing to learn about ancient Greek heroes if the reader relies on archaic and classical Greek literary sources alone. The relationship portrayed in Philostratus's *On Heroes* between the pious vinedresser and the charismatic cult hero Protesilaos illustrates most vividly the practice of hero cult as a personal experience, thereby offering students and experts alike an unparalleled insight into what

---

[49] For *timê* see Nagy, *Best of the Achaeans*, 72–83 and 118. For *sêma* see Nagy, "The Sign of Protesilaos."

was for the ancient Greeks the everyday life-sustaining practice of worshipping heroes.

Introduction

On Heroes is a dialogue set in Elaious, a town on the southern tip of the Thracian Chersonesus, the peninsula that runs along the European side of the Hellespont. There are only two participants in the dialogue: the man who tends the vineyard and gardens around the tomb of the hero Protesilaos and a Phoenician merchant, whose ship awaits favorable winds. After exchanging introductory pleasantries (the Phoenician seems to sound out the vinedresser[1] as a potential business contact), the merchant is surprised to learn that the vinedresser is an intimate of Protesilaos, the first Greek warrior to die in the Trojan War (*Il.* 2.695–710). Protesilaos not only aids the vinedresser in gardening, but discusses the Trojan War and Homer's poems, while inculcating in him a philosophic approach to life (*Her.* [= *On Heroes*] 2.6–5.5). At this opportunity to discuss heroes, the Phoenician realizes the meaning of a dream he had upon arriving at Elaious. As he had dreamed of reading the so-called catalogue of the ships (from *Iliad* 2), so now he must converse about the heroes in order to obtain favorable winds and be on his way (*Her.* 6.3–6). Although he is apparently a believer in signs, dreams, and other kinds of supernatural phenomena, the Phoenician voices skepticism about the ongoing existence of the heroes until the vinedresser offers as "proofs" of their existence the discovery of giant skeletons throughout the Greek world, but especially near Troy, which lies within sight of Protesilaos's tomb, just across the Hellespont (*Her.* 6.7–8.18). The rest of the dialogue is dedicated to a discussion of the heroes, but not simply as a retelling of Homer. Protesilaos is, after all, a more trustworthy witness not only of the

---

[1] We have chosen "vinedresser" to translate *ampelourgos*, a word rich in associations. This term designates one who tends, prunes, cultivates, and otherwise cares for the grapevines in a vineyard. In the context of a sanctuary of a hero, where abundant vegetation signals the immortality of the hero, as well as the justice and prosperity that derive from the hero, *ampelourgos* implicitly designates one whose work, agricultural or otherwise, entails the cultivation of the hero's cult.

events prior to landing at Troy (when he died), but also of those
that occurred afterward, since he is "free from the body and diseases" and thus can "observe the affairs of mortals" (*Her.* 7.3).
From this privileged vantage point, Protesilaos the hero is both
reader and critic of Homer.

With the Phoenician's initial doubts about the existence of
heroes overcome, the vinedresser launches into a description of
Protesilaos's appearance, character, and way of life, in addition
to the rituals at his sanctuary, his oracular pronouncements to
athletes, and his vengeance on adulterers (*Her.* 9.1–17.6). Protesilaos, however, is not the only hero who continues to be involved
in human affairs. Across the Hellespont at Troy, Ajax, Hektor, Palamedes, and Patroklos have recently appeared, bringing
fertility and prosperity to those who are devoted to them, but ex-
acting terrifying vengeance upon those who show them dishonor
(*Her.* 18.1–23.1). This section concludes with a lengthy tale of
Protesilaos's exploits in the battle of Mysia (*Her.* 23.2–30), an
elaborate celebration of a hero slain too early in life and slighted
by what *On Heroes* regards as Homer's scant praise (*Il.* 2.695–710;
cf. *Her.* 14.2).

The center section of the dialogue, the catalogue of Achaean
and Trojan heroes (*Her.* 25.18–42.4), ostensibly fulfills the Phoenician's dream. The vinedresser relates what Protesilaos knows
about the heroes' physical appearance, their bravery in war, and
their cleverness in speech and deed, and whether the poets have
actually gotten the stories about them right. The vinedresser discusses some heroes individually and some in groups for the purpose of contrast or comparison, allotting praise and blame where
due, while correcting Homer. At times the criticisms are minor,
at times more significant. Perhaps the most important critique of
Homer from the perspective of the dialogue is Protesilaos's praise
of Palamedes over his rival Odysseus (*Her.* 33.1–34.7). Palamedes,
who is never mentioned by Homer, stands with Protesilaos and
Achilles as one of the most important heroes of the dialogue.

Framing this section are two short discussions explicitly on
Homer and his portrayal of the heroes (*Her.* 24.1–25.17; 43.1–
44.4). In general, Protesilaos has many positive things to say
about Homer's talents as an epic singer (*Her.* 24.1–25.9). Yet,
in addition to the common complaint that Homer portrays the
gods poorly (*Her.* 25.10), he also faults Homer for his treatment

of Helen (*Her.* 25.10–12) and Odysseus (*Her.* 25.13–17). Homer's
credibility as a source of the events at Troy is attacked on a number of fronts: not only did he live considerably later than the war,
but he also tinkered with the truth in order to enhance the poetic appeal of his composition (*Her.* 43.1–5). Furthermore, while
Homer collected stories from the various cities of the heroes, his
"inside source," not surprisingly, was Odysseus himself, conjured
from the dead. In return for telling all, Odysseus makes Homer
promise to compose a song about his wisdom and bravery and
to leave out any reference to his more virtuous rival Palamedes
(*Her.* 43.11–16). The homeland of Homer, another common sophistic *topos*, although known to Protesilaos, is not revealed, since
the Fates have decreed that Homer be "without a city" (*apolis*;
Her. 44.1–4).

The last major section of the dialogue is devoted to the hero
Achilles (*Her.* 44.5–57.17). As in the earlier section on Protesilaos,
the life, physical appearance, character, cult, and ongoing activity of Achilles are celebrated. Achilles excelled in warfare, musical
skill, and wisdom, and is portrayed as self-sufficient, suspicious
of possessions, and a devoted friend. Ambushed at the sanctuary of Thymbraion while negotiating his marriage to Polyxena,
he was mourned by all and entombed on the Trojan shore. The
vinedresser describes in detail the yearly offerings to Achilles
required of the Thessalians; the improper enactment of these rituals and their occasional neglect altogether by the Thessalians
incited Achilles' implacable wrath and ultimately brought about
the economic destruction of Thessaly (*Her.* 52.3–54.1). Achilles
now inhabits Leukê in the Pontus (the Black Sea); there he and
Helen dwell together, singing of Troy and their love for each
other and receiving offerings from sailors who anchor at the island (*Her.* 54.2–55.6). Achilles' vengeance continues unabated
even in this idyllic setting. The vinedresser relates two brief stories: Achilles' dismemberment of the last descendant of Priam
(*Her.* 56.1–10) and his bloody slaughter of Amazons who invaded Leukê (*Her.* 56.11–57.17). After these gory stories of heroic
vengeance, the dialogue abruptly ends, with a promise of further
stories the next day, if the winds are still unfavorable, and an ad-
monition to pour a libation to Protesilaos if the Phoenician should
set sail.

PHILOSTRATUS AND *ON HEROES* AS A SOPHISTIC WORK

Flavius Philostratus[2] was born into a prominent and wealthy family at Lemnos. Although the date of his birth remains conjectural, there is little reason to doubt that he spent his youth on Lemnos (*Life of Apollonius* 6.27). He then studied rhetoric with Proclus in Athens and may have studied in Ephesus or Smyrna as well. During the first decade of the third century c.e. he was an active sophist in Athens, at which time he held the important position of hoplite general; he thus moved among the cultural and political elite of Athens. He later practiced as a sophist in Rome and was introduced to the Severan court during the reign of Septimius Severus, probably between the middle of 203 and early 208. Philostratus's association with the court was as a member of the so-called circle of Julia Domna (*Life of Apollonius* 1.3).[3] Near the end of the second century, Julia Domna, wife of Septimius Severus and mother of Caracalla and Geta, began to gather around her intellectuals of varying interests. Certainly the empress was interested in rhetoric (*Life of Apollonius* 1.3; *Epistles* 73). Her coterie also included "geometricians and philosophers" (*Lives of the Sophists* 622), the former of which may be

---

[2] Decisive determination of the dialogue's author has been complicated by the disparity between a confusing entry in a Byzantine lexicon (A. Adler, ed., *Suidae Lexicon* [5 vols.; Leipzig: Teubner, 1928–1938], 4:734) and evidence internal to the writings attributed to the Philostrati. For recent discussions of the problem of the Philostrati and their relationship, see Jaap-Jan Flinterman, *Power*, Paideia *& Pythagoreanism: Greek Identity, Conceptions of the Relationship Between Philosophers and Monarchs and Political Ideas in Philostratus'* Life of Apollonius (Amsterdam: Gieben, 1995), 5–14. The author of *On Heroes* was most likely also the same Philostratus who authored the *Lives of the Sophists* and the *Life of Apollonius*. Friedrich Solmsen, "Some Works of Philostratus the Elder," *TAPA* 71 (1940): 556-72. Teresa Mantero, *Ricerche sull'Heroikos di Filostrato* (Genoa: University of Genoa, Istituto di Filologia Classica e Medioevale, 1966), 9 n. 4. Ludo de Lannoy, "Le problème des Philostrate (État de la question)," *ANRW* 34.3:2391. The following summary of Philostratus' career is indebted to the detailed investigations of Flinterman (*Power*, 15–28) and Graham Anderson (*Philostratus: Biography and Belles Lettres in the Third Century A.D.* [London: Croom Helm, 1986], ch. 1).

[3] For a careful evaluation of the circle, see G. W. Bowersock, *Greek Sophists in the Roman Empire* (Oxford: Clarendon, 1969), ch. 8.

a reference to astrologers or to Pythagorean/Platonic mathematicians.[4] Julia Domna's interest in Apollonius of Tyana led to her
commissioning his biography by Philostratus, although it was
completed only after her death. More important for the study
of *On Heroes* is Caracalla's imitation of Alexander the Great's
sacrifices at Achilles' tomb (214 C.E.; Dio Cassius *Roman History* 78.16.7). Philostratus probably traveled with the empress's
entourage until at least 217, the year of Caracalla's murder and his
mother's suicide. He may have then lived briefly in Tyre, but at
some point he returned to his career as a sophist in Athens, during which time he completed his two great works, the *Lives of the
Sophists* and the *Life of Apollonius*. According to the *Suda*, Philostratus died during the reign of Philip the Arab (ca. 244–249).

What exactly did a career as a sophist entail? Philostratus was part of a cultural phenomenon he termed the "Second
Sophistic."[5] In his day the designation "sophist," as Bowersock
observes, referred to "a virtuoso rhetor with a big public reputation."[6] Sophists were those skilled in forensic or public speaking
who seemed to have reached the pinnacle of rhetorical skill (Sextus Empiricus *Against the Professors* 2.18). Their reputation was
gained primarily through extemporaneous performances of their
rhetorical skills either to their students or in public; skilled in
improvisation (requiring tremendous versatility) and master of
rhetorical exercises and techniques, the sophist spoke in an or-
nate style and with a vigorous delivery. As with sophists of the
past, appearance was counted more highly than historical accuracy. Anderson describes the sophists as almost media hounds,
whose public pronouncements caused more serious intellectuals
to cringe.[7]

In addition to delivering public speeches and educating the
young, sophists participated in religious festivals and acted as ad-
visors to cities; the people of Lemnos honored Philostratus by
erecting a statue of him in Olympia, perhaps for the delivery of

---

[4] Astrologers: Karl Münscher, "Die Philostrati," *Philologus* suppl. 10/4
(1907): 477; philosophical mathematicians: Flinterman, *Power*, 23.

[5] For a discussion of Philostratus's construction of the Second Sophistic
and its descent from Gorgias, see Anderson, *Philostratus*, 11–12.

[6] Bowersock, *Greek Sophists*, 13.

[7] Anderson, *Philostratus*, 9–10.

speeches there.[8] Moreover, like Philostratus, most sophists came from wealthy families, and their reputation was also enhanced by holding public offices and acting as benefactors of their cities.[9]

The ethos of the Second Sophistic centered on the celebration and preservation of Greek culture in the context of a multicultural empire. The sophists about whom Philostratus wrote came from Greece, Asia Minor, Syria, and Egypt, but their culture and language were Hellenic. In the strict requirement that a sophist speak with perfect Attic diction and in the choice of historical themes treated, the Second Sophistic looked to the past to justify the prominence of the Greek educated elite in the Roman world and to maintain Greek identity through the promotion of *paideia*, which Flintermann defines as the "absolute familiarity with literary culture."[10] This glorification of things Greek should not be seen as necessitating a subversive attitude toward the Roman empire; Greek identity was a cultural concept, not a political one. Many sophists were connected with the imperial court or held prominent positions, such as the *ab epistulis* or the chair of rhetoric in Athens, as the result of imperial patronage; their social status, economic success, and freedom to express their cultural identity depended upon the multicultural ethos of the empire.

On Heroes is one of many dialogues composed during the Roman imperial period and is indebted to Plato and the development of the genre of the dialogue by writers such as Dio Chrysostom, Plutarch, Lucian, and Athenaeus. There seems little doubt that Plato's *Phaedrus*, a favorite among rhetoricians and sophists, influenced *On Heroes*. Reminiscences of the *Phaedrus*'s setting have often been noted, for example, in the combination of pastoral scenery and a discussion which is often philosophical.[11] There is also, as in Plato's dialogues, belief in the continued existence of human *psukhê* ("soul"), especially those of the heroes.[12] The interaction of the characters is also reminiscent of Plato's dialogues: as the mouthpiece of Protesilaos the vinedresser is the main source of information and insight (like Socrates), with

---

[8] Flinterman, *Power*, 18–19.

[9] Bowersock, *Greek Sophists*, ch. 2.

[10] Flinterman, *Power*, 233.

[11] Anderson, *Philostratus*, 250.

[12] This is a belief shared with Pythagoreanism. See Solmsen, "Some Works," 565–69.

the Phoenician contributing little except to ask leading questions or to exclaim at the beauty of the garden, the wisdom of the vinedresser, or the power of the heroes (not unlike many of Socrates' interlocutors). Influences of sophistic uses of the dialogue are also evident: in Lucian's *Charon* the discussion of the tombs of Achilles and Ajax takes place looking over the same waters, and in Dio's *Euboikos* a shipwrecked writer converses with a self-sufficient rustic.[13] *On Heroes* cannot be classified, however, simply as a dialogue, since it displays certain novelistic techniques and thematic interests: presenting fictional characters in a credible setting, describing the physical beauty of the characters, and the inclusion of erotic episodes.[14] There are also characteristic sophistic exercises: correction of Homer, the description of statues, the elaboration of speeches and chreia, and "the pictorial creation of vivid and memorable scenes."[15] Ultimately this text defies classification into a single genre, but should be seen as drawing upon various aspects of both popular and more sophisticated literature.

Many aspects of *On Heroes* reveal sophistic themes and concerns. First of all, the vinedresser himself is presented as a sophist, whose education, eloquence, and insight are immediately evident to the Phoenician (*Her.* 4.4–10). Early in the dialogue the Phoenician exclaims that the vinedresser's speeches "will fill the horn of Amaltheia" (*Her.* 7.7), an image that Philostratus uses elsewhere to describe the rhetorical skill of Dio Chrysostom (*Lives of the Sophists* 1.7). Similarly, Palamedes, whom Protesilaos rescues from obscurity (on Homer's silence on Palamedes, see below), is also portrayed as a sophist. Protesilaos focuses on his contributions to human culture and technology.[16] He is the most clever of all human beings, the inventor of every skill and science (*Her.* 33.1, 14–18). He is even called "sophist" (*sophistês*), albeit pejoratively by Odysseus in *Her.* 33.25, and elsewhere Philostratus affirms that Palamedes is the patron of the sophists (*Life of Apollonius* 3.13). Palamedes is especially good at

[13] Ewen Bowie, "Philostratus: Writer of Fiction," in *Greek Fiction: The Greek Novel in Context* (ed. J. R. Morgan and Richard Stoneman; New York: Routledge, 1994), 184; Anderson, *Philostratus*, 241–42.

[14] Bowie, "Philostratus," 185–86.

[15] Anderson, *Philostratus*, 241, 243; Bowie, "Philostratus," 186–87.

[16] Solmsen, "Some Works," 563; Mantero, *Ricerche*, 120–42; Anderson, *Philostratus*, 246.

FLAVIUS PHILOSTRATUS: *ON HEROES*

the sophistic repartee (*Her.* 33.5–12, 44–46),[17] and sophistic arrogance is not unknown to him either: he tells the centaur Kheirôn that he does not want to learn medicine, since it has already been discovered (*Her.* 33.2), and having been slandered by Odysseus and now being stoned by the Achaeans, he cries out, "I have pity on you, Truth, for you have perished before me" and, as Protesilaos relates, "he held out his head to the stones as though knowing that Justice would be in his favor" (*Her.* 33.37; cf. *Life of Apollonius* 4.13, 16).

We have already noted the similarity of the setting of *On Heroes* to other sophistic works. In addition, much attention is given to the heroes' physical appearance; there are elaborate descriptions of characters and fantastically painted scenes; and composed speeches are placed in the mouths of the heroes. All these reveal sophistic education and literary panache. Yet one of the central and most characteristic sophistic endeavors was the correction of Homer and his poems. Homeric criticism can be said to have its roots in the transmission of the Homeric poems, and particularly in the competition of local traditions and the emergence of the *Iliad* and *Odyssey* as panhellenic poetic performances. In the philosophical tradition, Plato's dialogues, especially the *Republic* and *Ion*, reveal Homer as the "educator of Hellas" (*Republic* 606e), although Socrates (or Plato) is very critical of Homer's influence on his contemporaries' minds. The questions raised about Homer from the fifth to the second centuries B.C.E. are more specifically related to the gradual process of the standardization of the Homeric text during that time.[18] By the time of the Roman empire, correction or emendation of Homer became a kind of "literary sport,"[19] particularly in matters of myth and ritual. As we have seen, Philostratus does not always follow Homeric tradition in treating the heroes of the Trojan War. Following a well-established *topos*, Philostratus constructed *On Heroes* around a new and more trustworthy informant about the heroes. Lucian had corrected details of Homer's text through the help of Euphorbus, the first to wound Patroklos in

[17] Other heroes also display this sophistic talent (e.g., Achilles in *Her.* 48.20–22).
[18] For a discussion of the evolution of Homeric text, see Gregory Nagy, *Homeric Questions* (Austin: University of Texas Press, 1996), 42–43, 65–112.
[19] Friedrich Solmsen, "Philostratos," PW 20.1 (1941): col. 156.

the *Iliad* (see *The Dream, or The Cock* 17), and through the help
of Homer himself via Charon (see *Charon* 7), while Dio cited
a different kind of authoritative evidence when appealing to inscriptions on temple columns translated by an old Egyptian priest
in Onuphis (*Troikos* 38; cf. Plato *Timaeus* 21d–24a). In true
sophistic fashion, logical and chronological problems within the
text of Homer are also raised (e.g., *Her.* 23.5–6; 25.10–13), ra-
tionalistic explanations are offered in place of the fantastic (e.g.,
Her. 48.11–13; 50.1–3; 51.7–11), and the traditional question of
Homer's birthplace is discussed, though not resolved (*Her.* 44.1–
4). Many of these "supplements" to Homer have a foundation
in literary tradition, e.g., Stesichorus and Herodotus both report
that Helen never went to Troy. Others seem to stem from local traditions, e.g., the claim that Philoktêtês was cured by the
Lemnian soil (*Her.* 28.5) may be a local Lemnian tradition which
Philostratus learned during his own youth on Lemnos.[20]

PROTESILAOS: ORIGINS AND TRAJECTORIES OF HIS
STORY IN LITERATURE, ART, AND CULT

It has been suggested that Protesilaos may have originally been
a nature divinity, closely identified with Demeter and perhaps
Dionysos.[21] Vestiges of these connections may remain in our text
in the vinedresser's acknowledgment of Demeter's and Dionysos's ownership of the land, his cultivation of fruits and nuts at the
sanctuary, the unusual behavior of the trees that surround Protesilaos's tomb, and the Bacchic frenzy that brings insight to dead
souls (*Her.* 1.5; 2.3–4; 9.1–3; 7.3). Rather than viewing this relationship genealogically, it is better to understand it in terms of the

[20] A descendant of Philostratus was later priest of Hephaistos there
(*IG* 12.8.27). Philostratus's familiarity with Lemnian rituals also informs his
description of the yearly purification of Lemnos (*Her.* 53.5–7); see Walter Burkert, "Jason, Hypsipyle, and New Fire at Lemnos: A Study in Myth and Ritual,"
CQ n.s. 20 (1970): 1–16. See also the discussion of Philostratus's Lemnian connections in de Lannoy, "Le problème des Philostrate," 2382–86.
[21] Deborah Boedeker, "Protesilaos and the End of Herodotus' *Histories*," *Classical Antiquity* 7/1 (1988): 37–40. More hesitantly, Walter Burkert,
Homo Necans: The Anthropology of Ancient Greek Sacrificial Ritual and Myth
(Berkeley: University of California Press, 1983), 245–47.

symbiosis between a hero and a god, whereby in cult they typically share many characteristics.

Protesilaos the hero hails from Phulakê, within Phthia of
Thessaly.   In the *Iliad* he is called "warlike," "valiant," and
"noble" (*Il.* 2.695–710).   Any critic of Homer might have justly
inquired how Protesilaos could have proved himself in this fashion considering that "a Dardanian man had killed him as he
leapt from his ship, far the first of all the Achaians" (*Il.* 2.701–
702 [Lattimore]).   Some ancient writers avoided this problem by
only affirming Homer's words that Protesilaos was the first of the
Greeks to land and the first to be killed, without any reference to
the exact timing of his death.   In fact, only Homer (and Protesilaos himself through the vinedresser; *Her.* 12.1–4) claims that
he was killed in midstep, without even engaging the enemy.   One
version explicitly states that before he died he slew many Trojans
(Apollodorus *Epitome* 3.30), and a Corinthian pyx depicts Protesilaos among the Greek contingent as they approach the Trojan
forces.[22]   The tale of the Mysian conflict (*Her.* 23.2–30), in which
Protesilaos gained his reputation as a valiant warrior, is another
solution to this Homeric puzzle.   Other elaborations upon Homer's text center on the name of Protesilaos's slayer: Hektor is
by far the most common one named (*Cypria*; Ovid *Metamorphoses* 12.66–68; Apollodorus *Epitome* 3.30; Sophocles frg. 497;
Lucian *Dialogues of the Dead* 28 [23]; Quintus of Smyrna *Fall of
Troy* 1.816–817).

Few images of Protesilaos are extant.   In addition to appearing on coins from Skionê in the fifth and fourth centuries
B.C.E.,[23] his image is shown on the coinage of Thessaly (early
third century B.C.E.) and Elaious (in the reign of Commodus, late

---

[22] 575–550 B.C.E.; Hans Christoph Ackermann and Jean-Robert Gisler,
eds. *Lexicon Iconographicum Mythologiae Classicae* (*LIMC*) (8 vols.; Zurich:
Artemis, 1981-1997), s.v. Protesilaos, no. 15.

[23] *LIMC*, s.v. Protesilaos, nos. 4–6; Cornelius C. Vermeule, "Protesilaos: First to Fall at Troy and Hero in Northern Greece and Beyond," in *Flo-
rilegium Numismaticum: Studia in Honorem U. Westermark Edita* (Stockholm:
Svenska Numismatiska Föreningen, 1992), 342–43, fig. 3. Not surprisingly, the
coins from Skionê do not portray any images that would be reminiscent of the
story of his death. According to Konon (133a3; Felix Jacoby, *Die Fragmente der
griechischen Historiker* [FGrHist] [Berlin: Weidmann, 1923–1958] 26 F 1, 13),
Protesilaos did not die in Troy at all, but founded Skionê on his return from the
war.

second century C.E.). These coins depict him in the act of dis-
embarking or standing on the prow of a ship.[24] Similar poses are
depicted on a late geometric vase,[25] an early classical intaglio,[26]
and a Roman copy of a Greek bronze.[27] A late fourth-century
B.C.E. relief, found in Sigeion and belonging to an Attic treaty inscription, possibly depicts Protesilaos in the company of Athena
and another heroic figure.[28]

Only two sanctuaries dedicated to Protesilaos are attested.
At the sanctuary in Phulakê athletic contests were held in his
honor (*Her.* 16.5; Pindar *Isthmian* 1.30, 58-59 and scholia). Better known is the sanctuary at Elaious on the Chersonesus, which
provides the setting for *On Heroes* (Herodotus *Hist.* 7.33.1; 9.116–
120; Thucydides *Peloponnesian War* 8.102.3; Strabo *Geography*
13.1.31; 7.frg. 51). According to Pausanias, the whole of Elaious
was dedicated to Protesilaos, and there he received divine honors (*Description of Greece* 1.34.2).[29] Although the wealth of the
sanctuary's treasury is presupposed by the story of its plunder-
ing by Artayktes (Herodotus *Hist.* 7.33.1; 9.116–120), according
to the vinedresser the foundations of the sanctuary are the only
remaining indications of its former greatness. The cult statue is
badly worn (disfigured?) and stands apart from its original base

[24] *LIMC*, s.v. Protesilaos, nos. 10–11. The coin from Elaious (no. 11) is
reproduced at the beginning of this volume (p. vi). Jean Babelon, "Protésilas
à Scioné," *Revue Numismatique* 5th ser. 3 (1951): 1–11; Louis Robert, *Études
de numismatique Grecque* (Paris: Collège de France, 1951). Vermeule identifies
the hero depicted on the reverse of an early third-century C.E. bronze coin from
Philippopolis in Thrace as Protesilaos, but we find this identification question-
able; see Vermeule, "Protesilaos," 341–42, figs. 1 and 2.

[25] *LIMC*, s.v. Protesilaos, no. 12.

[26] 470–460 B.C.E.; Vermeule, "Protesilaos," 342–44, fig. 4.

[27] *LIMC*, s.v. Protesilaos, no. 14; see below. Unfortunately we know
nothing about the pose of the bronze Protesilaos by Diomenes (early fourth century B.C.E.; see Pliny *Natural History* 34.76; cf. 34.50).

[28] See L. Budde and R. V. Nicholls, *A Catalogue of the Greek and Roman
Sculpture in the Fitzwilliam Museum Cambridge* (Cambridge: Cambridge University Press, 1964), 11–12, no. 27, plate 5; Vermeule, "Protesilaos," 344.

[29] Artayktes calls Protesilaos *theos* (Herodotus *Hist.* 9.120.3); Herodotus
is here employing the terminology of hero cult, whereby a hero becomes *theos*
when he or she is immortalized after death. The description of Protesilaos's
cult in *On Heroes* also suggests that he received divine honors; see Mantero,
Ricerche, 104–6, 115.

(*Her.* 9.5–6).[30] Surrounding the tomb were remarkable trees that
by their unusual life cycle imitated Protesilaos's fate (*Her.* 9.1–
3; cf. Pliny *Natural History* 16.238; Quintus of Smyrna *Fall of
Troy* 7.408–411). The oracle of Protesilaos to which Philostratus
refers is mentioned also by Lucian (*Parliament of the Gods* 12; see
also Aelius Aristides *Orations* 3.365).[31]

The tales of Protesilaos fall into two categories, both of
which center on Protesilaos's return from the dead.[32] In fact,
Protesilaos's resurrection was so well known in the ancient world
that Christian writers were compelled to downplay its duration
and even its possibility in order to highlight the uniqueness of Jesus' resurrection (Origen *Against Celsus* 2.55–56; Minucius Felix
Octavius 11). Homer mentions the wailing of Protesilaos's wife[33]
at his departure for war (*Il.* 2.700), and her grief was the subject
of Euripides' tragedy *Protesilaos*. In later literature Protesilaos returns from Hades for a brief reunion with Laodameia. Lucian
depicts Protesilaos as the devoted lover who entreats Hades to
allow him to return to his wife (*Dialogues of the Dead* 28 [23]).
More common, however, is the celebration of Laodameia's devotion to Protesilaos: the elements of the tales vary, with Laodameia
molding an image of Protesilaos and "consorting" with it, praying

[30] The vinedresser indicates certain features of the statue: it depicts
Protesilaos with a "perfect" nose, wearing a purple Thessalian cloak, and
standing on the prow of a ship (*Her.* 9.6; 10.3–5). Based in part on this description, Gisela Richter identifies a marble Roman copy of a Greek bronze,
reproduced at the beginning of this volume (p. v), as Protesilaos; see her
"A Statue of Protesilaos in the Metropolitan Museum," *Metropolitan Museum
Studies* 1 (1928–1929): 187–200; see also José Dörig, "Deinoménès," *Antike
Kunst* 37 (1994): 67–80. For alternative identifications, see *LIMC*, s.v. Protesilaos, no. 14.

[31] Excavation of the presumed tomb of Protesilaos has not yielded any
artifacts helpful for reconstructing the cult in the Greek or Roman periods;
see R. Demangel, *Le Tumulus dit de Protésilas* (Fouilles du corps d'occupation
français de Constantinople 1; Paris: De Boccard, 1926).

[32] On the motif of apparent death and resurrection in literature beginning with the Neronian period (with special emphasis on Protesilaos), see G. W.
Bowersock, *Fiction as History: Nero to Julian* (Berkeley: University of California Press, 1994), 99–119.

[33] Even though Homer leaves Protesilaos's wife unnamed, she is identified in the *Cypria* (cited in Pausanias *Description of Greece* 4.2.7) as Polydorê;
the more common name given is Laodameia.

for and achieving his restoration from Hades, and either dying in his arms or by self-immolation (Catullus 68; Apollodorus *Epitome* 3.30; Hyginus *Fabulae* 103–104; Servius *Commentary on Virgil's Aeneid* 6.447; Ovid *Heroides* 13.153–157). The story of Protesilaos and Laodameia's reunion was a common iconographic theme for sarcophagi in the Roman period.[34]

Another persona of Protesilaos is Protesilaos the *revenant*, the frightening ghost who brings vengeance and terror. Protesilaos acts as *revenant* in Herodotus's story of Artayktes, which strategically appears as the final episode of the *Histories* (9.116–120).[35] Not only has the Persian governor offended Protesilaos personally by looting his sanctuary and having sex within its boundaries, but Protesilaos also takes revenge upon him as a representative of Xerxes, the Asian invader, for all the Persian offenses against the Greeks. The image of the *revenant* is illumined by the resurrection of dried fish, which leap from the fiery grill as a sign of Protesilaos's resurrection and coming vengeance.[36] This story must have been well known, since Protesilaos the avenger of Greeks against non-Greeks also appears as a commonplace in Chariton's novel (*Callirhoe* 5.10). Protesilaos was also recognized as the hero to whom one should sacrifice before going to war with non-Greeks. According to Arrian's *Anabasis*, after Alexander arrived at Elaious he sacrificed to Protesilaos with the hope that he would be luckier during his time in Asia (1.11.5). No doubt Protesilaos was invoked to aid Alexander during his campaigns.[37]

[34] *LIMC*, s.v. Protesilaos, nos. 21–22, 26–27. See also scenes from the same story in other media, nos. 20, 24–25, 28.

[35] On the importance of this passage for understanding Herodotus's aims, see Boedeker, "Protesilaos," 30–48; see also the excellent discussion by Gregory Nagy, "The Sign of Protesilaos," *MHTIΣ: Revue d'anthropologie du monde grec ancien* 2/2 (1987): 207–13; reworked in Gregory Nagy, *Pindar's Homer: The Lyric Possession of an Epic Past* (Baltimore: Johns Hopkins University Press, 1990), 268–73.

[36] See *Her.* 9.5 and the accompanying note.

[37] Alexander is said to have imitated Protesilaos by being the first to disembark in Asia (Arrian *Anabasis* 1.11.7).

THE TWO GREAT HEROES: PROTESILAOS AND ACHILLES

No doubt Homeric criticism and the retelling of the heroes' stories are prominent themes in *On Heroes*; their importance is emphasized by their central placement in the text (sections III–V in the Table of Contents). An important and often overlooked emphasis of the dialogue, however, is revealed by the carefully designed structure of the text. Framing these central sections are two lengthy discussions of Protesilaos and Achilles (sections II and VI in the Table of Contents), an arrangement which reveals the complementarity of these two great heroes of the dialogue. At first one might think that no two heroes could be more dissimilar. Achilles, after all, saved the Achaeans from utter defeat, and the great theme of Homer's *Iliad* is Achilles' wrath, whereas Protesilaos died before the conclusion of even the first battle and so receives barely a mention by Homer. Nevertheless, numerous parallels and associations between the two heroes can be found both within Homer and in later literary sources.[38]

First of all, both heroes hail from Phthia in Thessaly (Strabo *Geography* 9.5.14), and their friendship is hinted at in a number of ways: according to Homer, it is only when the Trojans have laid hold of Protesilaos's ships and threatened to set them on fire that Achilles agrees to allow Patroklos to enter the battle (*Il.* 15.704–725; more explicitly in Apollodorus *Epitome* 4.6), and later versions of that first engagement at Troy imply that Achilles avenged Protesilaos's death by slaying the hero Kyknos, not unlike Achilles' revenge upon Hektor for the death of Patroklos (*Cypria*; Ovid *Metamorphoses* 12.71–145; Apollodorus *Epitome* 3.31). Their respective deaths, though divided by the bulk of the war, share certain similarities. Homer describes Protesilaos as leaving behind "a house half-built" (*Il.* 2.701; see note on *Her.* 12.3), that is, as one who died without fully experiencing adult life, marriage, and children. Achilles, although fated to die later in the conflict, is similarly lamented as one cut off in the

---

[38] Drawing primarily on other sources, Boedeker ("Protesilaos," 36) discusses many parallels between Achilles and Protesilaos; cf. Anderson, *Philostratus*, 247.

bloom of youth (*Il.* 9.410–416) and as the eternal bridegroom.[39] According to later authors, an oracle is said to have indicated that the first to land at Troy would be the first to die, and that both Protesilaos and Achilles were warned (Protesilaos by Laodameia; Achilles by Thetis) not to let their valor eclipse their better judgment (Apollodorus *Epitome* 3.29–30; Ovid *Heroides* 13.93–102). Protesilaos and Achilles are two of the few major Achaean heroes to die at Troy, and their tombs face each other across the Hellespont (*Her.* 51.12–13). Yet for neither hero was death the end of their amorous affairs: Protesilaos was well known for his return from Hades to be reunited with Laodameia (see above), while Achilles enjoyed a posthumous affair with Helen (*Her.* 54.2–55.6; Pausanias *Description of Greece* 3.19.11–13).

Both the structure and the specific details of *On Heroes* emphasize the parallel lives, deaths, cults, and concerns of Achilles and Protesilaos. According to Protesilaos, the two heroes were well matched in their physical prowess (*Her.* 13.3–4); at the battle of Mysia they fought side by side, with Protesilaos in fact outdoing Achilles (*Her.* 23.16, 24–25). Each hero's death is associated with his wedding: Protesilaos confirms Homer's statement that his house was "half-built" and attests that Achilles died while negotiating his marriage to Polyxena at Thymbraion (*Her.* 12.3; 51.1); their spouses were similarly devoted to the point of self-sacrifice, choosing death over separation from their lovers (*Her.* 2.10–11; 51.2–6). Likewise each hero is reunited on an ongoing basis with his lover (*Her.* 11.1; 54.2–55.6), although Achilles' affections have turned from Polyxena to Helen. The cults of both heroes have suffered neglect, and each has exacted vengeance upon those from whom honor was due (*Her.* 4.2; 9.5–7; 16.4; 52.3–54.1).

By their valor in war, the brevity and tragedy of their lives, and their ongoing existence after death Protesilaos and Achilles are typical Greek heroes. Yet a more particular characteristic of the two heroes emerges from this text: Protesilaos and Achilles are watchful defenders of all that is Greek from all that is not. Standing on the Hellespont, the symbolic division between Europe and

---

[39] See Gregory Nagy, *The Best of the Achaeans: Concepts of the Hero in Archaic Greek Poetry* (2d rev. ed.; Baltimore: Johns Hopkins University Press, 1999), 174–84.

Asia, these two heroes guard the Greeks from barbarian invaders. Protesilaos avenges himself on the former owner of his sanctuary, one tellingly named Xeinis ("stranger, foreigner"; *Her.* 4.2); likewise the adulterer, whose presence at the sanctuary offended Protesilaos, dies from a dog-bite (*Her.* 16.3–4). Protesilaos, moreover, comes to life again to exact vengeance upon Artayktes, the Persian governor who plundered and desecrated Protesilaos's sanctuary (see *Her.* 9.5; Herodotus *Hist.* 7.33.1; 9.116–120). Achilles is presented in the same fashion in *On Heroes*, which ends with two such tales of heroic vengeance. The first tale brings to a close Achilles' vengeance upon the house of Priam: in a fury that seems at odds with Achilles' otherwise idyllic existence on Leukê, he dismembers the Trojan maiden as her wails echo from the shore (*Her.* 56.1–10). The even more bloody destruction of the Amazons, who are explicitly identified as new enemies of Achilles (i.e., they were not at Troy according to Protesilaos), points again to Achilles as protector of the Greeks from the barbarians (*Her.* 56.11–57.17).

One result of this careful paralleling of Protesilaos and Achilles is the explicit elevation of Protesilaos's heroic status, apparent in the *Iliad*'s compressed version of his death, through his close association with Achilles. More significant is the way in which the similarities of the heroes allow for a more precise definition of Protesilaos's mythic importance in this text. Certainly he is a devoted lover and a bringer of fertility to the land, but these themes receive relatively little attention in the text. Especially in light of the ending of the dialogue with the two stories of Achilles' vengeance, greater emphasis is laid on Protesilaos the *revenant*. Strategically poised at the Hellespont, Protesilaos maintains the boundary between Asia and Europe by defending Greek civilization from barbarian threats. More importantly, however, Protesilaos's vengeance against the hubris of the outsiders or foreigners in this narrative serves as a warning to Philostratus's own audience against adopting similar behavior.

ON CRITIQUING HEROIC TRADITIONS

A central feature of *On Heroes* is the characterization of the hero Protesilaos as both a reader and a critic of Homer. Although

Protesilaos was the first Hellenic hero to die at Troy, his continued existence, "cleansed of the body," permits him to observe "the
affairs of mortals" and thus to know what happened at Troy and
thereafter (*Her.* 7.3). The hero is, moreover, among those who
"critically examine" (*dioraô*) the poems of Homer (*Her.* 7.4); he
is able to set his own definitive version of the events against what
Homer reports and to correct the Homeric tradition. Through
this narrative device of the hero who knows the truth, Philostratus engages in the practice of Homeric criticism which, as we have
seen, is a standard sophistic endeavor, rooted in earlier poetic tradition.

It is important, however, not to dismiss the critical strategies of *On Heroes* as simply another example of sophistic skill.
Rather, by looking at the specific ways in which the Homeric poems are critiqued, we gain insight into both the purposes of the
dialogue and its attitudes toward texts, practices, and experience
as authoritative. It is thus necessary to inquire how the dialogue
defines the sources of what is "true," as well as the content of that
truth. What does getting the story right entail and what are the
consequences of doing so? By attending to the dynamics of how
authority is constituted in this text we are able to locate the dialogue in relation to the poetics of the Homeric tradition. From
a perspective of the history of religions, it also becomes possible
to compare the dialogue's stance toward the "canon" of Homer
and variant traditions with the development of canonical texts in
cognate environments, for example, in ancient Christianity. In
particular, the relation between story and cultic practice displayed
in this text, with its concern for telling the right story and doing
the proper ritual actions, may help in understanding the formation of religious identity in the early third century.

Throughout the dialogue, the hero Protesilaos is treated as
a source of knowledge and instruction. He not only instructs the
vinedresser about gardening and farming techniques (*Her.* 4.9–
10), but also shares in the vinedresser's reflective, philosophical
lifestyle (*Her.* 2.6). He is said to "excel in wisdom," and his sanctuary to be fruitful in "divine and pure wisdom," as well as in
grapes and olives (*Her.* 4.10–11). The vinedresser's contemporaries treat Protesilaos's sanctuary as an oracle, going there to
consult the hero about such matters as the disposition of giants'
bones (*Her.* 8.9). Athletes visit the sanctuary regularly to receive

oracular advice about how to succeed in their upcoming contests (*Her.* 14.4–15.10). The vinedresser sometimes appears as a mediator of the oracle, relaying information from Protesilaos to the inquirer, and he exercises this mediating role in the dialogue as he reports what Protesilaos has told him, but says little on his own authority. The visiting Phoenician is permitted to consult his host Protesilaos through the medium of the vinedresser (*Her.* 58.1–3). The vinedresser has obtained this status by his choice of the simple, agricultural life devoid of economic interchange, a choice based on his interpretation of Protesilaos's enigmatic advice to him upon his return from the city, "Change your dress" (*Her.* 4.8). Receiving knowledge from Protesilaos is possible for the vinedresser because of his lifestyle and his devotion to the hero. Moreover, if the vinedresser did not report correctly what Protesilaos told him, he would dishonor the hero, especially because this hero values truth as "the mother of virtue" (*Her.* 7.8). Thus telling the truth and accurately conveying knowledge from the hero gain religious value and are equated with giving proper honor to the hero.

The vinedresser obtains his information through direct encounter with Protesilaos who appears regularly in bodily form and talks with the vinedresser. The hero has come to life again (*anabioô*), although he refuses to disclose how this has happened (*Her.* 2.9–10; 58.2). The vinedresser has no need of a cult statue, because he spends time with the hero and sees him. Such immediate engagement with the hero contrasts with other sources of similarly authoritative knowledge, such as dreams, visions, oracular utterances, ancient histories, and the interpretation of sacred texts. The word of the hero who has returned to life and speaks to his worshippers thus has ultimate truth value in the dialogue. This revealed knowledge functions here as the final authority.

In addition, however, other experiences are proffered as the basis for belief or as authorities upon which to critique Homer. Philostratus invokes folk beliefs as a basis for authority; for example, there are others besides the vinedresser who have seen the heroes returned to life as phantoms, including the shepherds in the plain of Troy who hear the clattering of the warriors and see their figures covered with dust or blood (*Her.* 18.1–2). Both Ajax and Hektor are mentioned as appearing in vengeance to those who insult them (*Her.* 18.3–19.7). The case of Ajax is instructive since a Trojan shepherd insults him with the words of Homer, "Ajax stood firm no longer" (*Il.* 15.727); in reply Ajax shouts from the tomb that he did stand firm. Here the *revenant* himself corrects the account of Homer, just as Protesilaos does. Devout worshippers of the heroes also receive appearances, as in the case of the farmer devoted to Palamedes and the girl who falls in love with Antilokhos (*Her.* 21.1–22.4). The vinedresser hears about the experiences of the inhabitants of the Troad because they are his nearest neighbors (*Her.* 22.4). Likewise the merchants who sail the Black Sea bring back stories from Achilles' sanctuary on Leukê (*Her.* 56.1–4).

Certain experiences are available to all who care to look. In this regard, we may note the frequent references to cult statues of various heroes. Philostratus introduces these into the dialogue through the technique of *ekphrasis*, by which a visual representation is described in such detail as to make it appear before the eyes of the audience. In many cases, the vinedresser supplements discussion of a hero with Protesilaos's description of the cult statue (*agalma*); the depiction of Nestor is a good example (*Her.* 26.13). Even when a statue is not mentioned, as in the case of Palamedes, the discussion may include a similarly detailed *ekphrasis* of the hero (*Her.* 33.39–41). The heroes are thus available, through the techniques of verbal art, for the audience to see. Similarly, they may view the bones of the giants, about which the vinedresser tells the Phoenician in the process of convincing him that the marvels of myth really happened. Not only are there many reports from those who have seen the bones, but the Phoenician may go and see for himself (*Her.* 8.3–13). Common to reports about the bones and the appearance of the heroes is an appeal to the authority of the eyewitness and experiential knowledge. Just as the vinedresser sees and experiences the hero Protesilaos and thus receives wisdom and truth, so others see phenomena and have experiences that are not to be doubted. The audience is thus encouraged to attend to what is before their eyes.

What Protesilaos knows is similarly grounded in experience, albeit partially in the experience of a soul (*psukhê*) free from the body and its diseases (*Her.* 7.3). He can, however, relate events in the battle with the Mysians—a tale not told in Homer—because he was there: this conflict took place before his death in Troy (*Her.* 23.7–30). Similarly he reports what Achilles and Helen do on Leukê because he frequently visits them there, talks with Achilles, and sees for himself. Indeed, according to the vine-dresser, Protesilaos visited Achilles as recently as four years ago and tried to persuade him to temper his wrath against the Thessalians (*Her.* 53.19).

The discussion of Homer in *On Heroes* is considerable and not confined to correction and emendation of Homer's account. The central section of the dialogue, which is concerned with the Hellenic and Trojan heroes, is framed by two expositions of Protesilaos's opinions about Homer and his poetic technique (*Her.* 24.1–25.17; 43.1–44.4). Despite the corrections of Homer's account, Protesilaos has only the highest praise for Homer's skill. Homer is the preeminent poet, outdoing Hesiod and all the other poets, expert in the widest range of subjects, and working with divine assistance (*Her.* 25.2–5). Sensitive to the poetic conventions which seek divine inspiration for the singing of epic and lyric poetry, the dialogue makes it clear that although Homer's poems seem divine, they were not composed by Apollo or the Muses, but by a mortal with the aid of a god (*Her.* 43.3–6). The dialogue wrestles with the questions of when and where Homer lived, remaining in the end equivocal on these matters (*Her.* 44.1–4). Clearly this text utilizes Homer as the culture hero of poetry, attributing to him the poems of the Trojan War and excellence in song.

What the dialogue regards as the "poems of Homer" appears to encompass the *Iliad* and *Odyssey*, although these names are not used. Philostratus, however, does not present an account of the Trojan War, but of its heroes and of various episodes of their time at Troy and elsewhere. The Phoenician and Protesilaos both "read" (*anagi[g]nôskô*; *Her.* 6.3; 7.4) the verses of Homer, but Homer is never said to "write" his poems; rather he regularly "sings" (*aeidô*). It is clear that Protesilaos is presented as primarily concerned with the poems of Homer (i.e., the *Iliad* and the *Odyssey*) and critiquing them, and that matters contained in the so-called Epic Cycle are not included under the umbrella of Homer's poems. Nevertheless, *On Heroes* contains numerous references to what "many other poets" sing (*Her.* 8.16; 11.2; 23.4, 10; 26.16; 33.4; 39.4; 51.2; 56.11), and frequently the stories in question are found in the Epic Cycle. Defining the relationship of *On Heroes* and its stories to these

epics precisely is difficult due to our fragmentary knowledge of
the specific details of many of the stories. For example, the
death of Odysseus at the hands of his son by Circe is found in
the *Telegonia*, but, since Proclus's summary does not specify the
manner of his death, it is not clear whether Protesilaos is expressing agreement with the *Telegonia* or is drawing upon a variant
tradition that also appears in Apollodorus (see *Her.* 25.15; *Epitome* 7.36–37). What is clear, however, is that their stories are
subject to the same kind of critique as the *Iliad* and the *Odyssey*.
At times Protesilaos expresses disagreement with some details
of an epic's story, while agreeing with its general truth. Two
examples of this will suffice: Protesilaos discusses at length the
sack of Mysia, a story found in the *Cypria*, but disagrees with
its claim that the Achaeans mistook Mysia for Troy (*Her.* 23.5–
8). The retelling of the slaying of Antilokhos proceeds similarly:
according to the hero, the *Aithiopis* tells this story rightly, except for the mistaken identification of this Memnôn as the son of
Eos (*Her.* 26.16). Protesilaos also can completely repudiate a tale
from the Epic Cycle (the Amazon presence in Troy is flatly denied in contrast to the *Aithiopis*; *Her.* 56.11; likewise, the story
of Odysseus's feigned madness found in the *Cypria*; *Her.* 33.4),
as well as introduce a story "unknown to Homer and all poets" (*Her.* 23.1). Of particular interest and worthy of further
investigation is Protesilaos's emphasis on the tales of Palamedes
(*Her.* 21.2–8; 33.1–34.7; 43.11–16) and Philoktêtês (*Her.* 28.1–14),
both of whom figure prominently in the *Cypria* and the *Little Iliad*.

The dialogue also shows particular awareness of the tradition of the contest between Homer and Hesiod (*Her.* 25.2–7; 43.7–
8), a contest that the vinedresser heard reenacted more recently
at Protesilaos's sanctuary by two visiting poets (*Her.* 43.9–11).
The comparison with Hesiod is not surprising, not only because
of Hesiod's stature in antiquity, but also because there are clear
affinities between the vinedresser's way of life at Elaious and
the agricultural and economic ideals promoted in the *Works and
Days*.[40] Besides Hesiod only a few other poets are named: in

---

[40] Compare *Her.* 1.5–2.5 with Hesiod *Works and Days* 110–120, 170–
173, 320–326. Nagy (*Best of the Achaeans*, 152–54, following Erwin Rohde,
Psyche: Seelencult und Unsterblichkeitsglaube der Griechen [2 vols.; 2d ed.;
Freiburg: Mohr, 1898], 1:111–45) argues that Hesiod's characterization of the

praising Homer Protesilaos quotes the verses of a certain Pam-phôs (*Her.* 25.8), whom Pausanias (*Description of Greece* 8.37.9) knows as a pre-Homeric poet, although the extant fragments would appear to be somewhat later. On two occasions plays of Eu-ripides are mentioned by title and author; we find reference to his *Oineus* (*Her.* 4.1) and a quotation from the *Palamedes* (*Her.* 34.7), both of which are no longer extant.

In a dialogue in which a hero appears as the chief authority on subjects taken up by epic poetry, it should come as no surprise that the heroes are themselves singers of epic and lyric. Prote-silaos is said to "sing" of the Trojan events that took place after his lifetime, as well as other events in the history of the Hellenes and the Medes (*Her.* 7.6). Achilles, however, is the heroic poet *par excellence*. He is said to have learned music from his tutor, the cen-taur Kheirôn, and received "musical skill and mastery of poetic composition" from the muse Calliope (*Her.* 45.7). Lamenting the death of Palamedes, he composed the "Palamedes," apparently a song about his heroic deeds (*Her.* 33.36). On Leukê, Achilles and Helen occupy themselves with epic and lyric in a symposium-like setting; Protesilaos reports that they sing the poems of Homer, as well as love songs to one another. In a reversal of roles, Achilles also sings a song in praise of Homer, which the vinedresser quotes to the Phoenician (*Her.* 55.3).

Philostratus here presents a brief chronology of poetic his-tory. Epic recitation (*rhapsôidia*) began only with Homer and did not exist before the Trojan War. There was, nonetheless, some poetry, namely, "about prophetic matters"—the setting of orac-ular utterances in poetic form—and about Herakles (*Her.* 7.5). Herakles himself is credited with the composition of a poetic epi-gram in dactylic hexameter (*Her.* 55.5), which the vinedresser cites as evidence of the great age of poetic composition. By at-tributing such activities to the heroes, the dialogue implies that those who are engaged in poetic composition and in performance that remembers the deeds of the heroes are imitators of the heroes themselves. Just as the hero Protesilaos is the source of the ac-curate content for the performance, so too the heroes are the prototypical performers.

generation of the Golden Age matches closely the description of heroes "as they are worshipped in cult" (p. 152). Thus *On Heroes* is drawing upon the motifs of hero cult in depicting this way of life.

The primary trajectory for Protesilaos's correction of Homer lies in his assertion that Homer left Palamedes out of his account and favored Odysseus (*Her.* 24.2). By omitting events concerning Palamedes, Homer distorts key matters. Protesilaos maintains that the cause of Odysseus's wanderings was Poseidon's wrath, not over the blinding of his son, the Cyclops Polyphemos (whom indeed Homer invented), but over the death of Palamedes, his grandson (*Her.* 25.13–15). Likewise, Achilles' wrath is not the result of being deprived of Khrysêis, but because of the unjust death of Palamedes (*Her.* 25.15–17). In this way, Protesilaos reshapes the motives underlying the plots of both the *Iliad* and the *Odyssey*. Odysseus becomes "Homer's plaything" (*Her.* 25.14), promoted along with Achilles at the expense of other heroes. Moreover, to heighten appreciation of Odysseus and Achilles, Homer is accused of inventing characters such as the Cyclopes, the fabulous stories of Odysseus's wanderings, the immortality of Achilles' horses, and even Achilles' divinely wrought armor. Some of these Protesilaos regards merely as unnecessary, poetic hyperboles; the omission of Palamedes is more serious, since it perpetuates the injustice and dishonor rendered to the hero.

In *Odyssey* 11, Odysseus conjures up spirits of the dead by making a libation of blood at the entrance to the Underworld; in this way he learns the post-war fate of many of his companions at Troy. In *On Heroes*, it is Homer who makes such a libation and summons Odysseus from the dead in order to hear what really happened at Troy. Odysseus, from whom Palamedes demands justice for his murder, threatens to withhold the entire account from Homer unless Homer promises to say nothing at all about Palamedes and so erase him from the story. If Homer's account is favorable toward Odysseus and mortals come to believe that Odysseus had nothing to do with Palamedes, then the demands for Odysseus's punishment will lessen (*Her.* 43.12–16). In other words, Odysseus bribes Homer with the promise of revealing knowledge in return for a biased account. Protesilaos, in what he reveals to the vinedresser and hence to the audience, unmasks the deception.

Two episodes involving women leaders are notable examples of Protesilaos's correction and emendation of the poetic accounts. The first concerns Hiera, the warrior queen of the Mysians who led the Mysian women into battle with the Achaeans alongside the male warriors. Protesilaos, who fought in that battle on the Achaean side, maintains that she was the most beautiful of all women, surpassing Helen, and that to exalt Helen Homer omitted all mention of Hiera from his poems (*Her.* 23.28–29). Although revision of the events surrounding the presence of Helen at Troy is a common theme of Homeric criticism, the removal of Hiera from the story in connection with Homer's fondness for Helen is a surprising twist. It is tempting to suppose that Philostratus emphasizes the stature of Hiera either from an interest in the local traditions of the region surrounding the Troad or, as we shall explore below, as a model for the prominent women in the imperial family, such as Julia Domna.

The second example concerns Achilles and the Amazons. Protesilaos reports that Achilles did not fight the Amazons at Troy, and indeed the vinedresser maintains that it would not be plausible that the Amazons who earlier had been allied with the Phrygians against Priam would have come to Troy as Priam's allies (*Her.* 56.11). The Amazons then were never at Troy, according to this emendation. This permits Philostratus, on the supposed authority of Protesilaos, to locate Achilles' brutal encounter with the Amazons on Leukê, Achilles' home in the Black Sea, when the Amazons decide to invade the island in order to seize its wealth, Achilles' mares, and even Achilles himself. The result of this revision is to make the Amazons appear as aggressors without warrant, foreigners who threaten a focal point of Hellenic cultural identity by attempting to despoil the home and sanctuary of Achilles. Again the question of the relation between putting forward such a version of the story and the historical situation of Philostratus's work arises. We may speculate that the repelling of such an impious foreign invasion, matched by Protesilaos's reaction to similar foreigners elsewhere in the dialogue, corresponds in some fashion to the perception of threats to the Roman empire and Hellenic culture from outsiders (see below).

We may also examine Protesilaos's critique of Homer from the perspective of the relation between local tradition and panhellenism.[41] This text presents Homer's poems as the official version of events, known and accepted by all people. Homer's poems

---

[41] On panhellenism, see Nagy, *Pindar's Homer*, chs. 2 and 3; Nagy, *Homeric Questions*, 40–41.

are, to this extent, canonical and panhellenic; such a presentation corresponds well to the way in which the *Iliad* and *Odyssey* were regarded in Greek and Roman culture from the second century B.C.E. onward. The dialogue also recognizes the centripetal process by which local versions of epic are gathered into a centralized account.[42] It does so by attributing that process to the figure of Homer himself, who, according to the vinedresser, traveled around Greece and collected from each city the names and deeds of their local heroes (*Her.* 43.11). From these, combined with what he learned from Odysseus, Homer composed his poems.

Protesilaos's apparent reliance upon and revival of stories from the Epic Cycle is an important aspect of *On Heroes* insofar as it represents a reassertion of the more local traditions of the Epic Cycle in contrast to the panhellenic tendencies of the *Iliad* and the *Odyssey*. Protesilaos's critiques of these local epic traditions on the basis of his own authority and on-going ritual tradition represent an even more radical localization of mythic authority. In a sense what we seem to be observing is the deconstruction of the panhellenic ideals found in the *Iliad* and the *Odyssey* and a reconstruction of a new Greek identity on the basis of local traditions, both epic and ritual. The particular local connections of the various poems of the Epic Cycle (e.g., the connection of the *Aithiopis* with Miletus) need further investigation in order to attempt to localize Philostratus's own cultural and political commitments.

As we have seen, the dialogue questions the authority of Homer as soon as it introduces Protesilaos as the definitive bearer of the story and compares Homer's account to what Protesilaos has to say. It also does so by recognizing that there are stories that have been forgotten or neglected because of Homer's emphasis on Achilles and Odysseus. There may also be heroes whom Homer mentions in passing but with little remembrance of their deeds. In other words, Protesilaos is presented as bringing to light forgotten stories, much as the action of the sea brings to light the buried bones of the giants (*Her.* 8.5–6). They are not simply stories that are exclusively accessible to Protesilaos because of his supernatural knowledge; the implication is that had Homer not shaped his composition as he did, had the process of remembering

---

[42] On this phenomenon, see Nagy, *Homeric Questions*, esp. 43.

lxviii   FLAVIUS PHILOSTRATUS: *ON HEROES*

in song occurred differently, the audience would be familiar with a broader, as well as more accurate set of stories.

It is therefore important to examine how *On Heroes* links the alternative stories that Protesilaos recounts with the local tradition.[43] We have seen already the emphasis placed on the experience of the inhabitants of the Troad, the Chersonesus, and the Hellespont, especially around the tombs of the heroes and the giants. The vinedresser knows about the oracle of Orpheus not only from Protesilaos, but also from the inhabitants of Lesbos (*Her.* 28.9–10). Likewise, when he speaks about the sanctuary of Palamedes on the mainland across from Lesbos, he describes the practice of the Aeolians and the inhabitants of nearby coastal cities, including mention of their sacrifices (*Her.* 33.48). Remembering the exploits of Philoktêtês, the vinedresser mentions the healing powers of Lemnian soil and provides an etiology for the place name "Akesa" (*Her.* 28.6). The implication here is that local tradition is a source for correcting or emending the account of Homer. It is likely, moreover, that at this point and in the description of the rituals of purifying the sacred fire on Lemnos (*Her.* 53.5) Philostratus is drawing upon his own expertise in the Lemnian myth and ritual.[44]

Issues of regional ritual practice also arise in the lengthy discussion of the cult of Achilles at Troy, which Philostratus includes in his description of Achilles. Distinct from Achilles' sanctuary on Leukê, the site of his burial at Sigeion in the Troad possesses its own rites, decreed, according to the vinedresser, by the oracle at Dodona (*Her.* 53.8). At this point in the dialogue, the vinedresser appears to speak on the authority of his own knowledge; there is scant reference in this section to what he heard from Protesilaos. The cult seems, moreover, to be distinctively Thessalian; in relating the history of full observance, neglect,

---

[43] Simone Follet argues that Philostratus appeals to traditions local to the northern Aegean and the Troad ("Philostratus's *Heroikos* and the Northern Aegean," in *Philostratus's* Heroikos: *Religion and Cultural Identity in the Third Century* C.E. [ed. Ellen Bradshaw Aitken and Jennifer K. Berenson Maclean; SBLWGRW 4; Atlanta: Society of Biblical Literature. Forthcoming). Samson Eitrem ("Zu Philostrats Heroikos," *Symbolae Osloenses* 8 [1929]: 1) maintains that Philostratus came from this region and was familiar with the hero cults of the Hellespont from personal experience.

[44] Burkert, "Jason, Hypsipyle, and New Fire," 2.

resurgence under Alexander the Great, and its current status of observance, the vinedresser links it at each point to Thessalian and Macedonian political history (*Her.* 53.14–23). The ultimate authority for the proper observance of the cult is Achilles himself, endorsed by the witness of Protesilaos.

The dialogue's focus on the figure of Protesilaos similarly draws our attention to regional concerns. In making Protesilaos the ultimate authority for getting the story right, the dialogue grounds the "right" version of myth in the witness of a hero who enjoyed particular devotion in Thessaly and the Chersonesus. We have noted above the parallel treatment of Protesilaos and Achilles throughout the text. In matters of myth and ritual, the two heroes function rhetorically in like fashion. Discussion of the cult of Achilles provides an argument for the right performance of the cult of the hero, whereas the overarching conceit of *On Heroes* concerns the authority of Protesilaos for the right telling of the story. It is striking, therefore, that in both aspects of the phenomenon of proper cultic observance—story and ritual—the dialogue turns not to such institutions as the canon of Homer or the panhellenic festivals, but to regional and local experiences.

If these observations are correct, then we may understand them within a context of the continued awareness of the multiformity of epic tradition, supported by the religious practices of cities and regions. If we suppose a world in which a standardized Homeric version of events, albeit of some antiquity by the early third century C.E., has obliterated variant traditions, then it becomes impossible to account for their emergence in art and literature, as well as their persistence in localized religious practice.[45] Rather when we recognize that local and regional stories and ritual practices continued alongside the poems of Homer and the panhellenic festivals and institutions, then we can understand the text as drawing upon the strength of that multiformity while seeking a different authority for adjudicating the truth. *On Heroes* finds that authority in the experience of immediate engagement with the heroes, made possible by giving them proper honor which includes not only observance of the cult, but also the cultivation of an ethical and truth-loving life.

---

[45] On this question, see, among other works, Thomas H. Carpenter, *Art and Myth in Ancient Greece* (London: Thames & Hudson, 1991).

We should be careful to distinguish, however, between the rhetorical claims of this text and Philostratus's compositional practices. When the dialogue, through the character of Protesilaos, claims to draw upon local stories at variance with Homer, the authenticity of this claim needs to be evaluated in each case. Indeed those variant traditions may well have been available to Philostratus in the works of other writers or his own literary creation. Nevertheless, Philostratus makes a strong argument for taking local tradition seriously as a source of truth over against the poems of Homer. He is saying, in effect, that if you consult those who live on the Hellespont, in the Chersonesus and the Troad, as well as those who live near the sanctuaries of the heroes, you will obtain knowledge more accurate than that which you hear from the poets, including Homer. Moreover, if you go to the tombs of the heroes and worship properly, you will receive knowledge and insight. This is a central message of *On Heroes*. It does not mean necessarily, however, that Philostratus is an indubitable source of local stories about the Homeric heroes or the cult practices of his time. The fact that he makes such a rhetorical appeal, however, strongly suggests continuing tension between the canonicity of the Homeric poems, on the one hand, and stories and practices associated with local cult sites, on the other.

On Heroes raises important issues about the authority upon which stories and practices are founded. Its rhetorical strategies thus provide a useful foil against which to read the concerns central to the developing identities of early Christian communities, roughly contemporary with this text. That is, within formative Christianity of the second and third centuries C.E. we find concerns with the formation of the canon of scripture that are comparable to the interest here in telling the "right" story and that likewise reflect growing tensions among a diversity of memories about Jesus and his followers.[46] We may also compare the interest of *On Heroes* in proper observance of ritual with the varieties of cultic expression in early Christianity, including the proper way to perform and interpret actions such as eucharist and baptism. Similarly, we find both in *On Heroes* and in early

[46] For an introduction to these questions, see Harry Y. Gamble, "Canon: New Testament," *ABD* 1:852–61; see also Hans von Campenhausen, *The Formation of the Christian Bible* (Philadelphia: Fortress, 1972); Helmut Koester, "Apocryphal and Canonical Gospels," *HTR* 73 (1980): 105–30.

Christian texts discussion of the attitude or confession of the individual, the value of immediate experience of the divine world,
and the appropriate ethical and ascetic practices. Questions such
as these were by no means answered uniformly within the diversity of Christian communities before the middle of the third
century. We raise the comparative questions between this text
and early Christianity not to ignore the several differences, but
so as to illumine the particular strategies by which each text
constitutes and claims authority for its tradition.[47] For example,
whereas *On Heroes* presents a hero returned to life who provides
the "true" version of the epic tradition and critiques Homer, the
late first-century C.E. Gospel of Luke asserts that authoritative
interpretation of scripture is available through association with
Jesus after his resurrection, and the second-century C.E. *Apoc-
ryphon of James* shows the disciples receiving "sayings" from the
risen Jesus. The strategy of establishing authority through a figure who has returned from the dead is common to each, but the
nature of the utterance is significantly different: the epic tradition, the interpretation of a set of sacred texts, and enigmatic
sayings. It has also been argued that although early Christians
avoided veneration of Jesus as a hero, this text has "parallels" to
early Christian literature and indirectly furnishes evidence for a
confrontation between Christian and non-Christian beliefs about
heroes.[48] Whether one agrees with such an interpretation, *On
Heroes* may be read from a comparative perspective as a text that
sheds light upon the various means of creating and promoting religious identity in antiquity.

[47] For example, Eitrem ("Zu Philostrats Heroikos," 23–24) draws a comparison between the recounting of supernatural marvels in *On Heroes*, the
summary of miracle stories in the *Pseudo-Clementine Homilies*, and Lucian's
Menippus, or the Descent into Hades.

[48] This interpretation has been advanced strongly by Hans Dieter Betz,
"Heroenverehrung und Christusglaube: Religionsgeschichtliche Beobachtun-
gen zu Philostrats *Heroicus*," in *Griechische und römische Religion* (ed. Hubert
Cancik; vol. 2 of *Geschichte—Tradition—Reflexion: Festschrift für Martin Hen-
gel zum 70. Geburtstag*, ed. Hubert Cancik, Hermann Lichtenberger, and Peter
Schärfer; Tübingen: Mohr/Siebeck, 1996), 119–39. English translation forth-
coming in Aitken and Maclean, *Philostratus's Heroikos: Religion and Cultural
Identity*.

THE AIMS OF THE DIALOGUE

The foregoing observations about the literary, religious, and cultural setting of *On Heroes* lead us necessarily to inquire into dating of this work and the purposes for which Philostratus composed it. One piece of evidence for dating[49] the text is the mention of the athlete Aurelius Helix in *Her.* 15.8–10. The date of Helix's competitions provides an initial *terminus post quem*. His second victory took place in either 213 or 217 C.E.[50] The second clue for dating *On Heroes* is the allusion to the Roman punishment of the Thessalians for their illegal participation in the purple trade (*Her.* 53.23). A revised *terminus post quem* would then be 222–235 C.E., since the purple trade only became a state monopoly under Alexander Severus.[51] No *terminus ad quem* can be established other than the death of Philostratus (244–249 C.E.), although the immediacy of the reference to Helix suggests the early years of Alexander Severus's reign.[52] Given the remaining uncertainty about the date of the dialogue and even its authorship, our proposals are tentative. We particularly recognize that this work may have had several purposes and have spoken in a multivalent fashion to various parts of its audience.

[49] Solmsen argues that *On Heroes* was composed after the *Life of Apollonius*. This assumption has been rightly criticized, since the presence of similar themes cannot yield a clear indication of chronological priority: the shorter text may just as plausibly be the summary as the longer text may be the elaboration. Anderson, *Philostratus*, 294; Flinterman, *Power*, 26.

[50] Münscher ("Die Philostrati," 497–98, 554) argued for 213 C.E. Julius Jüthner's proposal of 217 C.E. (*Philostratos über Gymnastik* [Leipzig: Teubner, 1909], 87–88) is followed by Luigi Moretti, *Olympionikai: I vincitori negli antichi agoni olimpici* (Rome: Accademia Nazionale dei Lincei, 1957), nos. 911, 915.

[51] See Georges Radet, "Notes sur l histoire d'Alexandre: II. Les théores Thessaliens au tombeau d'Achille," *Revue des études anciennes* 27 (1925): 92.

[52] The conclusion of Münscher ("Die Philostrati," 497–98; followed by Solmsen, "Some Works," 571–72) that *On Heroes* was completed prior to 219 C.E. was based on the text's silence on Helix's double victory at the Capitoline games in 219 C.E. But this argument from silence can hardly stand. The point of the passage is the truthfulness of Protesilaos's oracular pronouncement, which only concerned Helix's victories at Olympia. Flinterman, *Power*, 25. Jüthner, *Philostratos*, 88.

Samson Eitrem argues at length that the dialogue is an attempt to encourage belief in heroes among the educated, and to promote worship of them.[53] In this context it is often noted that Caracalla visited Achilles' tomb circa 214–215 C.E. during his expedition to the East and made an elaborate commemoration of Achilles in the Troad, and that as part of Julia Domna's entourage, Philostratus would have been present.[54] Although the emperor's devotion to Achilles probably arose from his desire to emulate Alexander the Great, Caracalla's mother Julia Domna had great interest in Apollonius of Tyana, and to satisfy this, Philostratus wrote his *Life of Apollonius*. Caracalla also had a temple built in honor of Apollonius. Given these historical considerations and the relationship between the *Life* and *On Heroes*, Eitrem regards *On Heroes* as a serious effort to promote hero worship which, unlike the official cult of the Olympian gods, still had great popularity among the ordinary populace.[55] Despite misgivings about Philostratus's intentions, Eitrem claims that the text had a "national purpose," and by presenting ideal men, indeed "supermen" of the past, figures familiar to Greeks from their childhood, Philostratus indirectly combated anything anti-Hellenic, and thus promoted Hellenic culture.[56]

Following Eitrem, Teresa Mantero also argues that Philostratus had a religious purpose in composing *On Heroes*, namely, the revitalization of hero cults. Her analysis points out the likely influence of Neoplatonic and Neopythagorean ideas on Philostratus's presentation of the heroes and their cults. As a result, her interpretation of the dialogue tends to subordinate literary approaches to a religio-philosophical and folkloric reading.[57] Mantero also discusses the pro-Hellenic tendencies in the text, suggesting that Philostratus was here promoting a Greek identity with ancient roots in the stories and cults of the heroes in the face of the syncretistic tendencies of the Severan dynasty.[58]

---

[53] See Eitrem, "Zu Philostrats Heroikos," 1–56.

[54] Dio Cassius *Roman History* 78.16.7; Herodian *History* 4.8.3.

[55] Eitrem, "Zu Philostrats Heroikos," 2.

[56] Eitrem, "Zu Philostrats Heroikos," 5-6.

[57] See, for example, Mantero, *Ricerche*, 12–13, and esp. her concluding remark on p. 18. See also Mantero, *Aspetti del culto degli eroi presso i greci* (Genoa: Tilgher, 1973).

[58] Mantero, *Ricerche*, 227–28.

A far less positive evaluation of Philostratus's intentions is made by Graham Anderson. Contrary to the view that Philostratus is providing some kind of "propaganda for a genuine popular piety" and a "serious vindication of hero cults,"[59] Anderson observes that it is not always easy to see a "pious purpose" in Philostratus's reworking of myth. There is, however, what appears to be a sophistic penchant for the archaic and literary, and many details seem related to the repertoire of sophistic literature (see above).[60] Anderson concludes that Philostratus's commitment to the hero cults cannot be deduced from *On Heroes* alone and that whatever piety is found in the dialogue seems quite compatible with the *paideia*, or literary culture, of Philostratus and his audience.[61] Indeed Anderson argues that the interest in hero cult and Protesilaos is only "a preliminary excursus before the main subject—the correction of Homer."[62]

Without reference to Anderson's book on Philostratus, Hans Dieter Betz, inspired by Eitrem's work, claims that although Philostratus never mentions Christianity, he knew of it. Moreover, *On Heroes* is to be taken seriously as evidence for non-Christian religions in the second and third centuries, and given the popularity of hero worship, the early Christians "consciously" avoided the veneration of Jesus as a hero.[63] The evidence of Origen's *Against Celsus*, in which Celsus is said to ask about the similarity between Jesus' resurrection and the returning to life of various heroes, including Protesilaos,[64] indicates that early Christianity encountered the religious and philosophical categories of hero cult. Betz finds various parallels in early Christian literature—for example, Protesilaos and Jesus both walk over water (*Her.* 13.3),[65] and the risen Jesus' associations with his

[59] Anderson, *Philostratus*, 247–48.
[60] Anderson, *Philostratus*, 241–42.
[61] Anderson, *Philostratus*, 248.
[62] Anderson, *Philostratus*, 253.
[63] See Betz, "Heroenverehrung und Christusglaube," 119.
[64] Origen *Against Celsus* 2.55; Betz, "Heroenverehrung und Christusglaube," 119.
[65] Although it is true that a number of divine humans are said to walk on water (see Betz, "Heroenverehung und Christusglaube," 129 n. 44), as Protesilaos, however, exercises on the running tracks around the sanctuary, he is simply likened to one who floats upon the waves.

disciples—which suggest that the Gospel writers knew "about the possibility of an existence of the risen Jesus as a hero."[66] To be sure, Betz does not claim that early Christian writers knew *On Heroes*, but rather were acquainted with what it reflects about heroes and hero cults at the time Christianity was taking root.

Betz argues that one of the major themes of *On Heroes* is the movement from skepticism to belief on the part of the Phoenician merchant.[67] In the initial section of the dialogue, he is "unbelieving" (*apisteô*; *Her.* 3.1).[68] Under the influence of the vinedresser and his stories he gradually relinquishes his skepticism about the legends of the heroes and especially about the possibility of their appearance to mortals in his own time, until he exclaims, "By Protesilaos, I am convinced" (*peithomai*; *Her.* 16.6) and then, "Finally, I am with you, vinedresser, and no one hereafter will disbelieve such stories" (*Her.* 18.1). Only at this point then does the vinedresser, on the authority of Protesilaos, begin to relate the characteristics and deeds of the heroes. This reading of the dialogue's rhetoric thus supposes a correspondence between the narrative movement of the dialogue and the position to which the text seeks to persuade its audience. The vinedresser seeks to bring the Phoenician to believe that what the hero says is true and that the heroes really do appear and associate with humans; likewise the dialogue seeks to persuade its audience of the value of stories and practices associated with the cult of the heroes.

Against this interpretation and in keeping with a reading that emphasizes correction of Homer as the primary point of the text, it may be objected that the Phoenician is indeed not "skeptical" at the outset of the dialogue: he has a propensity to believe in omens and dreams, as well as a solid knowledge of Homer already. At the end of the dialogue, accordingly, he is not so much "converted" as simply pleased at listening to the vinedresser's corrections of Homer and looks forward to hearing more stories.

---

[66] See Betz, "Heroenverehung und Christusglaube," 129.

[67] Betz, "Heroenverehrung und Christusglaube," 122–23. Like Mantero, Betz indicates that *On Heroes* needs to be read in a religious-political framework and not only a literary-aesthetic one.

[68] He is "inclined to disbelieve legends" and thinks that stories such as those about the great stature of the heroes are "false and unconvincing for one who observes things according to nature" (*Her.* 7.9).

To be sure, his initial disbelief about the appearances of Protesilaos and other Trojan heroes is overcome, but, according to this
perspective, this is simply a narrative device to establish the credibility of the vinedresser and Protesilaos.

Resolving this debate depends in part upon how one assesses
the rhetorical conventions of the Second Sophistic. Moreover, because we lack any information about the commissioning of the
dialogue, it is difficult to be certain of the ends for which it was
written. We are, however, inclined to take *On Heroes* with some
seriousness as seeking to persuade its audience of the value of
hero cults. That it reflects "mocking doubt" about ghosts, mira-
cles, and other superstitious elements of popular belief,[69] cannot
be fully demonstrated. The categories of conversion, belief, and
disbelief are, however, not the most precise for understanding
the dialogue.[70] Rather, we find a contrast in sources of authority, illustrated at the very beginning of the dialogue, when the
vinedresser asks the Phoenician why he is "ignoring everything
at his feet"; the Phoenician replies that he is seeking a sign and
an omen, presumably in the sky, for fair sailing (*Her.* 1.2). This
contrast is again illustrated in the dispute between Odysseus and
Palamedes over an eclipse of the sun: Odysseus tells Palamedes
that he "will be less foolish by paying attention to the earth rather
than by speculating about what is in heaven." To this Palamedes
responds, "If you were clever, Odysseus, you would have understood that no one is able to say anything learned about the heavens
unless he knows more about the earth" (*Her.* 33.6–8).   Since
Palamedes is presented with characteristics of the true sophist, we
may recognize in Palamedes' words an attitude that the dialogue
is advocating. The Phoenician in the course of the dialogue is encouraged to look at what is "at his feet," namely, the tombs of the
heroes and their appearances to mortals, and from that to learn
higher truths and an enlightened way of life. The dialogue's emphasis on immediate experience and encounter is in keeping with
this attitude. Thus it is possible that Philostratus was not only interested in a revitalization of hero cults, but also in a particular
way of approaching the heroes as the basis of a reflective life.

[69] See Solmsen, "Philostratos," cols. 124–77, esp. col. 157.
[70] Cf. A. D. Nock, *Conversion: The Old and the New in Religion from
Alexander the Great to Augustine of Hippo* (Oxford: Clarendon, 1933; repr.,
Lanham, Md.: University Press of America, 1988), 90–91.

Aside from situating *On Heroes* in connection with Caracalla's visit to the Troad in 214–215 C.E. and Julia Domna's
patronage of Philostratus, discussions of the purposes of the dialogue tend to speak little of its historical and political aspects,
in favor of religious and literary questions. Recognizing that the
religious and political were inseparably intertwined in the early
third century C.E. and that many sophists held religious and political offices, we think that it is appropriate to inquire into the
political dimension. We can do no more than sketch an avenue of
approach here.[71]

One of Protesilaos's most prominent appearances in Greek
literature is at the end of Herodotus's *Histories* where he defends Greek territory against the outrages of the Persian governor Artayktes. It is important to recognize, however, that
Herodotus's account of Protesilaos as *revenant* against the Persian
governor does not convey a simplistic anti-Persian or ethnocentri-
cally pro-Greek message. Rather the story stands as a warning for
Herodotus's own Greek audience against hubris and tyranny.[72]

Looking at Philostratus's work in terms of its treatment of
foreignness raises a distinct set of questions about its purpose.
Throughout the dialogue, as we have seen, a parallelism is drawn
between Achilles and Protesilaos, and both appear at times as
avenging *revenants*. A wrathful Protesilaos regained his sanctuary from the possession of a man named Xeinis ("foreigner";
Her. 4.2). The dialogue ends with two stories of Achilles' brutal
wrath: in the first case upon a young girl, one of the last of Priam's
descendants (*Her.* 56.6–10); in the second upon the Amazons who
invade Achilles' island in the Black Sea (*Her.* 56.11–57.17). These
stories appear, at first reading, to be an abrupt shift from the relatively peaceful descriptions of Protesilaos's and Achilles' current
lifestyles, but their position as the climax of the dialogue suggests
their importance for its overall purpose. Anderson, moreover,
stresses "the element of similarity between the vengeance of

---

[71] A similar direction is indicated by T. J. G. Whitmarsh, "Performing
Heroics: Language, Landscape and Identity in Philostratus' *Heroicus*," in
Philostratus (ed. E. Bowie and J. Elsner; Cambridge: Cambridge University
Press, forthcoming) in which he discusses the text in terms of the cultural poli-
tics of its time.

[72] Nagy, *Pindar's Homer*, 308–13. Boedeker ("Protesilaos," 37, 42–44)
emphasizes Protesilaos's role in defending civilization against barbarian threats.

Achilles at the end of the *Heroicus* and that of Protesilaos at the
end of Herodotus's *Histories*: both have the last blood."[73]

It is important to notice not only the wrath of the heroes
but also at whom it is directed: in each case at those who are
quintessentially foreign or "other" from the Hellenic perspective.
Hektor, to cite another instance, returns as *revenant* to avenge the
insults hurled at him by the offending *Assyrian* youth (*Her.* 19.5–
9). It is also worth noting that Achilles' victims are women, a
point to which we shall return. Being a foreigner is also essential
to the construction of character in the dialogue: we are introduced at the outset to a *Phoenician* merchant, from the region
of Tyre and Sidon (*Her.* 1.1), who is realistically depicted as a
"hellenized" Phoenician: he wears an Ionic style of dress, knows
all about Homer, and speaks Greek. In addition to his skepticism, however, about the heroes of old, from the beginning of the
dialogue the Phoenician is associated with the values of luxury
and love of money (*Her.* 1.1–7), values which are typically understood as non-Greek, but which can also be employed to critique
Hellenic behavior.[74] Throughout he is called *xenos* ("stranger,
foreigner, guest"), and it is possible to read his passage from foreign stranger to guest, within the hospitality of the vinedresser
and Protesilaos, as taking place in tandem with his growing ac-
ceptance of the matters to do with the heroes. This foreigner,
moreover, ends up being a listener devoted to Protesilaos, prepared to abide by the hero's reluctance to speak of certain matters,
and ready to pour a libation to Protesilaos (*Her.* 58.1–6). It is perhaps not going too far to say that this foreigner, unlike Artayktes
and Xeinis, becomes subject to Protesilaos.

The composition of *On Heroes* in the early third century
C.E., during the later Severan period, situates it in a time when
the government of the Roman empire was strongly influenced by
such imperial women as Julia Domna, Julia Maesa, Julia Mamaea, and Julia Soemias, all from the Syrian religious aristocracy.
Religious practices were redefined, not only by a new wave of syn-
cretism, but also by the introduction into Rome of the Syrian sun
god and Elagabalus's installation of the Black Rock of Emesa on

[73] Anderson, *Philostratus*, 247.

[74] Thus, Nagy argues that in Herodotus the story of Artayktes is directed at the Athenians and "signals the threat of *hubris* from within, not from
without" (*Pindar's Homer*, 308).

the Palatine. One result was a heightened awareness of issues of the relationship between foreignness and what was perceived as authentically "Hellenic" or Greek. It is therefore striking that the Phoenician merchant in this text is, like Julia Domna and her family, a Syrian,[75] and that the Phoenician swears by Helios—a solar deity (*Her.* 20.3; cf. *Her.* 33.6). It is perhaps not coincidental that in the stories of Achilles' wrath the victims were women who broke the taboos of the sanctuary. As we have seen, the dialogue develops a contrast between two opposing stances toward the heroes of Hellenic culture, that is, between proper honor, as exemplified by the attitude of the Phoenician (Syrian) merchant by the end of the dialogue, and the extremes of dishonor exemplified by the quintessential foreigners—the Amazons, the Trojan girl, Xeinis, and the Assyrian youth. Such a contrast, therefore, may well serve to highlight attempts by the Syrian women of the Severan dynasty to present themselves as authentically "Greek" by engaging in the practices proper to the cult and culture of the Hellenic heroes. *On Heroes* may thus demonstrate the Hellenic piety of the emperor Alexander Severus and his highly influential mother, Julia Mamaea.

Dating the dialogue to the reign of Alexander Severus, moreover, suggests a political situation in which the dialogue's themes would have had specific resonance, namely, renewed threats and campaigns from the East against the Romans. In the 220s, after the accession of Alexander Severus as emperor in 222, the Parthian empire was overthrown by the Sassanid ruler Ardashir I.[76] This new Sassanid emperor not only ruled formerly Parthian territory but also, during the attack on the Mesopotamian city of Hatra, declared an intent to reclaim the full extent of the Persian empire under the Achaemenids, namely,

---

[75] Phoenicia was considered part of the Roman province of Syria Phoenice (founded in 194 C.E.); the city of Emesa, the home of Julia Domna, Julia Mamaea, and Julia Soemias, was located in eastern Syria Phoenice.

[76] When Gessius Alexianus Bassianus became emperor, he adopted the name M. Aurelius Severus Alexander, which combined elements from the Antonine and Severan dynasty and the name Alexander. Fergus Millar points out (*The Roman Near East 31 BC—AD 337* [Cambridge, Mass.: Harvard University Press, 1993], 149) that this is the sole use of the name Alexander by a Roman emperor, suggesting that he was drawing upon the memory of Alexander the Great as the "liberator" of Greece from the Persians and presenting himself as the deliverer of the Roman empire from the renewed Persian threat.

to the Aegean Sea.[77] Alexander Severus launched a campaign
against the Persians in the early 230s, in response to their invasion
of Roman Mesopotamia. In order to understand the particular
valence Protesilaos may have had in this political situation, it is
instructive to recall Herodotus's use of Protesilaos as the protector of Greece against the Persians. *On Heroes* may then have been
written around the time of Alexander Severus's Persian campaign
in order to promote Greek (and hence Roman) identity and piety,
by recalling not only the memory of the preeminent heroes of the
Trojan War but most notably that of Protesilaos.[78]

The episode of the Amazons' attack on the abode of Achilles
on the island of Leukê can also be understood within this political
framework. In the fifth century B.C.E., at the time of the Persian
Wars, the story of the Amazons' invasion of Attica and their defeat by Theseus was added to earlier stories about the Amazons
and was used as pro-Athenian propaganda against the Persian invasion.[79] Thus Philostratus may employ the literary *topos* of the
Amazons in order to represent a contemporary foreign threat to
Greek identity. Achilles' destruction of the Amazons, like their
defeat by Theseus, would then communicate the certainty of Roman success against the Sassanids, so long as the heroes receive
due honor.

Given this interpretation, *On Heroes* exhibits a strong anti-
Persian perspective, which coheres well with Alexander Severus's
campaign against the Sassanids. The difficulty is that we know
nothing about imperial patronage for Philostratus in the period
after the death of Julia Domna and during the reign of Alexander
Severus. Nevertheless, the heroes' reaction to foreign threats in
this dialogue means that questions of cultural identity in historical

[77] Millar, *The Roman Near East*, 146–47; G. W. Bowersock, *Roman Arabia* (Cambridge, Mass.: Harvard University Press, 1983), 126–28.

[78] See Dio Cassius *Roman History* 80.4.1–2.

[79] See Josine H. Blok, *The Early Amazons: Modern and Ancient Perspectives on a Persistent Myth* (Religions in the Greco-Roman World 120; Leiden:
Brill, 1995), 182, 441; John Boardman, "Herakles, Theseus, and the Amazons,"
in *The Eye of Greece: Studies in the Art of Athens* (ed. D. C. Kurtz and B.
Sparkes; Cambridge: Cambridge University Press, 1982), 1–28. According to
Herodotus (*Hist.* 9.27), before the Battle of Plataea the Athenians referred to
the Amazons' invasion. The story also appears in Aeschylus's *Eumenides* (657–
666), first performed ca. 460–458 B.C.E., during the Persian Wars; see Blok, *The
Early Amazons*, 182.

and political context must be set alongside discussion of religious and literary dimensions.

To the modern reader *On Heroes* may appear opaque at first, as though one were eavesdropping on a conversation about some-what familiar topics but conducted with a knowledge one does not share. Philostratus's portrayal of the conversation between the vinedresser and the Phoenician relies upon a detailed body of as-sumed knowledge and experience. In the first place, the reader is expected to be intimately conversant with the poems of Homer and the numerous other traditions about the Homeric heroes. Without such "Homeric" fluency, the corrections of Homer which the vinedresser offers on the basis of what Protesilaos has told him remain incomprehensible and meaningless. The references to Homer's poems are seldom made through direct quotation, but rather by allusion to an episode, use of a key phrase, or inclu-sion of a recognizable epithet. Homer is referred to here not only as one who recounts stories of the Hellenic and Trojan heroes at Troy, but also as a source of practical information, such as the best way to plant trees (*Her.* 11.4–6). *On Heroes* thus demonstrates a number of the uses to which the epic traditions were put.

The dialogue assumes, in addition to such familiarity with the *Iliad* and *Odyssey*, that the audience has further knowledge about the heroic age. The heroes' ancestry and birth, the exploits of their fathers, their deeds before the Trojan War, as well as sto-ries of their fate at the end of the war, their death and burial or their return to their homeland—all these are drawn into the dia-logue, rendering it a rich resource for traditions about the heroes. Many of these traditions are attested elsewhere, in the summaries of the lost poems of the Homeric cycle, such as the *Aithiopis* or the *Cypria*, or in allusions in Pindar or the tragedians. Herodotus and Pausanias, chief among the Greek authors, frequently include information about the heroes found in *On Heroes*. Moreover, it is not only the heroes of the Trojan War with which the dialogue is concerned but also others, such as Herakles and the Seven Against Thebes, inasmuch as their exploits impinged upon the history of the warriors at Troy.

The dialogue displays a special concern with heroes' tombs and sanctuaries; here the reader is expected to be familiar with the burial of the heroes, the rites appropriate in each sanctuary, and the particular interests each hero has. In what way has a hero been offended, either in life or in death, that he or she might seek vengeance upon the living? In this respect, the knowledge that the audience has or acquires from the dialogue has important consequences. It is vital to know the right story about each hero, not least so that one does not offend or do violence to their memory. The consequences of ignorance and offense are great, from the perspective of the dialogue, since each hero is a *revenant*, still possessing the capacity to avenge injustice. The consequences of proper knowledge about the heroes and their ways are also great, with blessing and prosperity bestowed by the heroes upon those who maintain a right relationship with them. *On Heroes* thus assumes a certain inculturation into the basic patterns of hero cult.

On Heroes also refers at times to pieces of Greek literature other than the poems of Homer, most notably the poems of Hesiod and the dialogues of Plato. Consideration of Hesiod is included chiefly through comparison with Homer's compositional technique and skill, with the introduction of the motif of the contest between Homer and Hesiod (known as the *Certamen*). References to Plato are more complex and less foundational to the worldview of the text. *On Heroes* contains no explicit references to Plato and yet by its genre draws upon the tradition of philosophical dialogue begun by Plato (see above). Philostratus also alludes to Platonic discussions about education, the acquisition of knowledge, the relation of the body and soul, and the role of sense perception (e.g., *Her.* 1.2; 7.3). A thorough analysis of the relation of *On Heroes* to Platonic ideas and writings is not possible here, but a preliminary examination suggests that the dialogue is critical of certain Platonic perspectives (e.g., see *Her.* 1.2 and the discussion there).

References to contemporary events and figures are also found throughout the dialogue. The deeds of certain Olympic athletes and various events in Roman fiscal policies, although obscure and tantalizing to the modern historian, are cited in a way that assumes the ancient audience was quite familiar with them. In order to understand, for example, the full impact of Achilles'

avenging wrath upon the Thessalians when they were overly ca-
sual about their sacrifices, it is necessary to be acquainted with the
imperial monopoly on extraction of purple dye and the sanctions
placed upon the Thessalians in the reign of Alexander Severus
for their violation of the monopoly. Such references to imperial
edicts suggest an interest in complimenting the imperial family,
whose policies thus fulfill the wishes of the heroes; combined with
discussion of contemporary athletes they render a dialogue that is
otherwise about events of long ago quite up-to-date.

   As one might expect in a dialogue in which a major characters is a Phoenician merchant who sails the Aegean and the
Black Sea, *On Heroes* is replete with geographical references. Like
the merchant, the audience is expected to recognize the names
of cities, regions, islands, mountains, and rivers associated with
the heroes, their sanctuaries, or where supernatural marvels are
to be found. The majority of these are in the northern Aegean,
the Hellespont, and the Troad, but the world circumscribed by
the dialogue extends from India to Spain and from Ethiopia to the
banks of the Danube (the ancient Istros). The dialogue conveys a
strong sense of place, emphasized by the present-day appearance
of the heroes in particular localities and especially the appearance of Protesilaos in his sanctuary at the tip of the Thracian
Chersonesus.   An underlying message of the dialogue is that
part of obtaining true knowledge entails being in the right place.
Moreover, as we have observed above, the role of Protesilaos as
guardian of Greece against foreign invasion is connected with the
location of his sanctuary on the western coast of the Hellespont,
at the ancient gateway between Europe and Asia. Thus the geo-
graphic dimension of the dialogue cannot be ignored, and in many
cases geography holds the key to the significance of an episode.

   These observations about the knowledge that *On Heroes*
assumes on the part of its audience locate the dialogue in an intertextual web of stories, traditions, and practices. We have already
explored the relation between this dialogue and the epic traditions; here it is sufficient to say that this web should not be limited
to what the audience could have obtained from written sources.
Rather, as we consider how to read this text, we may suppose as
a starting point that numerous stories about the heroes continued
to be told alongside the poems of Homer. These stories may have
been told in connection with the legends about the foundations

of cities and about cult sanctuaries; they may have enjoyed local
prestige, even as they contradicted or complemented the panhellenic epics of the *Iliad* and *Odyssey*. Inasmuch as these stories
surface in Greek and Roman literature and art, the modern reader
gains some access to them. We should emphasize, however, that
references in *On Heroes* to such traditions need not be thought of
as resulting solely from literary dependence. The same may be
said of the references to cultic practice. Although descriptions of
cultic activity cannot be taken simplistically as eyewitness reports,
we may suppose that Philostratus was well informed about certain
ritual practices and crafted them in ways that suited his aims. In
other words, we suggest that *On Heroes* is read best if it is seen as
situated within a world of performance, that is, the performances,
including those in written form, of stories and ritual practices associated with the heroes of the epic traditions.

On Heroes demands a certain expertise on the part of its audience. Thus, in producing the following translation,[80] we have
tried to provide the reader with what is needed to understand the
text. We have, above all, attempted to produce a translation that
is fairly transparent to the Greek idiom, with a minimum of para-
phrase; the translation is also sensitive to word-play and aware
of the technical vocabulary of Greek poetics, rhetoric, and cultic practice. Second, we have supplemented the translation with
notes, an extensive glossary, and maps. The notes do not pre-
tend to provide a full commentary on the text; they are limited to
elucidating obscure points, clarifying matters of translation, and
supplying references to the *Iliad*, the *Odyssey*, and other ancient
literature. A few notes contain a fuller discussion of phenomena
or practices mentioned in the text. We have avoided extensive ci-
tation of secondary literature in the notes, reserving discussion of
scholarship on Philostratus and *On Heroes* for the Introduction.

The Glossary contains an entry for every proper name mentioned in the text itself. The extent of this list indicates the
high degree to which the dialogue is concerned with the people
and places of epic tradition and of the ancient world in general.

---

[80] We have adopted the following system of transliteration: Names that
have passed into common English usage appear as they are generally familiar:
for example, Corinth, Euripides, Helen, Cassandra, and Achilles. Names that
are much less familiar are strictly transliterated, according to the guidelines in
the *Chicago Manual of Style*, 14th edition.

Because of the oblique quality of many references, readers are encouraged to make use of the Glossary alongside the text. In the entries we briefly identify the person or place and discuss those portions of the mythic or historical tradition most relevant to the present work. Following Philostratus's lead, we have been particularly attentive to variant traditions about the heroes. The Glossary, however, should not be considered encyclopedic, but rather as an introductory aid to the reader of this text. This volume also contains brief topical bibliographies intended to aid student research (pp. 151–160).

Since most modern readers are not as familiar with the geography of the ancient Mediterranean as the Phoenician merchant, we have included two maps (pp. 91–93). These maps show the location of all place names that occur in the text with the exception of strictly mythological locales (such as Aiaia) and the Ilissos river in Athens. One provides a general view of the Mediterranean, with indications of other, more distant sites mentioned in the text. The other map focuses on Greece and western Asia Minor, reflecting the dialogue's concern with this area.

This Student Edition of *On Heroes* is derived from our published translation *Flavius Philostratus: Heroikos*.[81] The full edition includes the Greek text, critical apparatus, index of Greek words, and a more detailed Introduction. Students interested in the manuscript history and textual variants are advised to consult the full version and de Lannoy's critical edition.[82]

[81] Jennifer K. Berenson Maclean and Ellen Bradshaw Aitken, trans., *Flavius Philostratus: Heroikos* (SBLWGRW 1; Atlanta: Society of Biblical Literature, 2001).

[82] Ludo de Lannoy, *Flavii Philostrati Heroicus* (Leipzig: Teubner, 1977).

Philostratus *On Heroes*

I. THE PHOENICIAN'S QUEST (1.1–8.18)

The Vinedresser and the Phoenician Meet (1.1–6.6)

VINEDRESSER. Stranger, are you an Ionian, or where are **1** you from?

PHOENICIAN. I am a Phoenician, vinedresser, one of those who live near Sidon and Tyre.

V. But what about the Ionic fashion of your dress?

PH. It is now the local dress also for those of us from Phoenicia.

V. How then did your people come to change their fashion?

PH. Ionian Sybaris[1] held sway over all Phoenicia at once, and there, I think, one would be prosecuted for not living luxuriously.

V. Where are you going so proudly and ignoring every- **2** thing at your feet?[2]

---

[1] "Ionian Sybaris" is a reference either to Ionia as a whole or, more likely, to Miletus in particular. The Ionians were well known as dedicated to luxury no less than were the Sybarites (Diodorus Siculus *Library* 8.18.2; *Suda*, s.v. Sybaritikais). A number of ancient authors single out Miletus as the center of Ionian extravagance and attest that Miletus and Sybaris were bound together by their common way of life (Herodotus *Hist.* 6.21; Athenaeus *Deipnosophists* 12.518; Diodorus Siculus *Library* 8.20; see also Juvenal *Satires* 6.296). The possible allusion to Thales (a Milesian) in the following line supports the identification of Miletus. Note Plutarch's similar reference to a "Parthian Sybaris" (*Crassus* 32.4).

[2] The vinedresser's question is reminiscent of Plato's anecdote about the philosopher Thales (*Theaetetus* 174a [Fowler, LCL]), "While Thales was studying the stars and looking upwards, he fell into a pit, and a neat, witty Thracian servant girl jeered at him, they say, because he was so eager to know the things in the sky that he could not see what was there before him at his very feet." Socrates' comment, "The same jest applies to all who pass their lives in philosophy," situates the anecdote in a description of the characteristics of those who are *sophoi* and engage in *philosophia*, a matter also discussed by the vinedresser and the Phoenician in this dialogue. The vinedresser's question is

PH. I need a sign and an omen for good sailing,[3] vine-dresser. For they say that we shall sail into the Aegean itself, and I believe the sea is dangerous and not easy to sail.[4] What's more, I am going against the wind. With this objective, Phoenicians seek omens for good sailing.

3   V. You people are at any rate skilled[5] in nautical affairs, stranger, for you have also, I suppose, designated Cynosura[6] as a sign in the sky, and you sail by reference to it. Yet just as you are praised for your skill in sailing, so you are slandered as money-lovers and greedy rascals for your business dealings.[7]

4   PH. But are you not money-loving, vinedresser, living among these vines and presumably seeking someone who will gather grapes after paying a drachma for them, and seeking some-one to whom you will sell sweet new wine or wine with a fine

---

ironic, since as the dialogue unfolds it is the vinedresser and not the Phoenician who is the source of knowledge and skill, which he has gained not by looking at the sky but by observing his surroundings. If the Phoenician wants to gain use-ful knowledge, he must, in the vinedresser's opinion, look down and observe the world of the heroes.

[3] As Rossi (*Filostrato: Eroico*, 193) notes, a "sign" (*sumbolon*) is any div-ination understood by the eyes, whereas an "omen" (*phêmê*) is a divination by either the voice of an oracle or the voice of a human appointed for the oracle.

[4] Whenever possible ancient sailors followed the coastline rather than sailing across the sea. On the dangers of navigation, see "Seewesen," *Der Kleine Pauly: Lexicon der Antike* 5 (1979): cols. 67–71. On the turbulent waters of the Aegean, see Philostratus *Life of Apollonius* 4.15.

[5] The adjective *sophos*, as well as the related noun *sophia* and adverb *sophôs* all designate the height of cultural achievement in the ancient world. Although *sophos* is commonly translated "wise," because achievement can be gained in various types of endeavors (not just abstract intellectual inquiry), at times the translation "skilled" or even "clever" is more appropriate. This "skill" or "cleverness," however, is not simply technical skill, but reveals the possession of "higher knowledge, exceptional understanding, insight into sub-jects far above the comprehension, though not the respect, of the common herd" (Werner Jaeger, *Paideia: The Ideals of Greek Culture* [3 vols.; 2d ed.; New York: Oxford University Press, 1943–1945], 1:219).

[6] Cynosura is the Greek name for Ursa Minor (literally, "the little bear"). The Phoenicians used this star for navigation, while the Greeks set their course by Helikê (Ursa Major; Aratus *Phaenomena* 24–44; Ovid *Fasti* 3.107–108).

[7] This reputation of the Phoenicians is first mentioned in Homer (*Od.* 14.288–289).

bouquet—a wine that, I believe, you are going to say you have hidden, just as Marôn did?

V. Phoenician stranger, if somewhere on the earth there 5 are Cyclopes, whom the earth is said to nourish, though they are lazy, neither planting nor sowing anything, then things would grow unattended, even though they belong to Demeter and to Dionysos, and none of the produce of the earth would be sold.[8] Instead, everything would be by nature without price and common to all, just as in the Marketplace of Swine.[9] Wherever it is necessary, however, for one bound to the land and subject to the seasons to sow, plow, plant, and suffer one toil after another, there it is necessary to buy and sell as well. For money is needed for 6 farming, and without it, you will feed neither a plowman nor a vinedresser nor a cowherd nor a goatherd, nor will you have a *krater*[10] from which to drink or pour a libation. In fact, the most pleasant thing in farming, namely, gathering grapes, one must contract out for hire. Otherwise, the vines will stand idle and yield no wine, as though they had been cursed.[11] These things, 7 stranger, I have said about the whole crowd of farmers, but my own way is far more reasonable, since I do not associate with merchants, and I do not know what the drachma is. But I either buy or

---

[8] That is, it would otherwise be expected that Demeter, the goddess of the grain, and Dionysos, the god of the vine, would tend the crops; compare Homer *Od.* 9.109 and the reference to the Cyclopes in Philostratus *Life of Apollonius* 6.11 (cf. *Imagines* 2.18).

[9] The Marketplace of the Swine is probably a reference to the Forum Suarium in the city of Rome. While the free distribution of meat in Rome is well attested under Aurelian, literary and epigraphic references to the Forum Suarium suggest that there was such a distribution already in the time of Caracalla. See Rossi, *Filostrato: Eroico*, 194 n. 7; Muth, "Forum Suarium," 227–36; S. Mazzarino, *L'Impero Romano* (Rome: Laterza, 1976), 441.

[10] General term for a vessel used to mix water and wine.

[11] This final phrase, "as though they had been cursed" (*hôsper gegrammenai*), most likely refers to the magical practice of inscribing a curse upon papyrus or a tablet; such a curse would render the vines barren (see LSJ, 360, s.v. γράφω). Compare another reference to magical practice in viticulture (*Her.* 21.8). It is equally possible to translate the phrase, "as though in a painting," suggesting that in artwork the grapes hang permanently upon the vines and are never made into wine. Similar uses of *gegrammenai* include Philostratus *Life of Apollonius* 2.20, referring to the deeds of Alexander inscribed on a tablet, and Ps.-Cebes *Tabula* 1.2, used of a painting on a tablet.

myself sell a bull for grain and a goat for wine and so forth, without much talking back and forth.

2   PH. You mean a golden marketplace, vinedresser, which belongs to heroes rather than to humans.[12] Hey, what does this dog want? He keeps going all around me, whining at my feet and offering his ear gently and tamely.

2   V. He explains my character[13] to you, stranger—and that we are so moderate and gracious to those who arrive here that we do not allow the dog to bark at them, but rather to welcome and to fawn before those who arrive.

3   PH. Is it permissible to approach a vine?

       V. No one is stingy, since there are enough grapes for us.

4   PH. What about picking figs?

       V. This is also allowed, since there is a surplus of figs too. And I could give you nuts, apples, and countless other good things. I plant them as snacks among the vines.

5   PH. What might I pay you for them?

       V. Nothing other than to eat them with pleasure, to be satisfied, and to go away rejoicing.

6   PH. But, vinedresser, do you live a reflective way of life?[14]

       V. Yes, indeed, with the handsome Protesilaos.

7   PH. What connection is there between you and Protesilaos, if you mean the man from Thessaly?

       V. I do mean that man, the husband of Laodameia, for he delights in hearing this epithet.

8   PH. But what, indeed, does he do here?

       V. He lives here, and we farm together.

9   PH. Has he come back to life, or what has happened?

       V. He himself does not speak about his own experiences, stranger, except, of course, that he died at Troy because of Helen, but came to life again in Phthia because he loved Laodameia.

[12] That is, the marketplace belongs to the golden age described by Hesiod (*Works and Days* 109–126).
[13] "Character" (*êthos*) includes not only a person's disposition and traits, but also one's habits and customs.
[14] *philospheô*: To engage in philosophy in the ancient world consisted in more than simply abstract intellectual pursuits; philosophy consisted in a whole manner of life ruled by the key insights and principles of that philosophy.

PH. And yet he is said to have died after he came to life 10 again and to have persuaded his wife to follow him.

V. He himself also says these things. But how he returned 11 afterwards too, he does not tell me even though I've wanted to find out for a long time. He is hiding, he says, some secret of the Fates. His fellow soldiers also, who were there in Troy, still appear on the plain, warlike in posture and shaking the crests of their helmets.

PH. By Athena, vinedresser, I don't believe it, although I 3 wish these things were so. But if you are not attending to the plants, nor irrigating them, tell me now about these matters and what you know about Protesilaos. Indeed, you would please the heroes if I should go away believing.

V. Stranger, the plants no longer need watering at midday, 2 since it is already late autumn and the season itself waters them. Therefore, I have leisure to relate everything in detail. Since these matters are sacred to the gods and so important, may they not escape the notice of cultivated people! It is also better for us to sit down in the beauty of this place.

PH. Lead the way; I will follow even beyond the interior of Thrace.

V. Let us enter the vineyard, Phoenician. For you may 3 even discover in it something to cheer you.

PH. Let us enter, for a scent that is, I suppose, pleasant comes from the plants.

V. What do you mean? Pleasant? It is divine! The blos- 4 soms of the uncultivated trees are fragrant, as are the fruits of those cultivated. If you ever come upon a cultivated plant with fragrant blossoms, pluck rather the leaves, since the sweet scent comes from them.

PH. How diverse is the beauty of your property, and how 5 lush the clusters of grapes have grown! How well-arranged are all the trees, and how divine is the fragrance of the place! Indeed, I think that the walkways which you have left untilled are pleasing, but, vinedresser, you seem to me to live luxuriously since you use so much uncultivated land.

V. The walkways are sacred, stranger, for the hero exer- 6 cises on them.

4   PH. You will discuss these things once we sit down where you are leading us. But now tell me this: do you farm your own property, or is someone else the owner, and "do you provide food for the one who feeds you," like Oineus in Euripides' tragedy?[15]

2   V. This one small plot of land out of many has been left to provide for me—as befits a free person. But powerful men have left me completely bereft of the other fields. Protesilaos took for himself this small piece of land, which was actually owned by Xeinis the Chersonesian. He took it for himself by projecting some kind of apparition of himself at Xeinis. The apparition so damaged Xeinis's eyes that he went away blind.

3   PH. I suppose you have acquired an excellent guard over your estate, and because your friend is so alert, you do not even fear attack by any wolf.

4   V. You speak the truth. No beast is allowed to enter the premises. No serpent, or poisonous spider, or extortionist[16] attacks us here in the field. This last beast is exceedingly shameless; it even kills in the marketplace.

5   PH. Vinedresser, how were you trained in speaking? You do not seem to me to be among the uneducated.

6   V. At first, we spent our life in a city, and we were provided with teachers and studied. But my affairs were really in a bad way because the farming was left to slaves, and they did not bring anything back to us. Hence it was necessary to take loans with the **7** field as security and to go hungry. And yes, on arriving, I tried to make Protesilaos my advisor, but he remained silent, since he was justifiably angry at me because, having left him, I lived in a **8** city. But when I persisted and said that I would die if neglected, **9** he said, "Change your dress." On that day, I heard this advice but did nothing; afterwards, examining it closely, I understood that he **10** was commanding me to change my way of life. From that point on, after I was suitably dressed in a leather jacket, carrying a hoe, and no longer knew my way to town, Protesilaos made everything

---

[15] August Nauck, *Tragicorum graecorum fragmenta* (2d ed.; Leipzig: Teubner, 1889), frg. 561.

[16] Extortionists or sycophants were those who for personal gain often prosecuted others without just cause, a practice that ironically became a prosecutable offense itself. The term may also be translated "informers," "slanderers," or "swindlers."

in the field grow luxuriously for me. Whenever a sheep, a beehive, or a tree became diseased, I consulted Protesilaos as a physician. Since I spend time with him and devote myself to the land, I am becoming more skilled than I used to be, because he excels in wisdom.

PH. You are fortunate indeed with such company and land, 11 if you not only gather olives and grapes in it, but also harvest divine and pure wisdom. I equally do an injustice to your wisdom by calling you a "vinedresser."

V. Do call me so, and indeed you would please Protesi- 12 laos by addressing me as "farmer" and "gardener" and things like these.

PH. Do you then spend time with each other here, vine- 5 dresser?

V. Yes, right here, stranger. How did you guess?

PH. Because this portion of the land seems to me to be most 2 pleasant and divine. I do not know whether anyone has ever come to life again here, but if someone were to, he would live, I suppose, most pleasantly and painlessly after coming from the throng of battle. These trees are very tall, since time has reared them. This 3 water from the springs is varied in taste, and I suppose you draw it as though drinking first one vintage wine and then another. You also produce canopies by twining and fitting together the trees, as one could not even weave together a crown from an unmown meadow.[17]

V. Stranger, you have not yet even heard the nightingales 4 that sing here both when evening comes and when day begins, just as they do in Attica.[18]

PH. I suppose that I have heard and that I agree that they 5

[17] This comparison implies that the vinedresser's canopies surpass in piety and sanctity garlands woven for divine offerings from a sacred meadow. See Euripides *Hippolytus* 72–83. The implication may also be that an unmown meadow would contain a great variety of flowers, and hence that because the canopies in the hero's sanctuary are made from a variety of trees, they represent the full range of beauty and color.

[18] In Greek poetic tradition, the nightingale is the typical song bird of lament; see, for example, Penelope's comparison of herself to the nightingale (Homer *Od.* 19.518–523), as well as the story of Procne and Philomela (Apollodorus *Library* 3.14.8). The nightingale thus becomes a metaphor for the poet

do not lament, but only sing. But say something about the heroes, for I would rather hear about them. Do you want to sit down somewhere?

V. The hero, who is a gracious host, agrees to offer us these seats of honor.

6 PH. Look, I am at ease, for hospitality is pleasant for one listening to serious discourse.

6 V. Ask whatever you wish, my guest,[19] and you will not say that you came in vain. For when Odysseus, far from his ship, was perplexed, Hermes, or one of his clever followers, had an earnest conversation with him (the subject was probably the *moly*[20]). And Protesilaos by means of me will fill you with information and make you more content and wise. For knowing many things is worth much.

2 PH. But I am not perplexed, my good friend. By Athena! I have come under the auspices of a god, and I finally understand my dream.

V. How do you interpret your dream? You hint at something divine.

(e.g., Hesiod *Works and Days* 203–208 where Hesiod compares himself as a poet to the nightingale) and a symbol of the poetic composition and performance (see especially Aeschylus *Suppliants* 60–67). In Aelian *On the Characteristics of Animals* 5.38, the nightingale has the epithet *philomousos* ("lover of the Muses"; see Gregory Nagy, *Poetry as Performance: Homer and Beyond* [Cambridge: Cambridge University Press, 1996], especially 7–38, 57–66, where he argues well that the nightingale functions as a model of the rhapsode). The mention of nightingales here, as the vinedresser undertakes to narrate the deeds of the heroes, is an important reference to the variability of the heroic poetic tradition. For association of the nightingales with Attica, compare Sophocles *Oedipus at Colonus* 672: Attica is the place where the nightingale most likes to sing.

[19] Up to this point, *xenos* has been translated "stranger." Now that some customs of hospitality have been observed, it seems appropriate to translate *xenos* as "my guest" for the rest of the dialogue.

[20] The *moly* is a magical herb with a black root and white flower. Hermes gave it to Odysseus as an antidote to Circe's enchantments (Homer *Od.* 10.274–306). Pliny (*Natural History* 25.8) identified the *moly* with a plant that grew in Arcadia and Campania. Although he agrees with Homer that it is difficult to dig up, he disputes Homer's description of it. In the *Odyssey* (10.278–279) Hermes appears in the guise of a young man, never revealing himself as Hermes. This part of the story leads to an ambiguity voiced by the vinedresser, which is an early hint of the critique of Homer, particularly the stories about Odysseus developed later in the dialogue.

PH. This is already about the thirty-fifth day, I suppose, 3
that I have been sailing from Egypt and Phoenicia. When the ship
put in here at Elaious, I dreamed I read the verses of Homer in
which he relates the catalogue of the Achaeans,[21] and I invited
the Achaeans to board the ship, since it was large enough for all.
When I awoke with a start (for a shuddering came over me), I at- 4
tributed the dream to the slowness and length of the voyage, since
apparitions of the dead make no impression on those who travel
in haste. Because I wished to be advised about the meaning of the 5
dream (for the wind has not yet allowed our sailing), I have disembarked here. While walking, as you know, I encountered you 6
first, and we are now talking about Protesilaos. We shall also converse about the catalogue of the heroes, for you say that we shall
do so, and "cataloguing them on the ship" would mean that those
who have compiled the story about them would then embark.

The Phoenician's Doubts Overcome (6.7–8.18)

V. My guest, you have truly arrived under the auspices of 7
a god, and you have described the vision soundly. Let us then recount the story, lest you say that I have corrupted you by diverting
you from it.

PH. You know at least what I long to learn. I need to un- **7**
derstand this association which you have with Protesilaos, what he
is like, and if he knows a story about Trojan times similar to that
of the poets, or one unknown to them. What I mean by "Trojan 2
times" is this sort of thing: the assembling of the army at Aulis and
the heroes, one by one, whether they were handsome, brave, and
clever, as they are celebrated. After all, how could he narrate the
war round about Troy when he did not fight to the end, since they
say that he was the first of the entire Hellenic army to die, the in-
stant he disembarked there?

V. This is a foolish thing for you to say, my guest. To be 3
cleansed of the body is the beginning of life for divine and thus
blessed souls.[22] For the gods, whose attendants they are, they then
know, not by worshipping statues and conjectures, but by gaining visible association with them. And free from the body and its

---

[21] Homer *Il.* 2.484–760.
[22] The tomb-like nature of the body is characteristic of Platonic philosophy; see Plato *Phaedo* 80e–84b.

diseases, souls observe the affairs of mortals, both when souls are filled with prophetic skill and when the oracular power sends Bacchic frenzy upon them.

4   At any rate, among those who critically examine Homer's poems, who will you say reads and has insight into them as Prote-
5   silaos does? Indeed, my guest, before Priam and Troy there was no epic recitation, nor had anyone sung of events that had not yet taken place. There was poetry about prophetic matters and about Herakles, son of Alkmênê, recently arranged but not yet developed fully, but Homer had not yet sung. Some say that it was when Troy was captured, others say it was a few or even eight generations later that he applied himself to poetic composition.
6   Nevertheless, Protesilaos knows everything of Homer and sings of many Trojan events that took place after his own lifetime, and also of many Hellenic and Median events. He calls at any rate the campaign of Xerxes the third destruction of mortals, after what happened in the time of both Deucalion and Phaethôn, when a great many nations were destroyed.

7   PH. You will fill the horn of Amaltheia, vinedresser, since your companion knows so much. I suppose you will report them correctly, even as you heard them.

8   V. By Zeus, I would wrong the hero, who is both learned and truth-loving, if I did not honor the truth, which he is accustomed to call the "mother of virtue."

9   PH. I think that I have confessed my own experience to you from the beginning of our conversation: I am inclined to disbelieve legends. This is the reason: Until now I have not met anyone who has seen such fabulous things, but rather one person claims to have heard it from another, that other person believes it, and a third one a poet convinces. What is said about the great size of the heroes—how they were ten cubits tall[23]—I consider pleasing in storytelling, but false and unconvincing for one who observes things according to nature, for which contemporary humans provide the measure.

[23] A unit of measure equivalent to the distance from the elbow to the tip of the middle finger (approximately eighteen inches). The heroes would thus be ca. 15′ tall, much taller than the biblical Goliath who, according to the MT of 1 Sam 17:4, was 6.5 cubits, or 9′ 9″ tall. The LXX and 4QSam^a give by contrast a height of 4.5 cubits, or only 6′ 9″ tall.

V.   When did you begin to consider these things unconvinc-   10
ing?

PH.   Long ago, vinedresser, while yet a young man. When
I was still a child I believed such things, and my nurse cleverly
amused me with these tales, singing and even weeping over some
of them.[24] But when I became a young man, I did not think it necessary to accept such tales without question.

V.   But concerning Protesilaos, have you ever happened to   11
hear that he appears here?

PH.   Vinedresser, how could I when I do not believe what I
am hearing from you today?

V.   Then let the ancient things which you find unconvinc-   12
ing be the beginning of my story. You say, I suppose, that you
disbelieve that human beings were ten cubits tall. When you can
sufficiently accept this, you ought to demand the rest of the story
about Protesilaos and whatever else you want about Trojan matters. You will disbelieve none of these things.

PH.   You speak well. Let us proceed this way.

V.   Listen now, my friend. I had a grandfather who knew   **8**
many of the things you do not believe. He used to say that the
tomb of Ajax was destroyed by the sea near which it lies, and
that bones appeared in it of a person eleven cubits tall. He also
said that upon his arrival at Troy the emperor Hadrian embraced
and kissed some of the bones, wrapped them up, and restored the
present tomb of Ajax.[25]

PH.   Not without reason, vinedresser, am I likely to doubt   2
such things, since you say that you have heard something from
your grandfather and probably from your mother or nurse; but
you report nothing on your own authority unless you would speak
about Protesilaos.

V.   Indeed, if I were versed in legendary lore, I would de-   3

---

[24] See Plato *Republic* 376e–378e, on the use of stories in the education of
the young.

[25] Pausanias (*Description of Greece* 1.35.5) relates a Mysian story of the
poor condition of Ajax's grave and huge size of his bones. Hadrian's visit may
have been during his tour of the province of Asia in 124 C.E.; see Anthony R.
Birley, *Hadrian: The Restless Emperor* (New York: Routledge, 1997), 164.

scribe the seven-cubit-long corpse of Orestes, which the Lacedaemonians found in Tegea,[26] as well as that corpse inside the bronze
Lydian horse, which had been buried in Lydia before the time
of Gyges.[27] When the earth was split by an earthquake, the marvel was observed by Lydian shepherds with whom Gyges then
served. The corpse, appearing larger than human, had been
4 laid in a hollow horse that had openings on either side. Even if
such things can be doubted because of their antiquity, I do not
5 know anything from our own time that you will deny. Not long
ago, a bank of the river Orontes, when it was divided, revealed
Aryadês—whom some called an Ethiopian, others an Indian—a
6 thirty-cubit-long corpse lying in the land of Assyria.[28] Moreover,
not more than fifty years ago, Sigeion—right over here—revealed
the body of a giant on an outcropping of its promontory. Apollo
himself asserts that he killed him while fighting on behalf of Troy.
When sailing into Sigeion, my guest, I saw the very condition of
the earth and how big the giant was. Many Hellespontians and Ionians and all the islanders and Aeolians sailed there as well. For
two months the giant lay on the great promontory, giving rise to
one tale after another since the oracle had not yet revealed the true
story.

7   PH. Would you speak further, vinedresser, about his size,
the structure of his bones, and the serpents, which are said to have
grown together with the giants, and which the painters sketch below the torso of Enkelados and his companions?

8   V. If those monstrous beings existed, my guest, and if they
were joined with snakes, I do not know. But the one in Sigeion
was twenty-two cubits long, and it was lying in a rocky cleft with
its head toward the mainland and its feet even with the promontory. But we did not see any sign of serpents around it, nor is there

[26] The majority of manuscripts read "Nemea" here, but the variant
"Tegea" is to be preferred following Herodotus *Hist.* 1.66–68 and Pausanias
Description of Greece 3.3.5–7; 8.54.4, who recount a story of how in the time of
Lycurgus, the Lacedaemonians were instructed to seek the bones of Orestes in
Tegea.

[27] See the story of Gyges in Plato *Republic* 359d–e.

[28] According to Pausanias (*Description of Greece* 8.29.3–4), an unnamed
Roman emperor wanted to build a canal from the Orontes near Antioch to the
sea. A corpse was discovered, and the oracle at Klaros revealed his name to be
Orontes, an Indian.

anything different about its bones from those of a human being.
Furthermore, Hymnaios of Peparêthos, who is on friendly terms 9
with me, sent one of his sons here some four years ago to consult
Protesilaos through me about a similar marvel. When Hymnaios
happened to dig up vines on the island of Ikos (he alone owned
the island), the earth sounded somewhat hollow to those who
were digging. When they opened it up, they found a twelve-cubit
corpse lying there with a serpent inhabiting its skull. The young 10
man then came to ask us what should be done in his honor, and
Protesilaos said, "Let us cover the stranger completely," without
doubt urging those who were willing to rebury the corpse and not
to leave it exposed. He also said that the giant was one of those
who were hurled down by the gods. But the corpse that came to 11
light on Lemnos, which Menekratês of Steiria found, was very
big, and I saw it a year ago when I sailed from Imbros, only a short
distance from Lemnos. Its bones, however, no longer appear in
their proper order: the vertebrae lie separated from each other,
tossed about by earthquakes, I suppose, and the ribs are wrenched
out of the vertebrae. But if one imagines the bones together as a
whole, the size seems to make one shudder and is not easily described. Certainly when we poured two Cretan amphoras[29] of
wine into the skull, it was not filled. Now, there is a headland 12
on Imbros called "Naulokhos" facing the south, under which a
spring is found that turns male animals into eunuchs, and makes
females so drunk that they fall asleep. At this spot, when a piece of
land was severed from the mainland, the body of a very large giant was pulled out. If you disbelieve me, let us set sail. The corpse
still lies exposed, and the sea journey to Naulokhos is short.

PH. I would gladly go beyond Okeanos, vinedresser, if I 13
could find such a marvel. My business, however, does not allow
me to stray so far. Rather, I must be bound to my ship, just like
Odysseus.[30] Otherwise, as they say, the things in the bow and the
things in the stern will perish.

V. But do not yet regard as credible what I have said, my 14

[29] An amphora is a large-bellied clay vessel with two handles. As a Greek
liquid measure it held approximately nine gallons.

[30] Compare Homer *Od.* 12.154–200 where Odysseus is bound to the
mast of his ship to prevent him from following the Sirens' singing.

guest, until you sail to the island of Cos, where the bones of earth-
born men lie, the first descendants of Merops, they say, and until
you see the bones of Hyllos, son of Herakles, in Phrygia[31] and,
by Zeus, those of the Alôadai in Thessaly, since they are really
nine fathoms long and exactly as they are celebrated in song.[32]
15 The Neapolitans living in Italy consider the bones of Alkyoneus a
marvel. They say that many giants were thrown down there, and
16 Mount Vesuvius smolders over them. Indeed in Pallênê, which
the poets call "Phlegra," the earth holds many such bodies of giants encamped there, and rainstorms and earthquakes uncover
many others. Not even a shepherd ventures at midday to that
17 place of clattering phantoms[33] which rage there. Disbelief in such
things probably existed even at the time of Herakles. Hence, after
he killed Geryon in Erytheia and was alleged to have encountered the most enormous creature, Herakles dedicated its bones at
Olympia so that his contest would not be disbelieved.

18   PH. I consider you fortunate for your knowledge,[34] vine-
dresser. I was ignorant of such great bones, and out of ignorance
I disbelieved. But what about the stories of Protesilaos? It is time,
I suppose, to come to those, since they are no longer unbelievable.

II. PROTESILAOS (9.1–23.30)

The Sanctuary of Protesilaos at Elaious (9.1–7)

9   V. Listen to such stories now, my guest. Protesilaos does

---

[31] Pausanias (*Description of Greece* 1.35.6) offers an alternative identification: the inhabitants of a Lydian city called the Doors of Temenos discovered a
huge corpse, which they at first claimed to be the body of Geryon; sacred officials later declared it to be the body of Hyllos, the son of Gê. A river was named
after him, and Pausanias says that Herakles named his son Hyllos after the Lydian river.

[32] Homer *Od.* 11.305–320. One fathom is equivalent to the length of
arms outstretched, or about six feet. These giants are described in the *Odyssey*
(11.311–312 [Lattimore]) as the "tallest men the grain-giving earth has brought
forth ever" and they grew "nine fathoms" tall.

[33] The phantoms (*eidôla*) here are apparitions of the shades of the dead;
see Homer *Odyssey* 11, where Odysseus summons the shades from Hades.

[34] Literally, *historia*, inquiry, observation, research, or the information
obtained from such a process of investigation; implied is accurate discernment
and the authority that accompanies it.

not lie buried at Troy but here on the Chersonesus. This large
mound here on the left no doubt contains him. The nymphs created these elms around the mound, and they made, I suppose, the
following decree concerning these trees: "Those branches turned 2
toward Ilion will blossom early and will then immediately shed
their leaves and perish before their season (this was indeed the
misfortune of Protesilaos), but a tree on the other side will live and
prosper." All the trees that were not set round the grave, such as 3
these in the grove, have strength in all their branches and flourish
according to their particular nature.[35]

PH. I see, vinedresser, and I am not surprised that I con- 4
tinue to marvel, because what is divine is cleverly devised.

V. Consider this sanctuary, my guest, where the Mede 5
committed a sacrilege in our forefathers' time. It was because of
this they say even the preserved fish came back to life.[36] You see
how little of the sanctuary is left. But back then it was lovely and
not small, as can be made out from its foundations. This cult 6
statue stood upon a ship, since its base has the shape of a prow,
and the ship's captain dedicated it. Time has worn it away and, by
Zeus, those who anoint it and seal their vows here have changed

[35] The strange life cycle of the trees planted around the sanctuary of
Protesilaos was well known. See *Anthologia Palatina* 7.141, 385; Pliny *Natural History* 16.88; Quintus of Smyrna *Fall of Troy* 7.408–411. Elms were often
planted around tombs, perhaps as symbols of the dead since they do not bear
fruit; see Homer *Il.* 6.420 for the elms planted around the tomb of Andro-
makhê's father, Êetiôn, and the discussion by Rossi (*Filostrato: Eroico*, 203).

[36] *tarikhos*, translated here as preserved fish, may also designate a corpse
embalmed according to Egyptian custom (see Herodotus *Hist.* 2.85–89), and
thus Philostratus retains an implicit reference to Protesilaos's return to life.
According to Herodotus, Artayktes, the Persian governor of Sestus and a subordinate of Xerxes, "brought women into the sanctuary of Protesilaos at Elaious
and committed sacrilegious acts" and stole the offerings to Protesilaos housed in
the sanctuary (*Hist.* 7.33; 9.116 [Godley, LCL]). Protesilaos performed a mirac-
ulous sign of bringing to life preserved fish (*tarikhoi*) to indicate the coming
vengeance that he would exact upon Artayktes. Despite his offer to compen-
sate Protesilaos with one hundred talents and the Athenians with two hundred,
he was nailed alive to a plank (*Hist.* 9.120). As Herodotus narrates the episode
in light of the Persian claim that all Asia belongs to them, it is Protesilaos's
preserved corpse (*tarikhos*) who exacts retribution from Artayktes not only for
these injustices, but also as vengeance for his own death as the first Hellene
to die on Asian soil (*Hist.* 9.120.2–3). See the discussion in Nagy, *Pindar's
Homer*, 268–73.

7 its shape. But this means nothing to me. For I spend time with him and see him, and no statue could be more pleasant than that man.

Protesilaos's Appearance, Character, and Way of Life (10.1–13.4)

10   PH. Why don't you describe him to me and share what he looks like?

2   V. Gladly, my guest, by Athena. He is about twenty years old at most. Because he sailed to Troy at such a young age, he has a full, splendid beard and smells sweeter than autumn myrtles. Cheerful eyebrows frame his eyes, which gives him a pleasant, friendly manner. When he exerts himself, he looks intense and determined. But if we meet him at ease, ah, how lovely and
3 friendly his eyes appear! He has blond hair of moderate length. It hangs a little over his forehead rather than covering it. The shape of his nose is perfect,[37] like the statue's. His voice is more
4 sonorous than trumpets and comes from a small mouth. It is most enjoyable to meet him naked, since he is well built and nimble, just like the herms set up in race courses.[38] His height is easily ten cubits, and it seems to me that he would have exceeded this had he not died in his early twenties.

5   PH. I can envision the young man, vinedresser, and I admire you because of your companion. Is he armed as a soldier, or how is he attired?

V. He is clad in a riding cloak, my guest, in Thessalian style, just like this statue. The cloak is sea-purple, of a divine luster, for the luster of purple cannot be expressed.

11   PH. And his passionate love for Laodameia—how is it now?

---

[37] *tetragônos*, literally, "four-sided," "square," hence, "perfect as a square" (LSJ, 1780, s.v. τετράγωνος). The vinedresser here refers to a cult statue of Protesilaos visible in the shrine. The statue would by custom have been painted and clothed. The way in which the Phoenician in his description of the hero refers to the statue is reminiscent of Philostratus's *Imagines*, in which the visual arts are depicted verbally.

[38] A herm was a tall oblong stone, often with a bearded human head at the top and a phallus halfway up; it represented the god Hermes and was placed as a boundary stone or distance marker. Vase paintings show sacrifices being made at herms (Burkert, *Greek Religion*, 156).

V. He loves her, and he is loved by her, and they are disposed toward one another just like those hot from the bridal chambers.

PH. Do you embrace him when he arrives, or does he escape you like smoke, as he does the poets?[39]   2

V. He enjoys my embrace and allows me to kiss him and cling to his neck.

PH. Does he come often or only once in a great while?   3

V. I think that I converse with him four or five times a month, whenever he wishes to plant some of these plants, to gather them, or to cut flowers. When someone is garlanded, he makes the flowers even sweeter, whenever he is around them.

PH. You say the hero is cheerful and really married.   4

V. And self-controlled, my guest. For loving laughter because of his youth, he does not act with arrogance. If I chance on a rock while digging somewhere, he often takes up a hoe and assists me with difficult jobs, and if I don't know something about farming, he corrects me. Because I heard from Homer about   5 "long trees," I used to plant them by putting into the ground less of the tree than was above, and when Protesilaos stopped me, I quoted the verses of Homer to him. He, understanding, said, "Yet Homer commanded the opposite of what you are doing. For from his skill he knew that the depths are 'long' so that somewhere he called the cisterns 'long' since they are deep." He said that the trees take better root in the earth if a great part is firmly rooted and only a little bit is able to move.[40] Standing near me as I wa-   6 tered the flowers, he said, "The perfume, my good friend, does not need water," presumably teaching me not to drench the flowers.

PH. Where does he spend the rest of the time, vinedresser?   7

V. He says that sometimes he lives in Hades, other times in Phthia, and even sometimes in Troy, where his companions are.

[39] When Achilles tried to embrace the ghost of Patroklos he disappeared like a vapor (*Il.* 23.65–101). Likewise in Hades Odysseus tried unsuccessfully to hold his dead mother and Agamemnon (*Od.* 11.204–222, 390–394).

[40] This passage is a discussion about the meaning of the word *makra* ("long") in Homer. The vinedresser recalls from Homer the phrase *dendra makra* (e.g., *Od.* 18.359), which he understands to mean "tall trees." Protesilaos, however, refers to Homer's use of *makra* to mean "deep" (*Il.* 21.197).

And when he hunts wild boar and deer, he arrives here at midday, stretches out, and falls asleep.

8   Ph.   Where does he spend time with Laodameia?

V.   In Hades, my guest. He says that she fares most favorably among women, since she is numbered with such women as Alcestis, the wife of Admêtos, and Euadnê, the wife of Kapaneus, and others equally chaste and worthy.

9   Ph.   Do they eat together, or is that not their custom?

V.   I have not yet met him when he is eating, my guest, nor have I observed him drinking. Indeed, I make a drink-offering[41] for him every evening from these Thasian vines, which he himself planted, and I dedicate seasonal sweetmeats every day at noon, whenever summer has come and fall stands at the door. When the moon becomes full in the season of early spring, I pour milk into this chilled vessel and say, "Behold, here is the flowing essence of the season for you. Drink." When I have said this, I go away, and the things are eaten and drunk faster than the blink of an eye.

12   Ph.   What does he say about his dying at such a young age?

V.   My guest, Protesilaos regrets his suffering, and the daimon[42] who was against him at that time he considers unjust and malicious since, although his foot was compliant, it was not fixed firmly in Troy. As a fighter, he would not have been inferior in

2   any way to Diomedes, Patroklos, or the lesser Ajax. He says that,

---

[41] That is, a libation or the outpouring of liquid (wine, water, honey, or oil) as a ritual act. The verb used here (*spendô*) is usually associated with a libation of wine, which was made whenever wine was drunk. The libation was accompanied by invocation of a god or hero. Libations were also a part of prayer and supplication, occurring at both the beginning and the conclusion of animal sacrifices. They were also made to mark the cessation of hostilities, as for an armistice or ceremonial games. Libations for the dead were poured into offering pits (*bothroi*) around the graves. See Burkert, *Greek Religion*, 70–73.

[42] An unpredictable, unnamed, and sometimes frightening manifestation of supernatural power, "daimon" designates more a "mode of activity" rather than a category of god (Burkert, *Greek Religion*, 180). In Homer, gods and heroes are called "daimones." From Hesiod on, the term "daimon" was used to refer to heroes from the past who bring prosperity or destruction to humans; prominent figures are honored after death as daimons. To be "eudaimon," that is, happy or fortunate, is to be possessed of and influenced by a favorable daimon; hence "daimon" came to be a rough synonym for *tukhê*, "good fortune."

compared with the descendants of Aiakos, he lacked military skills because of his youth, since he was in late adolescence, but Achilles was a young man and Ajax a grown man. He confirms Homer's 3 verses about him,[43] although he does not confirm all of them: how, for example, Homer says that his wife's cheeks were torn on both sides, that his house was half-built,[44] that the ship upon which he sailed was under attack, and that he calls him warlike. He grieves that he accomplished nothing at Troy, and how he fell 4 in a land that he had not even assaulted.[45] He is marked with a scar on his upper thigh, for he said that his wound was washed together with his body.

PH. Vinedresser, how does he train his body, since you **13** claimed that he also practices this activity?

V. My guest, he practices all warlike exercises except archery, and all kinds of sports except wrestling. He considers archery for cowards and wrestling for the lazy.

PH. How good is he at the pancratium,[46] and how well does 2 he box?

V. My guest, he practices these with a shadow,[47] and he throws the discus farther than a mortal can. He tosses the discus

---

[43] Homer *Il.* 2.695–710.

[44] The meaning of the phrase, "his house was half-built (*hêmitelês*)" was debated in antiquity. According to Lucian (*Dialogues of the Dead* 27.1), it referred to Protesilaos's death; according to Strabo, however, a "half-built house" is one that is bereft of women (Strabo *Geography* 7.3.3). Other interpreters took it to mean that Protesilaos was childless or that his wedding-chamber was unfinished when he went to war (see R. O. A. M. Lyne, "Love and Death: Laodamia and Protesilaus in Catullus, Propertius, and Others," *Classical Quarterly* 48/1 (1998): 201 n. 6).

[45] Protesilaos here agrees with Homer's tale of his death. An alternative story portrays Protesilaos as the first of the Greeks to land in Troy and the first to die, but says that he slew many Trojans before his death (Apollodorus *Epitome* 3.30).

[46] An athletic contest in which each contestant tried to force his opponent to admit defeat. The tactics of wrestling and boxing, as well as kicking, were allowed; only biting and gouging of the eyes, nose, and mouth were prohibited.

[47] In other words, since Protesilaos has no real opponent with whom to train, he competes against his own shadow, a practice corresponding to *skiamakhia* or shadow-boxing (compare 1 Cor 9:26). See Rossi, *Filostrato: Eroico*, 207–8 n. 52.

above the clouds, and he casts it more than one hundred cubits, and that, you see, with it being twice the Olympic weight! When he runs, you would not find a trace, nor does his foot leave any impression on the ground.

PH. But there are huge footprints on the walkways, which suggest that the hero is ten cubits tall.

3   V. Those prints, my guest, are from his walking or doing some other exercise; but when he runs, the earth remains unmarked because he is raised off the ground and like someone floating on the waves. He said that in Aulis, when Hellas was training for war against Troy, he outran Achilles in the
4   competitions and that he jumped farther than Achilles. But in warlike exercises he yields to Achilles, as he said, except in the fight against the Mysians, for there he killed more Mysians than Achilles and carried away the rewards of valor. He also outdid Achilles in the contest over the shield.

Suppliants at Protesilaos's Sanctuary (14.1–17.6)

14   PH. And, vinedresser, what would be the contest over the shield? No poet has mentioned it, nor does it appear in any story of the Trojan War.

V. That, my guest, you will say about many matters, because the hero tells many things about warriors as well as deeds
2   of battle that are not yet known to most people. This is the reason. He says that, in their passion for the poems of Homer, most people, looking only at Achilles and Odysseus, neglect good and brave men, so that some are not remembered at all, and for others Homer dedicates a trireme[48] of four verses. He says that Achilles is celebrated in song worthily but Odysseus at too great a length.
3   But I shall tell you a little later whatever was left untold of Sthenelos, Palamedes, and other such men, lest you go away knowing nothing about them. In a moment we shall complete the Mysian
4   story, into which the matter of the shield enters. But now, since we mentioned the pancratium, boxing, and throwing the discus,

---

[48] A ship, usually with three banks of oars, often a warship; here the metaphor may refer to the way in which, within Homer's Catalogue of Ships (*Il.* 2.494–759), only a very few verses are devoted to some heroes (e.g., Telamônian Ajax, *Il.* 2.557–558) in contrast to the lengthier mention of other commanders. See Rossi, *Filostrato: Eroico*, 208 n. 55.

which will bring us back to the shield, hear the wonderful deeds performed by our hero for the athletes who consulted Protesilaos as advisor. For example, you have heard, I think, of the Cilician pancratic athlete, whom our fathers called "Halter,"[49] how small he was, indeed much smaller than his opponents.

PH. I certainly am aware of him, in view of his statues, for **15** bronze ones stand in many places.

V. He possessed excellence in skill and courage, and harmony of body made him very strong. When the young man 2 arrived at this sanctuary (he sailed directly to Delphi for the trial of strength) he asked Protesilaos how he might overcome his rivals. He said, "By being trampled upon." Faintheartedness im- 3 mediately seized the athlete, as if he had been struck down by the oracle. After he first discovered the heel maneuver during a contest, he later realized that the oracle ordered him not to let go of his opponent's foot. For the one who wrestles with the heel must be trampled upon repeatedly and lie under his opponent.[50] By doing so, the athlete gained an illustrious name for himself and was defeated by no one. Possibly you have also heard of the dexterous 4 Ploutarkhos?

PH. I have, for in all likelihood you mean the boxer.

V. On his way to compete in his second Olympiad, he pe- 5 titioned the hero to give him an oracular response about victory. The hero ordered him to pray to Akhelôos, presider over the games.

PH. What then was the riddle?

V. Ploutarkhos contended against Hermeias the Egyptian 6 in Olympia for the crown of victory. When both were exhausted— the one from wounds, the other from thirst (for the noonday sun

[49] Literally a jumping weight held in the hand and originally used for gaining momentum and greater distance in the long jump. These weights, made of metal or stone, ranged from two to ten pounds and were also used for muscle strengthening through lifting, swinging, and throwing them (Philostratus *On Gymnastics* 55; E. Norman Gardiner, *Athletics of the Ancient World* [Oxford: Clarendon, 1930], 145–53). Here the term is used as a nickname of an athlete, perhaps for his trademark method of training; modern equivalents might be "Weights," "Dumb-bell," or "Shot put."

[50] The vinedresser here describes a maneuver in which the pancratist, while lying on his back, holds his opponent's heel and throws him into a worse position. See Gardiner, *Athletics*, 215.

glared down on the boxing ring)—a cloud burst over the stadium, and the thirsty Ploutarkhos drank some water that the sheepskins around his forearms had soaked up.[51] When he reflected on the oracular response, as he said later, he screwed up his courage and
7 gained the victory. (You would equally marvel at the endurance of Eudaimôn the Egyptian if you had encountered him boxing somewhere.) When asked how he had not been defeated, he said, "By despising death."

PH. He does indeed trust the oracle, vinedresser, for by preparing himself in this way, he seems unconquerable and divine to the crowds.

8   V. The athlete Helix himself has not yet sailed toward this sanctuary, having sent one of his companions to ask how often he would win at the Olympic games. And Protesilaos said, "You will win twice, if you do not want three times."

9   PH. Amazing, vinedresser! I suppose you will relate what happened at Olympia. For he had won one victory already, when as a man among boys he won the wrestling contest.[52] At the Olympiad after that he stripped himself for wrestling as well as for the pancratium. The Eleans were displeased at this and decided to exclude him from both these events by making accusations that he had violated Olympic regulations. Nevertheless, they grudgingly
10 crowned him for the pancratium. And Protesilaos told him beforehand to be on his guard against this kind of envy, because he knew that Helix was a rival of choice athletes.

V. You have made a most excellent interpretation of the oracle, my guest.

16   PH. But what diseases does he heal? For you say that many pray to him.

---

[51] The vinedresser is referring to the "sharp thongs" worn by boxers. These thongs consisted of leather strips wrapped around the knuckles and forearms and ending in a thick strip of fleece near the elbow. The meaning of the oracle is, presumably, that praying to the river god, Akhelôos, resulted in a flow of refreshing water.

[52] There were two classes of competition at the Olympic games: boys and men. The phrase "man among boys" indicates that Helix was probably eighteen years old and that although he competed in the boys' division, his physique and strength made him appear older. Disputes about age were not uncommon. See Plutarch *Agesilaos* 13; Pausanias *Description of Greece* 6.14.1.

V. He heals all the illnesses there are, especially consumptions, edemas, diseases of the eyes, and quartan fever.[53] Lovers 2 can also gain his counsel, for he sympathizes deeply with those unlucky in erotic matters, and he suggests charms and tricks with which they enchant their boy lovers. But he neither converses with adulterers nor offers them any erotic advice. He says that he dislikes them because they give love a bad name. An adulterer 3 once arrived here with the very wife whom he was trying to seduce, and both of them wished to conspire against her husband who was present but did not yet realize the situation—for he was sleeping there at midday, but they already made their conspiracy while standing at the altar...

PH. What did Protesilaos do?

V. He egged on this dog, even though you can see that it 4 is good-natured, to attack them from behind and bite them while they were still conspiring. When he had frustrated the conspiracy in this way, Protesilaos stood near the husband and ordered him not to trouble himself about the adulterers, since their bites were incurable, but now at least to save himself as well as his own household. The gods know everything; but the heroes know less than the gods but more than humans. A great crowd of such ones 5 streams in—if only I could remember them all; they include at least even those who in Phthia and Phulakê have appeared to all the inhabitants of Thessaly. For you see, Protesilaos has an active sanctuary there, and he gives many benevolent and favorable signs to the Thessalians and wrathful ones if he is neglected.[54]

PH. By Protesilaos, I am convinced, vinedresser. It is 6 good, I see, to swear by such a hero.

V. You would be wrong to disbelieve, my guest. Since **17** you live near the mainland of Cilicia, perhaps you know more than I do about both Amphiaraos, whom the earth is said to

---

[53] One of three forms of malaria known in the ancient world; Hippocrates declared quartan fever "the safest, easiest to bear and yet longest of all" fevers (*Epidemics* 1.24 [Jones, LCL]).

[54] Pindar (*Isthmian* 1.58–59) mentions the sacred ground of Protesilaos in Phulakê.

hold in a cleverly devised and secret shrine, and his son Am-
2 philokhos.[55] But you might do injustice to Marôn, the son of
Euanthês, who haunts the vines at Ismaros and, by planting and
pruning them, makes them produce sweet wine, especially when
farmers see Marôn handsome and splendid, exhaling a breath
3 sweet and smelling of wine. You should also know something
about the Thracian Rhêsos. Rhêsos, whom Diomedes killed at
Troy,[56] is said to inhabit Rhodopê, where they celebrate many of
his wonders in song. They say that he breeds horses, serves as
4 a soldier, and hunts wild beasts. A sign that the hero is hunting
is that the wild boars, deer, and all the wild beasts on the mountain come to the altar of Rhêsos by twos or threes to be sacrificed
5 unbound and to offer themselves to the sacrificial knife.[57] This
same hero is also said to keep the mountains free of pestilence.
Rhodopê is extremely populous, and many villages surround the
6 sanctuary. For this reason I think even Diomedes will cry out
in defense of his fellow soldiers. If we believe this Thracian still
exists (whom Diomedes killed as one who had done nothing famous at Troy nor displayed there anything worthy of mention
other than his white horses[58]) and we make sacrifices to him while
traveling through Rhodopê and Thrace, then we would dishonor
those who have performed divine and brilliant works, believing
the fame surrounding them fabulous tales and idle boasting.

Recent Appearances of Heroes at Troy (18.1–23.1)

18   PH. Finally I am on your side, vinedresser, and no one
hereafter will disbelieve such stories. What about those heroes
on the plain at Ilion whom you said marched in warlike fashion?
When have they been seen?

2   V. They appear, I said. They still appear great and divine to herdsmen and shepherds on the plain, and they are seen
whenever there is evil upon the land. If they appear covered with

[55] A famous oracular shrine of Amphiaraos was located at Mallos in Cilicia (Pausanias *Description of Greece* 1.34.2).
[56] Homer *Il.* 10.469–502.
[57] The willingness of the victims to be sacrificed was considered a necessary sign for a successful sacrifice, and their spontaneous procession to the altar
was a common legendary motif. See Burkert, *Greek Religion*, 56; and Walter
Burkert, "Greek Tragedy and Sacrificial Ritual," *GRBS* 7 (1966): 107.
[58] Homer *Il.* 10.435–441.

dust, they portend drought for the land, but if they appear full
of sweat, they portend floods and heavy rains. If blood appears
on them or their weapons, they send forth diseases upon Ilion. If
none of these signs is perceived about their images, they immediately bring prosperous times, and then the herdsmen sacrifice
to them a lamb, a bull, a colt, or whatever each one tends. They 3
say that all deaths among the herds come from Ajax. I believe
they say this because of the story of his madness, when Ajax is
said to have fallen upon the herds and cut them to pieces as if
slaying the Achaeans because of their decision.[59] No one grazes
a herd near his grave for fear of the grass, since what grows there
is diseased and harmful to eat. There is a story that Trojan shep- 4
herds once insulted Ajax because their sheep became sick. As they
stood around the tomb, they called the hero an enemy of Hektor,
of Troy, and of the flocks. One said that Ajax had been driven
mad, another that he was in a warlike rage, but the most outra-
geous of the shepherds said, "Ajax stood firm no longer"[60]; up
until this point he used to recite the verse against him as a coward.
But shouting from his grave in a spine-tingling and shrill voice,
Ajax said, "But I did stand firm."[61] Then it is said that he even
clashed his weapons together, as is usual in battle. There is no 5
need to marvel at the suffering of those poor devils, if, since they
were Trojans and shepherds, they were panic-stricken at Ajax's
attack, and some fell, others ran, and still others fled from their
pastures. But it is worthwhile to admire Ajax, since he killed none
of them. Rather, he endured the drunkenness which possessed
them, only showing that he was listening to them. I suppose, my 6
guest, that Hektor is not acquainted with this virtue. For last year,
when some youth (they say he was quite young and uneducated)
offended Hektor, he rushed headlong at him and killed him on the
road, blaming the deed on a river.

PH. Vinedresser, you speak to someone who is ignorant and **19**
greatly astounded by this report, for I thought that this hero had
not appeared anywhere. When you told me things having to do

---

[59] Namely, the awarding of Achilles' armor to Odysseus rather than to
Ajax; this story is found in the *Little Iliad* and is the subject of Sophocles' *Ajax*.

[60] Quotation of Homer *Il.* 15.727, according to which Ajax had to give
way to the onslaught of the Trojans.

[61] See the similar exchange in *Anthologia Palatina* 9.177.

with the Hellenes, I grieved exceedingly for Hektor, because neither plowman nor goatherd says anything on his behalf, but he is
2 invisible to human beings and simply lies buried. I do not think
it worthy to hear anything about Paris, because of whom so very
many great men fell. About Hektor, however, who was the bulwark of Troy and of all their allies, who kept four horses under
control[62] (which no other hero could do), who attempted to burn
the ships of the Achaeans to ashes, who fought them all at once
while they were advancing and arrayed against him—would I not
ask something about such a hero? Would I not listen gladly, so
long as you do not pass over these things lightly, nor speak carelessly?

3   V. Keep listening, since you do not consider this careless
talk. The statue of Hektor in Ilion resembles a semidivine human being and reveals many delineations of his character to one
inspecting it with the right perspective.[63] In fact, he appears
high-spirited, fierce, radiant, and with the splendor of full health
and strength, and he is beautiful despite his short hair. The
statue is something so alive that the viewer is drawn to touch it.
4 The statue was dedicated in admiration of Ilion and accomplishes
many useful things both for the general public and for individu-
als. Therefore they pray to Hektor and hold games in his honor.
The statue becomes so heated and involved during the contest
5 that sweat flows from it. Now an Assyrian youth came to Ilion
and kept insulting Hektor, throwing in his face the draggings that
Achilles once afflicted upon him, Ajax's rock[64] with which he was
struck and died soon after, how he had initially fled from Patroklos, and that not he, but others killed Patroklos.[65] He disputed
the identity of Hektor's statue and claimed that it was Achilles on

---

[62] That is, he could drive a four-horse chariot. Homer *Il.* 8.184–185.

[63] On the existence of a statue of Hektor in Ilion, see Julian *Letters* 19;
Synesius *In Praise of Baldness* 82c; a discussion of the numismatic, archaeologi-
cal, and literary evidence can be found in "Hektor," PW 7 (1912): col. 2815; and
Rossi, *Filostrato: Eroico*, 211.

[64] The *Iliad* narrates two times when Ajax struck Hektor with a rock;
neither, however, is fatal; after the first (*Il.* 7.268–772) Apollo immediately re-
stores Hektor to the battle; after the second (*Il.* 14.409–432) Hektor is pulled
unconscious from battle but later revived by Apollo. The second is probably intended here, since Hektor is killed by Achilles a short time later.

[65] According to Homer (*Il.* 16.788–822), Apollo and Euphorbus wounded Patroklos first; Hektor gave the final blow. In his dying words Patroklos

the basis of the hair, which Achilles had shorn for Patroklos.[66]
After he had made these insults, he drove his chariot from Ilion, 6
and before he had gone ten stades,[67] a stream, so insignificant that
it did not even have a name in Troy, rose up to a great size. As
his attendants who escaped reported, an immense, heavily armed
soldier directed the river, commanding it vehemently in a foreign
language to flow into the road on which the youth was driving four
small horses. The river overtook them along with the youth just 7
as he was crying aloud, finally aware of Hektor. The river carried him back to its usual course and destroyed him so that it did
not yield his corpse for burial. It disappeared and I do not know
where it went.

PH. Vinedresser, it is not necessary to admire Ajax en- 8
during the outrages of the shepherds or to consider Hektor a
barbarian because he was not patient with those of the youth.
While it is perhaps forgivable that the shepherds, who were Tro- 9
jans, assaulted the tomb after their sheep had fared badly, what
forgiveness is there for the Assyrian youth who mocked the hero
of Ilion? After all, there was never any war between the Assyrians and the Trojans, nor did Hektor ravage the Assyrians' herds
as Ajax did those of the Trojans.

V. My guest, you seem to have a passion for Hektor, and I **20**
do not regard it worth disputing, but let us rather return to the affairs of Ajax, for there I think our digression occurred.

PH. Yes, let us resume from that point, vinedresser, as
seems best.

V. Now pay attention, my guest. Once when a ship put into 2
harbor near the sanctuary of Ajax, two of the strangers wandered
in front of the tomb and began to play with gaming stones.[68]
Ajax appeared and said, "By the gods, get rid of this game, for it

attributes his demise primarily to Apollo and Euphorbus; he degradingly calls
Hektor his "third slayer" (*Il.* 16.844–850).

[66] As part of the ritual of lamenting Patroklos' death (Homer *Il.* 23.45–
53).

[67] One stade equals approximately 200 yards.

[68] These are *pessoi*, oval-shaped stones used in a game roughly similar to
checkers or draughts, played on board with thirty-six squares. Palamedes is said
to have invented the game (see Gorgias *Palamedes*). In Euripides (*Iphigeneia at
Aulis* 195–199) Protesilaos and Palamedes play the game together.

reminds me of the deeds of Palamedes, my close and clever companion. A single enemy destroyed both him and me by bringing on us an unjust judgment."

3   Ph. By Helios, I have shed tears over this, vinedresser! Both of their experiences were comparable and properly evoke goodwill. Sharing good things sometimes brings forth envy, but those who share misfortunes are fond of each other and return

4 compassion for compassion. Could you say whether anyone has seen Palamedes' phantom in Troy?

21   V. When the phantoms appear, the identity of each is not immediately clear. Many appear sometimes one way, sometimes another, interchanging outward appearance, age, and armor. I

2 hear, nevertheless, stories about Palamedes. There was a farmer in Ilion, who did then what I do now. He had deep sympathy for Palamedes' suffering, and he used to sing a dirge for him when he visited the shore where it is said Palamedes was stoned by the Achaeans. And on the dust of Palamedes' grave he would place whatever people customarily bring to tombs.[69] After selecting sweet grapes for him, he gathered them in a *krater* and said that

3 he drank with Palamedes when he rested from his labors. He also had a dog that fawned slyly, while lying in wait for people. This dog he called "Odysseus" and, in the name of Palamedes, this Odysseus was beaten, hearing in addition a thousand bad names.

4 So it seemed good then to Palamedes to visit this admirer periodi-
5 cally and to give him something good. The farmer was, of course, at a certain grapevine, mending its joint, and Palamedes, standing by him, said, "Do you recognize me, farmer?" He answered, "How would I recognize you whom I have never seen?" "Then do

6 you love him whom you do not recognize?" said the other. The farmer realized that it was Palamedes, and he reported that the hero's image was tall, beautiful, and brave, although he was not yet thirty years old. The farmer embraced him and said with a smile, "I love you, Palamedes, because you seem to me to be the most sensible of all and the most fair champion in deeds of skill. You have endured most pitiful ordeals at the Achaeans' hands because of Odysseus's crafty designs against you. If Odysseus's tomb had been here, I would have dug it out long ago. He

---

[69] For a description of Palamedes' tomb, see Philostratus *Life of Apollonius* 4.13.

is blood-stained and more evil than the dog that I keep in his honor." "Let us spare Odysseus from now on," the hero said, 7 "because for these deeds I have exacted penalties from him in Hades. But you, since you love the grapevines, I suppose, tell 8 me what you are especially afraid could happen to them." "What else," said the farmer, "than that the hailstones will blind and break them?" "So then," said Palamedes, "let us fasten a leather strap to one of them, and the rest will not be hit."[70]

PH. The hero is ingenious, vinedresser, and always invents 9 something good for people. What could you say about Achilles, since we consider him the most godlike of the whole Hellenic army?

V. The events in the Pontus, my guest, if you have not yet 22 sailed to it, and all those things that he is said to do on the island there I shall tell you later in a longer story about Achilles, but his deeds in Ilion are nearly equal to those of other heroes. And he converses with some people, visits regularly, and hunts wild beasts. They conclude that it is Achilles from the beauty of his 2 physique as well as from the size and flash of his weapons. Behind him a windstorm whirls around, an attendant to his phantom. My guest, I shall lose my voice recounting such tales! For truly, 3 they sing something even about Antilokhos, how a girl from Ilion, wandering along the Scamander, came upon the phantom of Antilokhos: falling in love with the phantom, she clung to his tomb. They also sing of how, while young herdsmen were playing dice around the altar of Achilles, one would have struck the other dead with a shepherd's crook, had not Patroklos scared them away, saying, "One shedding of blood on account of dice is enough for me."[71] But it is possible to find out about these things from the 4 cowherds or anyone living in Ilion. Since we inhabit the banks of the Hellespont's outlets, we are in close contact with each other, and, as you see, we have turned the sea into a river. But let us re- 23

[70] Palamedes' invention seems to entail a kind of apotropaic magic. Leather straps (or thongs) were wound about the hands and forearms of boxers for protection (Philostratus On Gymnastics 10). Here the leather strap enables the grapevine to defend itself when struck by hailstones. Palamedes was also renowned as a boxer. The vines are "blinded" perhaps because when the grapes are knocked off, the vines look as though they have empty eye sockets.

[71] As a boy Patroklos accidentally killed another over a game of dice (Homer Il. 23.85–88).

turn, my guest, to the story of the shield, which Protesilaos says
was unknown to Homer and all poets.

The Battle at Mysia and the Contest of the Shield (23.2–30)

2   PH. Vinedresser, you tell the story to one who yearns for it.
I believe I will seldom hear it.

V. Very seldom. Listen and pay attention.

PH. Pay attention, you say? Not even the wild beasts listened as intently to Orpheus when he sang as I, listening to you,
prick up my ears, rouse my mind, and gather every detail into my
memory. I even consider myself to be one of those encamped at
Troy, so much have I been possessed[72] by the demigods[73] about
whom I speak.

3   V. Therefore, since you are so minded, my guest, let us set
out from Aulis since it is true that they assembled there. As we
4 embark on our story, let us make offerings to Protesilaos. How the
Achaeans before they came to Troy plundered Mysia, which was
then ruled by Têlephos, and how Têlephos, fighting for his own
people, was wounded by Achilles, you can also hear from poets
5 since they have not neglected these stories.[74] But the belief that
the Achaeans, in ignorance of the land, thought they were carrying off the spoils of Priam slanders Homer's account, which he
sings about Kalkhas the prophet. If they sailed under prophetic
skill and made his skill their guide, how could they have anchored
6 there unintentionally? And how, once they had anchored, could
they have been ignorant that they had not come to Troy, although
they met many cowherds there and many shepherds? For this region extends to the sea, and it is customary, I think, for those who
put into port to ask the name of a foreign country.

7   Even if they had not met any herdsmen or asked any such
questions, Odysseus and Menelaos had already been to Troy,

[72] The verb used here, *katekhô*, conveys the double sense of "to be de-
tained, held back"—that is, the Phoenician is prevented from continuing his
journey—and "to be possessed" (by a god or supernatural force); see LSJ, 926,
s.v. κατέχω.

[73] In Hesiod (*Works and Days* 155–173), the "demigods" (*hêmitheoi*) are
the heroes who inhabit the earth in the fourth of the five generations of humankind.

[74] The sacking of Mysia was narrated in the lost *Cypria*, which claims
that the Achaean forces mistook it for Ilion.

served as ambassadors, and knew the battlements of Ilion.[75]
It seems unlikely to me, therefore, that they would have overlooked these matters and permitted the army to go quite so astray
from the enemy's country. Indeed, the Achaeans plundered the 8
Mysians deliberately, because a report had come to them that the
Mysians fared best of those on the mainland. Moreover, they
feared lest those who were dwelling in the vicinity of Ilion might
somehow be called over as allies in the battles. To Herakles' 9
son Têlephos, an especially noble man and a leader of armed
men, these matters seemed intolerable. Hence, he drew many
infantry and cavalry into battle formation. He led troops from 10
the part of Mysia that he controlled (he ruled, I believe, all of
coastal Mysia), and fighting alongside him were those from upper Mysia, whom the poets call "Abians" and "horse shepherds"
and "drinkers of milk."[76] The intention of the Achaeans became 11
clear, as they made encircling maneuvers, and Tlêpolemos sent
a messenger to his kinsman[77] aboard a Rhodian merchant vessel. When he ordered him to report by word of mouth (for the
alphabet had not yet been invented) how many Achaean ships he
had seen at Aulis, the whole interior of the country formed an alliance, and the Mysian and Scythian peoples came in waves over
the plain. Protesilaos says that this was the greatest contest for 12
them, greater than both those at Troy itself and any subsequent
battles between Hellenes and barbarians. The alliance of Têle- 13
phos was highly esteemed by both the multitude and the warriors.
Just as the Achaeans celebrated in song the Aiakidai and heroes
as renowned as Diomedes and Patroklos, so the Mysians sang
the names of Têlephos and Haimos, son of Ares. But the most
renowned names were Heloros and Aktaios, sons of the river god
Istros in Scythia.

The Mysians prevented the Achaeans from landing by shoot- 14
ing arrows and hurling javelins from the shore, and the Achaeans,
though unyielding, were hard pressed. The Arcadians even ran
some ships aground since they were sailing for the first time and

[75] Homer *Il.* 3.205–224; 11.139–141.

[76] Homer (*Il.* 13.6) refers to the Mysians as "mare-milkers" and
"drinkers of milk"; see also Hesiod frg. 150.15 and 151 (in R. Merkelbach
and M. L. West, *Fragmenta Hesiodea* [Oxford: Clarendon, 1967]); Strabo
Geography 7.3.7, 9.

[77] That is, to Têlephos, who also was the offspring of Herakles.

15 were not prepared for the sea. As you perhaps know, Homer says
that the Arcadians were neither sailors before coming to Ilion, nor
were they skilled in navigation, but Agamemnon brought them
to the sea in sixty ships and himself gave vessels to those who
had never sailed.[78] Hence, they provided military expertise and
strength for land forces, but when sailing they were good nei-
16 ther as men at arms nor as rowers. On the contrary, they ran
the ships aground because of inexperience and daring, many of
them were wounded by those stationed on the rocky shore, and
a few died. But Achilles and Protesilaos, fearful for the Arcadians, leapt to the shore simultaneously, as if by mutual agreement,
and drove back the Mysians because these two heroes appeared to
be the most heavily armed and the noblest of the Hellenic force;
they even seemed quite supernatural to their most barbarian op-
17 ponents. But when Têlephos led his army into the plain and the
Achaeans sailed to the shore undisturbed, all on board except for
the pilot and petty officer immediately jumped out of the ships
and assembled for battle while keeping their feelings and thoughts
18 under control. Protesilaos says that Homer reported this about
them correctly, since he praised the manner of Hellenic warfare,[79]
19 of which he says Ajax, son of Telamôn, was the advisor. For
when Menestheus the Athenian, the most learned tactician among
the lords, came to Troy and taught the whole army at Aulis the
need for cooperation, he did not rebuke those who used the battle
cry, but Ajax dissented and criticized it as effeminate and undisciplined, for he said that the battle cry expresses courage poorly.
20 Protesilaos said that he and Achilles together with Patroklos were
arrayed against the Mysians, while Diomedes, Palamedes, and
Sthenelos faced Haimos, son of Ares; the Atreidai, the Locrian,[80]
and the remaining forces were drawn up against those coming
21 from the Istros. The greater Ajax considered those killing the
crowds "harvesters" since they were mowing down nothing remarkable, but those who prevailed over the bravest he called
"wood-cutters" and considered himself more worthy of this sort
22 of battle. Accordingly, he moved quickly against the sons of the

[78] Homer *Il.* 2.603–614. Arcadia was almost entirely land-locked, hence
its inhabitants had little nautical experience.
[79] Homer *Il.* 3.8–9.
[80] That is, the lesser Ajax, son of Locris.

river,[81] since they did not share his heritage and were fighting from a four-horse chariot, as Hektor also fought. Walking haughtily amid the confusion of battle, Ajax clanged his shield loudly in order to spook the horses, and the horses immediately panicked and rose up on their hind legs, at which point the Scythians, distrusting their chariot, leapt from it, since it was now in disarray, and fell upon Ajax; although both Heloros and Aktaios fought in a manner worthy of fame, they died.

Protesilaos also remembers how great the deeds of Palame- 23 des were when he, Diomedes, and Sthenelos killed Haimos and his companions. Palamedes did not consider himself worthy of any rewards of valor; rather he yielded them to Diomedes, since he recognized that Diomedes had done everything for the honor and glory of battle. If the Hellenes, however, had proposed a crown for intellectual skill, Palamedes would not have lost it to any other man, since from the beginning he desired wisdom and trained himself in it.

Protesilaos says that he himself fought Têlephos and strip- 24 ped him of his shield while still alive, but that Achilles fell upon the unprotected man, wounding him at once in the thigh. And although later in Troy he healed the wound,[82] at that time Têlephos lost heart because of it and would have died if the Mysians had not together run to Têlephos and snatched him out of the battle. So many Mysians are said then to have fallen for him that the Kaikos river ran red with their blood. Protesilaos says that 25 Achilles contended with him for the shield since Achilles was the one who wounded Têlephos. The Achaeans voted rather that the shield belonged to Protesilaos because Têlephos would not have been wounded had he not been stripped of the shield.

He says that even the Mysian women fought from horses 26 alongside the men, just as the Amazons do, and the leader of the cavalry was Hiera, wife of Têlephos. Nireus is said to have 27 killed her (for the young men of the army, who had not yet won honor, drew up for battle against the women). When she fell, the Mysian women cried out, scaring their horses, and were driven into the marshes of the Kaikos. This Hiera, Protesilaos says, 28 was the tallest woman he had ever seen and the most beautiful of

[81] Heloros and Aktaios, the sons of the river Istros.
[82] Apollodorus *Epitome* 3.19-20.

all who won a name for beauty. He does not claim that he saw
Menelaos's wife Helen in Troy, but that he now sees Helen herself and does not blame her for his death.[83] When he considers
Hiera, however, he says that she surpasses Helen as much as He-
29 len surpasses the Trojan women. Not even Hiera, my guest, won
the praise of Homer, who did not introduce this divine woman
into his own works because he favored Helen. Even the Achaeans
are said to have been afflicted with passion for Hiera when she fell
in battle, and the elders commanded the young soldiers neither to
30 despoil Hiera nor to touch her as she lay dead. In this battle, my
guest, many Achaeans were wounded, and an oracle prescribed
baths for them, namely, the hot springs in Ionia, which even today
Smyrna's inhabitants call the "Baths of Agamemnon."[84] They
are, I believe, forty stades from the city, and the captured Mysian
helmets were once hung up there.

III. PROTESILAOS'S OPINION OF HOMER (24.1–25.17)

24   PH. What then, vinedresser? Shall we say that Homer
deliberately or accidentally omitted these events, which are so
pleasing and worthy to be celebrated by poets?

2   V. Most likely deliberately, my guest. He wanted to sing
of Helen as the best of women with respect to her beauty, and to
praise the Trojan battles as the greatest of those fought anywhere.
But he deprived the divine Palamedes of any story because of
Odysseus and attributed the most warlike deeds to Achilles alone
so that he left out the other Achaeans whenever Achilles fought.
He did not compose a Mysian epic nor did he make a record of
this battle, in which may be found a woman more beautiful than
Helen, men no less courageous than Achilles, and a most illustrious contest. Had he remembered Palamedes, he would not have
found a place where he could have hidden Odysseus's disgraceful
deed against Palamedes.

---

[83] In Lucian's *Dialogues of the Dead* 27, Protesilaos blames Helen for his
death first, then Menelaos, then Paris, then Eros, then himself, before finally
placing full blame on Fate.

[84] These baths, located outside Smyrna, are mentioned by Pausanias (*Description of Greece* 7.5.11) and in an epigram of Agathias (*Anthologia
Palatina* 9.631).

PH. How then is Protesilaos disposed toward Homer, since **25** you claim that he examines his poems closely?

V. My guest, he says that just as Homer, in terms of mu- 2 sical harmonics, sang every poetic mode,[85] he also surpassed all the poets whom he encountered, each in the area of his expertise. For example, he fashioned verses more solemnly than Orpheus, excelled Hesiod in providing pleasure, and outdid other poets in other ways. He took the story of the Trojan War as his subject, in 3 which fate[86] brought together the excellent deeds both of all the Hellenes and of the barbarians. Homer introduced into the story battles involving men, horses and walls, rivers, as well as gods and goddesses. Protesilaos says that Homer also included all matters pertaining to peace: choral dances, songs, erotic encounters, and feasts; he touched on agricultural tasks and the appropriate seasons for performing them. He also described sea voyages, the making of arms in the "Hephaistos,"[87] and especially men's appearances and their various characteristics. Protesilaos says that 4 Homer accomplished all these things with divine power and that those who do not love him are mad. He also calls Homer Troy's 5 founder because the city gained distinction from his laments over it. Protesilaos marvels that even when Homer found fault with 6 those practicing the same art he did not correct them harshly, but unobtrusively. Homer corrected Hesiod both on other points 7 which were not minor and, by Zeus, about the relief figures on the shields. Once when Hesiod was describing the shield of Kyknos, he sang about the Gorgon's form carelessly and not poetically; hence, correcting him, Homer sang about the Gorgon in this way:

> And upon it, the grim-looking Gorgon was set as a crown
> Glaring terribly, and about her were Fear and Terror.[88]

In many details concerning divine stories, Homer outdid Or- 8

[85] Ancient writers on harmonics list thirteen, or alternatively fifteen, different poetic modes, the most common of which were Dorian, Ionian, Phrygian, Aeolian, and Lydian.

[86] *tukhê* designates fate, fortune, or providence as an agent beyond human control.

[87] The "Hephaistos" designates Book 18 of the *Iliad*, which recounts how Hephaistos made new armor for Achilles and describes the shield of Achilles.

[88] Homer *Il.* 11.36–37, describing Agamemnon's shield. This description of the shield of Kyknos is probably to be identified with the shield of

pheus, and in oracular odes he surpassed Mousaios. Moreover,
when Pamphôs insightfully regarded Zeus as the producer of all
living things and the one through whom everything from the
earth arises, he used this insight rather foolishly and sang despicable verses about Zeus (for these are the words of Pamphôs:

> Zeus, most glorious, greatest of gods, enfolded in dung
> Of sheep, horse, and mule).

Protesilaos says that Homer, however, sang a hymn worthy of
Zeus:

> Zeus, most glorious, greatest, enveloped by clouds, dwelling
> in the sky.[89]

While Zeus fashions the living things under the sky, he also in-
9 habits the most pure realm. He says that, like Orpheus, Homer
represented truly the battles between Poseidon and Apollo and
between Hermes and Leto, as well as how Athena fought with
Ares and Hephaistos with the river.[90] And these battles are divine
and not contemptible for their terror, even as the verse goes,

> Great heaven trumpeted on all sides,[91]

just as when Aidôneus leapt up from his throne, when the earth
was shaken by Poseidon.[92]

10   He finds fault with the following verses of Homer.[93] First,
because, after intermingling gods and mortals, Homer spoke
highly about mortals, but contemptibly and basely about the gods.
Next, clearly knowing that Helen was in Egypt, since she along
with Paris had been carried away by the winds, Homer kept her
on the wall of Ilion so that she would see the sorry events on the
plain. It is likely that, if these events had taken place because

---

Herakles; see Hesiod *Shield of Herakles* 138–318, including the description of
the Gorgon pursuing Perseus, in lines 223–237.

[89] Homer *Il.* 2.412. *aithêr* ("sky") can also be the "ether" or the "heaven"
above the sky. In *Life of Apollonius* 3.34, Philostratus uses the word to refer to
the divine element in the human soul (LSJ, 37, s.v. αἰθήρ).

[90] Homer *Il.* 20.67–74; see also 5.825–863; 21.328–382.

[91] Homer *Il.* 21.388.

[92] Homer *Il.* 20.57–67.

[93] Compare the complaints against the poets in Xenophanes frgs. 11–12;
and Plato *Republic* 377d–394e.

of any other woman, she would have covered her face and not
looked while her people were attacked.[94] Because Paris was not 11
even renowned in Troy itself for the seizure of Helen, Protesilaos says that neither would the most prudent Hektor have put up
with Paris's not giving her back to Menelaos,[95] had she been in
Ilion, nor would Priam have allowed Paris to live in luxury when
many of his other children had already perished.[96] Nor would Helen have escaped death at the hands of the Trojan women whose
husbands, brothers, and sons had already fallen. She probably
would have run off to Menelaos because she was hated in Troy.
Of course, then, the contest that Homer says Paris fought with 12
Menelaos when there was a solemn truce in the war must be ex-
cised.[97] Protesilaos says that Helen was in Egypt and that the
Achaeans, although knowing this for a long time, said that they
were eager to fight for her, but in reality they fought for the sake
of Troy's wealth.[98]

For the following reasons also Protesilaos does not com- 13
mend Homer, because though he chose the story of Troy as his
subject, he then digresses from it after Hektor's death,[99] as if has-
tening on to another set of stories, in which he gives credit to
Odysseus. While he celebrates in Dêmodokos's and Phêmios's
songs the destruction of Ilion and the horse of Epeios and Athena,
he discusses these apart from the story of Troy and dedicates
them rather to Odysseus. For Odysseus's sake Homer invented
the race of the Cyclopes, although they live nowhere on the earth,
and also imagined the Laestrygonians—no one knows where they
came from. Circe, a daimon who was clever with magic spells,
and other goddesses were made to fall in love with Odysseus, even
though he had already advanced to untimely old age, when he appeared even to have hyacinth-like curls,[100] which blossomed on
him in Nausicaa's presence! Hence, Protesilaos calls Odysseus 14
Homer's plaything. The young woman was not even in love with

[94] Homer *Il.* 3.121–242.
[95] Homer *Il.* 22.90–130.
[96] Homer *Il.* 6.312–324.
[97] Homer *Il.* 3.243–383.
[98] Herodotus cites similar arguments for his belief that Homer knew Helen never went to Troy (*Hist.* 2.116–120).
[99] Homer *Iliad* 22.
[100] Homer *Od.* 6.231.

his reputed wisdom, for what clever thing did he either say or do towards Nausicaa? He calls him Homer's plaything in his wandering as well, since he often comes to ruin because he is asleep,[101] and he is carried off the ship of Phaeacians as though he died during a fair voyage.[102] Moreover, Protesilaos says that Poseidon's wrath, because of which Odysseus was left without a single ship (and his men who filled the ships perished), did not come about because of Polyphemos. He says that neither did Odysseus come into such haunts, nor, if the Cyclops had been Poseidon's child, would Poseidon have ever been enraged for such a child, who used to eat human beings like a savage lion. Rather, it was because of Palamedes, who was his grandson, that Poseidon made the sea impossible for Odysseus to navigate, and, since Odysseus escaped the sufferings there, Poseidon later destroyed him in Ithaca itself, by thrusting, I think, a spear from the sea against him.[103] He also says that the wrath of Achilles did not fall upon the Hellenes because of the daughter of Khrysês, but that Achilles, too, was angry over Palamedes.[104] But let my account of Achilles' deeds be laid aside, for I shall indeed proceed through the heroes one by one, reporting what I have heard about them from Protesilaos.

IV. THE CATALOGUE OF THE HEROES (25.18–42.4)

Nestor and Antilokhos (25.18–26.20)

18   PH. You have come to my favorite kind of story. Already my "ears ring with the battle-crash"[105] of horses and men, and I predict that I shall hear something very good.

---

[101] For example, Homer *Od.* 10.31.

[102] Upon Odysseus's return to Ithaca (Homer *Od.* 13.117–119).

[103] In contrast to Homer's prediction of Odysseus's calm old age and a peaceful death (*Od.* 11.134–136), others tell of Têlegonos, son of Odysseus and Circe, who mistakenly killed his father with his stingray-pointed spear (Apollodorus *Epitome* 7.36–37; cf. the lost epic the *Telegonia*).

[104] Protesilaos here offers a different explanation of Achilles' wrath and withdrawal from the war from that which is found in Homer. The death of Palamedes and Achilles' withdrawal from battle are also linked in the *Cypria*.

[105] Homer *Il.* 10.535.

V. Listen, my guest. May nothing elude me, Protesilaos, nor may I forget anything that I have heard.[106]

So then, Protesilaos says that Nestor, son of Neleus, was **26** the oldest among the Hellenes when he came to Troy, trained in many wars waged in his youth, as well as by athletic contests in which he won prizes for boxing and wrestling. Of all mortals he knew infantry and cavalry tactics best, and from his youth he rose to leadership not by flattering the rank and file, by Zeus, but by chastening them. He did this at the right time and with pleasant words, so that his criticisms seemed neither coarse nor disagreeable.[107] And whatever has been said about him by Homer, **2** Protesilaos says has been spoken truthfully. Moreover, Protesi- **3** laos confirms as true and not fabricated what others have said about Geryon's cattle: that Neleus and his sons except for Nestor stole the cattle from Herakles. In truth, Herakles gave Messene to Nestor as a reward for his righteousness, since in the case of the cattle he did none of the wrongs that his brothers did.[108] Herakles is also said to have been captivated by Nestor, since he **4** was exceedingly prudent and handsome, and to have cherished him more than Hyllas and Abdêros. For these two were just little boys and quite young, but Nestor was already an ephebe[109] and practiced in every excellence of soul and body when Herakles met him, and they therefore cherished each other.[110] In truth, **5**

[106] The vinedresser invokes Protesilaos's inspiration, just as Homer invoked the Muses before embarking on his catalogue of the ships (*Il.* 2.484–493).

[107] For example, see Homer *Il.* 1.255–284; 7.124–160; 11.656–803.

[108] According to Hesiod (as preserved in a fragment from Stephanus of Byzantium, s.v. Gerenia = frg.34 [Merkelbach and West]; cf. Apollodorus *Library* 1.9.9), the reason for Herakles' wrath was that Neleus and his sons, with the exception of Nestor, refused to purify him from murder; luckily for Nestor, he was away with the Gerenians.

[109] In fourth-century B.C.E. Athens, the term ephebe designated boys sixteen to twenty years old, who spent two years in military training, followed by two years as frontier guards (Aristotle *Athenian Constitution* 42; O. W. Reinmuth, *The Ephebic Inscriptions of the Fourth Century B.C.* [Leiden: Brill, 1971]). In the centuries that followed, the ephebes' military training devolved to military exercises, while intellectual and cultural training dominated.

[110] In other versions Nestor is the sworn enemy of Herakles (Ovid *Metamorphoses* 12.536–576).

swearing by Herakles was not yet a custom among mortals; Protesilaos says that Nestor first instituted the custom and passed it on to those at Troy.[111]

6   He also had a child named Antilokhos, who arrived in the
7 middle of the war. Because Antilokhos was still young and not mature enough for war when they assembled at Aulis, his father did not agree to his wish to serve as a soldier. After the fifth year of the war, however, Antilokhos set forth on a ship; upon arrival he went to Achilles' tent, since he had heard that Achilles was very friendly with his father. He pleaded with him to intercede on his behalf with his father, lest Nestor be annoyed by
8 his disobedience. Achilles, pleased at Antilokhos's maturity and admiring his eagerness, said, "You don't yet know your own father at all, my boy, if you think that you won't be praised by him
9 for having done an ambitious and high-spirited deed." Achilles spoke accurately. With pride and joy in his child, Nestor presented him to Agamemnon, who immediately called together the Achaeans. Nestor is said then to have made his best speech ever.
10 They assembled, pleased to see Nestor's child (for he had had no son at Troy, neither Thrasymedes nor any other), and Antilokhos stood blushing and staring at the ground while he received no
11 less admiration for his beauty than Achilles had. For Achilles' physique appeared startling and divine, but that of Antilokhos
12 seemed to all to be pleasant and gentle. Protesilaos says that, although it had not otherwise utterly escaped the Achaeans' notice, what came most of all to his own mind was Antilokhos's resemblance to his own age and height. He says that tears came to the eyes of many out of pity for their tender age and that the Achaeans spoke auspicious words to Nestor, to which he responded, "They are disposed like children to a father."
13   It is also possible to portray the statue of Nestor for you. Protesilaos describes him as always appearing cheerful, beginning

[111] Divine beings were invoked as witnesses to ancient oaths. Herakles was one among a number of such witnesses to the Athenian ephebic oath. See P. Siewert, "The Ephebic Oath in Fifth-Century Athens," *JHS* 97 (1977): 102–16; Marcus Niebuhr Tod, *A Selection of Greek Historical Inscriptions* (2 vols.; Oxford: Clarendon, 1933–1948), 2:204. Herakles' name was invoked more colloquially as an exclamation; see Aristophanes *Acharnians* 284; *Clouds* 184. On oaths more generally, see Rudolf Hirzel, *Der Eid: Ein Beitrag zu einer Geschichte* (Leipzig: Hirzel, 1902).

to smile, and with a beard that is majestic and well-proportioned; his ears display what he went through at wrestling school, and his neck is restored to its strength. In truth, Nestor stands upright, not defeated by old age, with black eyes and without a drooping nose. And this, in old age, only those whom strength has not forsaken maintain. Protesilaos says that in other respects Antilokhos 14 resembled Nestor, but that he was swifter, trim in physique, and paid no attention to his hair. He gave me the following details 15 about Antilokhos: He was most fond of horses and hunting with dogs, even using times of truce in the fighting for hunting. At any rate, Antilokhos frequented Mount Ida with Achilles and the Myrmidons, and when he was on his own, he would hunt with the Pylians and Arcadians, who provided a market-place for the army because of the great number of animals caught. He was noble in battle, swift-footed, quickly moving when armed, easily understood orders, and did not lose his pleasant manner even in battle. He did not die at the hands of the Memnôn who had 16 come from Ethiopia, as the multitude of poets sing.[112] Memnôn was an Ethiopian, to be sure, and ruled there during the Trojan War; it is said that a sandy burial mound was raised up for him by the Nile, and Egyptians and Ethiopians also sacrifice to him at Meroê and Memphis; whenever the sun sends out its first ray the statue breaks out with a voice by which it greets the cult attendants. Protesilaos says, however, that there was another 17 Memnôn, a Trojan, the youngest of the Trojan army, who while Hektor was still alive seemed no better than the men around Deiphobos and Euphorbus, but after Hektor died this Memnôn was deemed both extremely ready for action and very brave, and Troy looked to him since it was already faring badly. This man, my 18 guest, is said to have killed the handsome and valiant Antilokhos when he was covering his father Nestor with a shield.[113] Indeed, Protesilaos says that when Achilles piled up a funeral pyre for Antilokhos and sacrificed much upon it, he burned both the armor and the head of Memnôn on it. Protesilaos says that the custom 19 of funeral games, which Achilles established for Patroklos {and

---

[112] Homer *Od.* 4.186–188; the *Aithiopis*; Pindar *Pythian* 6.28–43.
[113] In Homer (*Il.* 8.94–117) Diomedes defends and rescues Nestor.

Antilokhos[114]}, were observed above all for the best men. Therefore Protesilaos says that games were appointed here for himself,
but in Ilion for Achilles, as well as for Patroklos and Antilokhos.
20 It is said for Hektor there was established a contest of running,
shooting arrows, and throwing spears, but that none of the Trojans stripped for wrestling and boxing. The former sport they did
not know yet, and the latter, I think, they feared.

Diomedes and Sthenelos (27.1–13)

27 Diomedes and Sthenelos were the same age; the latter was the
son of Kapaneus, the former of Tydeus. Their fathers are said
to have died while laying siege to the Theban walls. Tydeus died
at the hands of the Thebans; Kapaneus, I think, was struck by
2 a thunderbolt. While their corpses were still lying unburied, the
Athenians won a contest for the bodies and buried them when
they were victorious. Their children, however, when they had
reached their prime, won a life or death battle on behalf of their
fathers, and the strength of battle entered Diomedes and Sthene-
3 los as men both excellent and well-matched.[115] But Homer does
not value them equally, for he likens the former to a lion[116] and
to a river sweeping away its dikes and other human constructions[117] (and so he fought), but the latter stood by like a spectator
4 of Diomedes, advising flight and inciting fear.[118] Yet Protesilaos says that even there Sthenelos performed deeds that were
not inferior to Diomedes'. For their bond of friendship was not
less than that between Achilles and Patroklos, and their rivalry
with each other was such that they returned from the battle de-
5 spondent, each one thinking himself inferior to the other. And
Protesilaos says that together they executed the attack against Aeneas and Pandaros: Diomedes fell upon Aeneas, the greatest of the
Trojans, and Sthenelos fought with Pandaros and prevailed over
6 him. But Homer assigned these deeds to Diomedes alone[119] as

[114] The games in *Iliad* 23 were celebrated for Patroklos alone.
[115] On the story of the Epigonoi (the sons of the seven princes who attacked Thebes) and their taking of Thebes, see Apollodorus *Library* 3.7.2–4.
[116] Homer *Il.* 5.161–164.
[117] Homer *Il.* 5.84–94.
[118] Homer *Il.* 5.239–250.
[119] Homer *Il.* 5.286–310.

if he had quite forgotten what he had said to Agamemnon in the
name of Sthenelos, namely,

> We boast that we are better than our fathers,
> We have taken even the foundations of Thebes.[120]

I suppose these deeds of Sthenelos are nearly equal to those which
he performed at Ilion as well.

You should also know other matters about Sthenelos: that 7
no wall was erected by the Achaeans at Troy, nor was there
any protection for either the ships or the booty, but these were
intended by Homer as songs of the siege,[121] because of which
the wall was also constructed by him. At any rate, the impetus 8
for building the wall is said to have come to Agamemnon when
Achilles was raging. Sthenelos first declared his opposition to this
when he said, "I, of course, am more fit for pulling down walls
than for erecting them." Diomedes also opposed building the wall
and said that Achilles was being deemed worthy of great deeds "if
we should then shut ourselves in while he rages!" Ajax is said to
have remarked, eyeing the king like a bull, "Coward! What then
are shields for?" Sthenelos deprecated the hollow horse as well, 9
alleging that this was not a battle for the city walls but a theft of
the battle.

In warlike matters, then, both men were similar and wor- 10
thy of equal fear in the eyes of the Trojans. Sthenelos, however,
lacked Diomedes' insight, his power of speech, and his patient
endurance which belong to both soul and body. He gave way
to anger, was contemptuous of the throng of battle, was savage
upon being rebuked, and was prepared for a more delicate lifestyle
than was needed for a military camp. Diomedes' conduct was just 11
the opposite. He was modest upon rebuke, checked the eruption
of his anger, and refused to insult the troops or to be disheart-
ened. He himself considered it appropriate for an army to appear
unwashed, and he commended sleeping in any opportune place;
his provisions consisted of what was available, and he did not
take pleasure in wine unless troubles came upon him. He praised 12
Achilles, but neither was in awe of him nor did service to him,
as many did. Protesilaos once cried out at those verses in which
Diomedes is represented as saying,

[120] Homer *Il.* 4.405–406.
[121] Homer *Iliad* 12, which is known as the Teichomachy.

You ought not to have supplicated the blameless son of
Peleus, by offering him innumerable gifts. He is haughty
even without this.[122]

He said that Homer had spoken these words like a fellow soldier,
and not as a composer of fiction,[123] but as though he himself had
been present with the Achaeans at Troy: for Diomedes upbraided
Achilles, since Achilles was being extravagant before the Hellenes
13 during his wrath. With respect to the appearance of the two men,
Protesilaos knows that Sthenelos is of a good size and towering,
gray-eyed, with an aquiline nose, fairly long-haired, ruddy, and
hot-blooded. He describes Diomedes as steadfast and having eyes
that are blue-gray and not black at all and a straight nose; his hair
was woolly and dirty.

Philoktêtês (28.1–14)

28 Although Philoktêtês, the son of Poias, served as a soldier late in
the Trojan War, he shot the arrow best among mortals, since, they
say, he learned how from Herakles, the son of Alkmênê. He is
said to have inherited Herakles' bow and arrows when Herakles,
departing human form, had him stand beside the funeral pyre on
2 Mount Oitê. They say that Philoktêtês was abandoned on Lemnos, dishonored in the sight of the Achaeans, after a water snake
darted at his foot.[124] He became ill from this bite and lay on the
rocky ledge of a high peak. It was foretold to the Achaeans by
an oracle that he would later come against Paris and, after he had
killed him, he would thereafter capture Troy with the bow and
arrows of Herakles, and he himself would be healed by the Ascle-
3 piades. Protesilaos says that these statements were not far from
the truth: the bow and arrows of Herakles are just as they are
told in song, Philoktêtês assisted him with the ordeal on Mount
Oitê, he went away in possession of the bow and arrows, he alone
among mortals knew how to draw the bow, and he obtained splen-
4 did rewards for prowess at the conquest of Ilion. But he relates

---

[122] Homer *Il.* 9.698–699.

[123] *hupotithêmi*: to assume, to suppose, or to compose fiction (LSJ, 1898,
s.v. ὑποτίθημι IV.2); for a discussion of the relation between fiction and history
in Greek and Roman literature, see Bowersock, *Fiction as History*.

[124] See the *Cypria*.

the matters of the disease and of the people who healed him differently: Philoktêtês was left behind on Lemnos, assuredly not
bereft of people to care for him, nor had he been rejected by the
Hellenes. Many of the Meliboians stayed behind with him (he
was their general), and tears came over the Achaeans because a
man left them who was warlike and worth just as much as many
men. He was healed immediately by the Lemnian soil, onto which 5
Hephaistos is said to have fallen. It drives away diseases that
cause madness and stanches bleeding, but the only snake bite it
heals is that of the water snake. While the Achaeans spent time 6
in Ilion, Philoktêtês helped Euneôs, son of Jason, take the small
islands by driving out the Carians by whom they were held, and
his recompense for the alliance was a portion of Lemnos, which
Philoktêtês called "Akesa" since he had been cured at Lemnos.
From there Diomedes and Neoptolemos brought him to Troy 7
willingly, beseeching him on behalf of the Hellenes and reading
to him the oracular utterance about the bow and the arrows, the
utterance which had come, so Protesilaos says, from Lesbos.[125]
The Achaeans customarily consulted their own oracles, both the 8
Dodonian and the Pythian, as well as all the renowned Boeotian
and Phocian oracles, but since Lesbos is not far from Ilion, the
Hellenes sent to the oracle there. I believe that the oracle gave its 9
answer through Orpheus, for his head, residing in Lesbos after
the deed of the women, occupied a chasm on Lesbos and prophesied in the hollow earth.[126] Hence, both the Lesbians and all 10
the rest of Aeolia, as well as their Ionian neighbors, request oracles there, and the pronouncements of this oracle are even sent
to Babylon. His head sang many prophecies to the Persian king, 11
and it is said that from there an oracle was given to Cyrus the
elder: "What is mine, Cyrus, is yours." Cyrus understood it in
this way, namely, that he would occupy both Odrysai and Europe,
because Orpheus, once he had become wise and powerful, had

[125] A red-figure kylix depicts the head of Orpheus prophesying, framed
by Apollo and a youth with tablet and stylus (Jane Harrison, *Prolegomena to the
Study of Greek Religion* [3d ed.; Cambridge: Cambridge University Press, 1922;
reprinted New York: Meridian 1955], 465–66). The writing down of oracular
inquiries and especially responses was not unusual. Needless to say, however,
the attribution of this practice to the heroic age is anachronistic.

[126] Philostratus narrates the visit of Apollonius of Tyana to the oracle of
Orpheus at Lesbos (*Life of Apollonius* 4.14).

ruled over Odrysai and over as many Hellenes as were inspired in his rites of initiation. But I think that he instructed Cyrus to be

12 persuaded by his own fate, for when Cyrus had advanced beyond the river Istros against the Massagetai and the Issêdonians (these tribes are Scythian), he died by the hand of a woman who ruled those barbarians, and this woman cut off the head of Cyrus just

13 as the Thracian women had done with that of Orpheus.[127] This much, my guest, I have heard about this oracle from both Prote-

14 silaos and the Lesbians. When Philoktêtês came to Troy, he was neither ill nor like one who had been ill, and although his hair was gray because of age (he was about sixty years old), he was more vigorous than many of the young men, his gaze was most fearsome among mortals, his words most brief, and he attended few of the councils.

Agamemnon, Menelaos, and Idomeneus (29.1–30.3)

29 Protesilaos says that Agamemnon and Menelaos were alike nei-

2 ther in appearance nor strength. Agamemnon was experienced in the arts of war, was inferior to none of the best in combat, and fulfilled all the duties of a king: he knew what was necessary for a ruler, was persuaded by whatever insight someone else had, and even by his very appearance was fit to lead the Hellenes. He looked majestic and magnificent and like the sort of person who offered sacrifice to the Graces.

3   But Menelaos, although he fought along with many of the Hellenes, abused his brother in every respect. And while having the goodwill and favor of Agamemnon, he nevertheless maligned him and what Agamemnon was doing for him by his desire to

4 rule, even though he was not deemed worthy. Orestes, at any rate, was held in honor in Athens and among the Hellenes since he had avenged his father. But when Orestes was in danger in Argos, Menelaos would have allowed his defeat by the Argives, had Orestes not fallen upon them with his Phocian allies and put them to flight. Thus he won for himself the realm of his father

5 and of Menelaos, although Menelaos was unwilling. Protesilaos says that Menelaos wore his hair boyishly long, as was the Spartan custom, and the Achaeans made allowance for him when he

---

[127] Cyrus's death at the hands of the Massagetai is narrated by Herodotus (*Hist.* 1.201–214).

was visiting, since they did not mock those who came from Euboea even though their hair was ridiculously long. He says he 6 conversed most easily and very concisely, mixing pleasant speech with his discourse.

Protesilaos did not see the Cretan Idomeneus in Ilion, but 30 he says that when they were in Aulis an embassy arrived from Idomeneus promising the Cretan forces as allies, if he were to share the command with Agamemnon. Agamemnon cautiously 2 listened to the proposal and introduced the ambassador, who proclaimed with a clear and self-confident voice, "Achaeans, a man who has command of Minos's Crete offers you a hundred cities as allies so that even playing like children we might capture Troy, and he requests that he be ranked with Agamemnon and rule you just as this man does." To this Agamemnon responded, "I am 3 prepared to cede the entire command if he should appear better than I." Then, he says, Ajax the son of Telamôn stepped forward and gave the following speech, "Agamemnon, we have given you supreme command for the discipline of the army and so that not many would be in command. And we are fighting not because we are slaves to either you or anyone else, but for the enslavement of Troy. May we capture it, O gods, after we have accomplished illustrious and noble deeds. We are so disposed toward excellent deeds that we are able to take Troy if we give it serious attention, but we could capture Crete for sport."

The Locrian Ajax (31.1–32.2)

Protesilaos says that the Locrian Ajax was as capable as Diomedes 31 and Sthenelos in the arts of war, but appeared less intelligent and paid no heed to Agamemnon. His father, the most powerful of the Locrians, commanded a significant army, and he would never willingly serve the Atreidai or anyone else, "So long as this flashes." He said this with his quick mind while showing the point of his spear, looking fierce, and throwing his long hair back. He 2 said that the others, who gave heed to Agamemnon, had come because of Helen, but he himself had come for the sake of Europe, since it was now necessary for the Hellenes to prevail over the barbarians. He also had a tame snake, five cubits long, who 3 drank with Ajax and accompanied him, either leading the way or following him like a dog. He dragged Cassandra away from the 4 statue of Athena, although she was clinging to the goddess and

beseeching her; assuredly he neither raped nor abused her as the stories falsely tell about him,[128] but he led her away to his own tent. And when Agamemnon saw Cassandra (for in addition to beauty she was crowned by skill), he was immediately captivated by the maiden and deprived Ajax of her. When a fight between them ensued over the division of spoils, Ajax claimed as his own whatever he had captured, but Agamemnon did not yield and said
5 that Ajax had committed sacrilege against Athena. Because of Agamemnon's on-going enmity toward Ajax, Agamemnon's storytellers produced tales for the Hellenes that the goddess gave many strange signs concerning the young girl and that the army
6 would be destroyed unless it destroyed Ajax. When this Ajax pondered how an unjust judgment had destroyed the other Ajax and that cleverness did not keep Palamedes from dying after being slandered, he ran away by night in a small ferryboat during a storm, and as it happened, when sailing straight for Tênos and
7 Andros, he died at the Gyrian rock. When news of this disaster reached the Achaeans, few of them touched their food and all lifted up their hands in honor of a good man, and turning toward the sea, they invoked him, lamented, and were angry at Agamemnon because he accomplished the destruction of Ajax all but by his
8 own hand. Ajax received offerings for the dead such as had never been offered previously or have been since for any mortal, not
9 even for all the many men whom naval battles destroyed. When they had piled wood, as for a funeral pyre, on the Locrian ship that carried Ajax, they sacrificed all the black animals, and when they had equipped the ship with black sails and with many other things invented for sailing, they secured it with cables until the wind blew from the land, the wind that Mount Ida sends forth particularly at dawn. When day appeared and the wind swept down, they set fire to the hollow ship. Buoyed up on the high seas, it sailed away, and before the sun had risen, the ship was consumed, along with all that it bore for Ajax.

32   Protesilaos says that Kheirôn, who lives on Mount Pelion, resembled a human and that he was skilled in words and deeds (for he participated in various kinds of hunts, taught the skills of

---

[128] The lost epic *Destruction of Ilion* may have depicted Ajax as intending to rape Cassandra.

war, trained physicians, "tuned" the musicians,[129] and made people just). He lived for a very long time, and Asclepius visited him as did Telamôn, Peleus, and Theseus; Herakles also often came to Kheirôn when his labors did not divert him. Protesilaos says that 2 he himself shared the company of Kheirôn at the same time with Palamedes, Achilles, and Ajax.

Palamedes and Odysseus (33.1–34.7)

Protesilaos reports the affairs of Palamedes as follows: Palamedes **33** arrived self-taught and already practiced in wisdom, knowing even more than Kheirôn. Before Palamedes, seasons as such did not yet exist, nor did the cycle of the months, and "year" was not yet a word for time; nor were there coins, nor weights and measures, nor numbering, and the desire for knowledge did not yet exist, because there were no letters of the alphabet yet.[130]

When Kheirôn wanted to teach him medicine, he said, 2 "Kheirôn, I would gladly have discovered medicine had it not existed, but since it has been discovered, I do not deem it worth learning. And besides, the extreme cleverness of your skill is loathsome to both Zeus and the Fates, and I would describe the deeds of Asclepius, if he had not then been struck dead." While 3 the Achaeans were in Aulis, he invented checkers,[131] which is not a frivolous pastime, but a shrewd and serious one.

The story, which has been told by many poets,[132] that, 4 when Hellas waged war on Troy and Odysseus feigned madness in Ithaca and yoked an ox together with a horse to the plow, Palamedes tested him by means of Telemachus—well, Protesilaos denies that this story is sound. He says indeed that Odysseus went to Aulis most eagerly, and his reputation for cleverness had already become legendary among the Hellenes. Odysseus, however, 5 disagreed with Palamedes from that time on: there was an eclipse of the sun at Troy, and the army lost courage, because they took it as a sign from Zeus for the future.[133] So Palamedes stepped for- 6

---

[129] That is, the lyric poets.

[130] See Gorgias *Palamedes* 30, on Palamedes as the inventor of tactics, law, letters, measures, numbers, beacon-fires, and checkers.

[131] *pessoi*; see the note on *Her.* 20.2 above for a discussion of this game.

[132] See the *Cypria*; Apollodorus *Epitome* 3.7; Hyginus *Fabulae* 95.2.

[133] The Athenian army, under the leadership of Nicias and the guidance of soothsayers, delayed their attack on the Syracusans after a lunar eclipse

ward and interpreted fully the very phenomenon of the sun, that, when the moon ran beneath it, it was obscured and drew down mist.[134] "If it should signify anything bad, perhaps the Trojans will be persuaded. For they began the injustices, and we have come as the injured party. It is fitting also to make a vow to Helios when he rises by sacrificing to him a foal, white and set free from labor." When the Achaeans applauded these remarks (for they were won over by Palamedes' words), Odysseus stepped forward and said, "Kalkhas will say what it is necessary to sacrifice, what to vow, and to whom, for such things require prophetic skill. What is in heaven and whatever is the improper or proper position of the stars, Zeus knows, by whom these have been arranged and invented. But you, Palamedes, will be less foolish by paying attention to the earth rather than by speculating about what is in heaven."

8 Then Palamedes replied, "If you were clever, Odysseus, you would have understood that no one is able to say anything learned about the heavens unless he knows more about the earth. That you are wanting in these matters, I have no doubt, for they say that you Ithacans have neither seasons nor land." Because of these words, Odysseus departed full of anger, and Palamedes went away to prepare himself against one who had already slandered him.

10 Once when the Achaeans were in their assembly, cranes happened to fly by in their usual manner, and Odysseus, looking at Palamedes, said, "The cranes bear witness to the Achaeans that the cranes themselves have discovered the letters of the alphabet, not you." Palamedes said, "I did not discover the letters of the alphabet, but I was discovered by them. Long ago, while lying in the house of the Muses, these letters needed such a man, and the gods reveal such letters through learned men. The cranes, then,

---

(Thucydides *Peloponnesian War* 7.50). The rivalry of Odysseus and Palamedes here is reminiscent of the attack by the seer Diopeithês upon Anaxagoras for his naturalistic explanation of heavenly phenomena and indirectly upon Pericles, Anaxagoras's pupil, for his refusal to consult the seers after an eclipse (Plutarch *Pericles* 32.1; 35.1–2).

[134] In the *Iliad*, *akhlus* ("mist") refers to a supernatural obscuring of sight, sometimes accompanying the visitation of a god (*Il.* 5.127; 20.321), as well as to the darkening of sight in death (*Il.* 5.696; 16.344; 20.421). In the *Odyssey* (20.357), the mist follows an eclipse of the sun, which forebodes evil and destruction for Penelope's suitors in Ithaca.

do not lay claim to the letters, but fly, commending their orderly arrangement. They travel to Libya in order to engage in war on small humans.[135] But you, now, should not be talking about order, for you are disorderly in battles."

I think this is the reason for Palamedes' charge, my guest: 12 Odysseus held that if he ever saw Hektor, Sarpêdon, or Aeneas, he would abandon his post and change his position to the easy places in the battle. In the opinion of the assembly he was youth- 13 ful, and although older he was bested by the young Palamedes, and he used Agamemnon as his bulwark against him while he made the Achaeans opposed to Achilles.

He says that once more they were brought through troubles 14 by Palamedes. When wolves descended from Mount Ida, they devoured the young pack animals and the yoked animals round about the tents. Odysseus then ordered men fitted with bows and arrows and javelins to go to Mount Ida against the wolves. But Palamedes said, "Odysseus, Apollo makes the wolves a pre- lude to plague, and though he then shoots them, just as he does both the mules and the dogs, he sends them beforehand among the sick, because of his goodwill toward mortals and so that they might be on guard. Let us pray therefore to both Apollo Lykios and Apollo Phyxios, for they say that the one kills the wild beasts with his own arrows, and the other diverts disease to goats. And let us, men of Hellas, take care of ourselves. To guard against the plague we must have a light diet and vigorous exercise. I did not take up medicine, but all things can be achieved by clever- ness." Saying this, he halted the supply of meat and ordered the 15 army to avoid grain; instead he sustained the army on sweetmeats and wild herbs, and they trusted him and believed everything from Palamedes to be both divine and oracular. For indeed the 16 plague that he foretold did strike the cities of the Hellespont, be- ginning, they say, from the Pontus, and it even fell upon Ilion, but it touched none of the Hellenes although they were encamped in the diseased land. Thus he instructed them in their diet and 17 exercises. After launching one hundred ships, he put the army on board in turns, rowing and competing with one another either

[135] The battle between the cranes and the Pygmies was well known in the ancient world (see, e.g., Homer *Il.* 3.4–6). The delta-shaped pattern in which cranes fly may have suggested a connection with the invention of the alphabet; see Marcel Detienne, *L'écriture d'Orphée* (Paris: Gallimard, 1989), 12.

to surround the promontory, or to touch the headland, or to run
before their neighbors into some harbor or shoreline, and he per-
18 suaded Agamemnon to offer them prizes for fast sailing. They
exercised gladly then and with an understanding of health, for
truly he taught them that, since the land was spoiled and was in
19 such a state, the sea was more pleasant and safer to breathe. In
addition to these things, Palamedes was crowned with rewards for
his wisdom by the Hellenes but Odysseus planned to act dishon-
orably, and whatever villainy he had he turned against Palamedes.
20   In addition to these stories, Protesilaos reports the following: Achilles, who was fighting against the islands and the coastal
21 cities, asked the Achaeans to fight along with Palamedes. They
did fight—Palamedes nobly and wisely, but Achilles fought without restraint. His fighting spirit rose up and led him away from
his post in battle, where he rejoiced at Palamedes who was fighting
alongside him; Palamedes, carrying him out of the rush of battle,
enjoined him how one ought to fight. And what is more, he resembled a lion tamer who calms and stirs up a well-bred lion, and he
did these things without even giving way, but while hurling darts
and being on guard against them, standing firm against shields,
22 and pursuing warriors in close formation. Then, after saying
farewell to one another, they sailed away, and both the Myrmidons
and the Thessalians from Phulakê followed them. Afterwards,
Protesilaos stationed his own force under Achilles, and thus all the
23 Thessalians are called Myrmidons. Indeed, the cities were being
captured and glorious deeds of Palamedes were reported: digging
of canals through narrow passages of land, rivers diverted into the
cities, pilings for harbors, forts, and a battle by night around Abydos. In this battle, when they were wounded, Achilles retreated
but Palamedes did not give up, and before the middle of the night
24 came, he conquered the place. Odysseus, however, was composing reports to Agamemnon in Troy, reports that were false,
but convincing to whoever foolishly listened, to the effect that
Achilles lusted after dominion over the Hellenes and that he was
25 using Palamedes as a go-between.[136] Odysseus said to Agamemnon, "They will arrive in a little while, paying you cattle, horses,

[136] *mastropos*; literally, a pimp or procurer of sexual encounters. Here the
term is used metaphorically for a middle-man or negotiator (for a similar usage,
see also Xenophon *Symposium* 4.61–67).

and captives, but keeping for themselves money with which they
will doubtless seduce powerful Hellenes against you. Thus, it is
necessary to keep away from Achilles, to be on guard against those
who know him, and to kill this schemer Palamedes. I have devised a plan against him by which he will be hated by the Hellenes
and killed by them." Protesilaos then related how the events sur- 26
rounding the Phrygian and the gold that had been received by the
hand of the Phrygian had been arranged by Odysseus.[137] Since 27
these things seemed to have been cleverly contrived, and since
Agamemnon agreed with the plot, Odysseus said, "Come, King,
keep Achilles for me around the cities where he is now, but sum-
mon Palamedes here on the pretense that he is going to lay siege
to Ilion and invent engines of war. Since he will come without
Achilles, he will be a captive not only to me but to anyone else who
is less clever than I." These matters seemed good, and the heralds
sailed off to Lesbos.

The entire island, however, had not yet been captured, but 28
Achilles blockaded it in this way. An Aeolian city, Lyrnêssos,
is naturally enclosed by walls and fortified; they say Orpheus
brought his lyre here and gave the rocks a certain echo, and that
even now at Lyrnêssos the area around the sea resounds with the
song of the rocks. While laying siege here until the tenth day 29
(for it was difficult to capture the place), the heralds proclaimed
the message from Agamemnon. It seemed that Achilles was persuaded to remain behind while Palamedes went, and so at once
they departed from one another with tears. When Palamedes 30
sailed back to the encampment and reported the events of the expedition, ascribing everything to Achilles, he said, "King, are you
ordering me to attack the walls of Troy? I believe the Aiakidai,
both the son of Kapaneus and the son of Tydeus, the Locrians,
and, of course, Patroklos and Ajax are excellent fighting machines. But if you also need lifeless fighting machines, believe
Troy already lies within my control."

[137] This episode is also narrated by Hyginus (*Fabulae* 105), who records
that Odysseus framed Palamedes by planting a large quantity of gold in
Palamedes' tent and forging a letter from Priam to Palamedes that promised
much gold for the betrayal of the Greeks. This letter was found on the body of a
Phrygian, murdered by Odysseus's order. Apollodorus (*Epitome* 3.8) recounts
a similar tale, except that in this version the letter was written by the captured
Phrygian and left in the camp.

31   But the wiles of Odysseus, which were already cleverly devised, had anticipated him. He was reputed to give in to gold
and was falsely accused of being a traitor, and so with his hands
twisted around behind his back, he was stoned to death, with both
Peloponnesians and Ithacans throwing stones at him. The rest of
Hellas had not seen these events, but were pleased with them too
32 even though they seemed to be unjust. The proclamation against
him was savage: neither to bury Palamedes nor to satisfy divine
law by throwing earth,[138] but rather to kill the one who took him
33 up for burial and performed funeral rites. After Agamemnon
had announced these things, the greater Ajax cast himself on the
corpse and shed many tears over it. Placing Palamedes upon himself, he burst through the crowd with his unsheathed and ready
sword. Then, after performing funeral rites for him who had been
denied them, as was appropriate, he did not approach the assembly of the Hellenes or participate in their council or purpose, and
34 he did not join in the battles. When Achilles arrived, after the
capture of the Chersonesus, both were enraged over the affair of
35 Palamedes. Ajax was not enraged for long, for when he perceived
that his allies were faring badly, he grieved and then changed his
36 disposition. Achilles, however, prolonged his wrath; he created a
song for the lyre called the "Palamedes" and praised him in song
just as much as he did the earlier heroes. He begged for a vision
to come to him in his sleep, by pouring out a libation for dreams
from a *krater* out of which Hermes drinks.[139]

37   Not only to Achilles, but also to all who possessed love of
strength and wisdom, this hero seemed to show himself worthy
of emulation and song. Whenever we return to the remembrance
of him, Protesilaos sheds floods of tears, praising the uncommon courage of the hero even in death. Indeed, he reports
that Palamedes did not make supplication, either saying anything
pitiable or lamenting, but after he had said, "I have pity on you,
Truth, for you have perished before me," he held out his head to
the stones as though knowing that Justice would be in his favor.

38   PH. Is it also possible to behold Palamedes, vinedresser,

---

[138] Here earth is thrown over the body in place of the funerary rites. See
the passionate speech by Antigone in defense of such an act even in defiance of
royal order (Sophocles *Antigone* 499–524).

[139] Compare the appearance of Patroklos to Achilles in Homer *Il.* 23.54–
107.

just as I beheld Nestor, Diomedes, and Sthenelos; or does Protesilaos describe nothing about his appearance?

V. It is possible, my guest, just look! So then in height he 39 was the same as the greater Ajax; in beauty, Protesilaos says, he vied with Achilles, Antilokhos, Protesilaos himself, and with the Trojan Euphorbus. His soft beard was springing up and with the promise of curls; his hair was cut close to his skin; his eyebrows were noble, straight, and came together above the nose, which was perfect as a square and stately. The resolve of his eyes ap- 40 peared unshaken and fierce in battles, but when he was at rest their gaze was full of comradely affection and affable; he also is said to have possessed the most marvelous eyes among mortals. And in 41 truth, Protesilaos also says that when he was naked, Palamedes weighed halfway between an athlete and a lithe person, and that he had a toughness about his face that was much more pleasant than the golden locks of Euphorbus. And he cultivated toughness by sleeping wherever he happened to be and by frequently encamping on top of Mount Ida during lulls in the battles, for the learned make direct observations of meteors from the highest elevations. He brought to Ilion neither ship nor armed men, but 42 he sailed on a ferryboat with his brother Oiax, considering himself, they say, to be worth as much as many strong arms. He had 43 no attendant nor companion [140] nor a Tekmêssa or Iphis to wash him or to make up his bed, but his life was simple and without furnishings. At any rate, Achilles once said to him, "Palamedes, you 44 appear rather boorish to many people because you do not possess a servant." He replied, "What then are these, Achilles?" stretching forth both hands. Once when the Achaeans gave him treasures 45 from the spoil and urged him to enjoy the riches, he said, "I do not accept them, for I myself urge you to remain poor, but you do not obey." Once when Odysseus asked him as he returned from ob- 46 serving the stars, "What more do you see in the sky than we do?" he said, "I perceive evil men." It would have been better, however, had Palamedes thoroughly instructed the Achaeans in what manner the evil men would someday be revealed. They would not

[140] *therapôn* in Homer refers to a hero's closest companion (as Patroklos to Achilles), who often fights and dies in place of the hero. The word is connected to the concept of a ritual substitute; see Nagy, *The Best of the Achaeans*, 33, 292–93.

then have believed Odysseus, who was in this way pouring a flood
47 of lies and villainous plots against Palamedes. He said that the
fire alleged to have been set by Nauplios against the Achaeans in
the valley of Euboea was real, and it had been done on behalf of
Palamedes by the Fates and Poseidon, my guest, probably even
though the ghost of Palamedes did not wish these things; indeed,
48 being clever, he joined, I suppose, in the trick with them. Achilles
and Ajax honored him with funeral rites on the mainland of the
Aeolians that borders Troy. The Aeolians also built a very ancient sanctuary to him and set up a noble and well-armed statue
of Palamedes. Those who settled the coastal cities come together
49 and sacrifice to him. His sanctuary must be sought across from
Methymna and Lepetumnos (this mountain appears high above
Lesbos).

34   Protesilaos speaks about Odysseus in this way. He was
extremely skilled in public speaking and clever, but he was a dis-
sembler, a lover of envy, and praised malice. His eyes were always
downcast, and he was the sort of person who engages in self-
examination. He appeared more noble than he was in military
matters; surely he was not well versed in preparing for war, in
commanding naval battles and sieges, or in drawing of spear and
2 bows. His deeds were many, but not worth admiration except for
one, namely, the hollow horse, whose builder was Epeios, with
Athena's help, but whose inventor was Odysseus. It is said that
while in the horse he appeared more daring for the ambush than
the rest inside.

3   Odysseus came to Ilion already past his prime and returned
to Ithaca when he was an old man. He experienced a longer wandering because of the war which was waged against the Kikones
4 when he was ravaging their lands by the sea of Ismaros.[141] Protesilaos does not even allow us to listen to the stories about Polyphemos, Antiphatês, Scylla, the events in Hades, and what the Sirens
sang, but he permits us to smear over our ears with beeswax and
to avoid these stories,[142] not because they are not full of pleasure

[141] Homer *Od.* 9.39–61.
[142] Odysseus was warned by Circe of the Sirens' seductive melodies;
she instructed Odysseus to put wax in his companions' ears, but if he himself
wished to listen to their song, he should have himself tied to the ship by his men
(Homer *Od.* 12.39–54). The emphasis here is not on what it takes to listen safely
to the stories, but rather on avoiding hearing them altogether.

and able to allure us, but because they are untrustworthy and fabricated.[143] He bids us to sail past the islands of Ôgugia and Aiaia 5 and the stories of how the goddesses made love to him, and not to cast our anchor among fables. Odysseus, he says, was too old for amorous affairs, was somewhat flat-nosed, short, and had shifty eyes because of his schemings and insinuations. He was like one 6 who was always plotting, and this gracelessness extended to his amorous affairs. Therefore, Protesilaos aptly teaches that a man like Odysseus killed a man like Palamedes, who was both more clever and more courageous than he. Thus he also praises the 7 dirge in Euripides, where Euripides says in the verses from the *Palamedes*:

> "You have killed," he says, "yes killed,
> the all-wise one, O Danaans,
> the nightingale of the Muses who caused no pain."[144]

He praised the succeeding verses even more, in which Euripides also says that they did these things in obedience to a terrible and shameless person.

The Telamônian Ajax (35.1–36.1)

The Achaeans called Ajax the son of Telamôn great, not because **35** of his size, nor because the other Ajax was smaller, but because of the things he did. They considered him a good advisor for the war because of his father's deed: along with Herakles, Telamôn pursued Laomedôn, when he had tricked Herakles, and captured Troy itself. The Achaeans delighted in Ajax even when he was 2 unarmed (for he was someone mighty even beyond the entire army and bore a disciplined and prudent spirit); they depended on him when he was armed, setting out proudly against the Trojans, handling his shield well even though it was so large,[145] and looking out from under his helmet with flashing eyes, like lions preparing to attack. He fought battles against the best men, and 3 although he said that the Lycians, the Mysians, and the Paionians

---

[143] Compare Socrates' justification for excluding the poets from his ideal society (Plato *Republic* 602c–608b.)

[144] Nauck, *Tragicorum graecorum fragmenta*, frg. 588.

[145] According to Homer (*Il.* 7.219–220), Ajax's shield consisted of seven layers of leather and one of bronze.

came to Troy for the sake of the sheer number,[146] he considered their leaders well worth combating and capable of giving fame to their slayer and not a disgraceful injury to the wounded. After killing an enemy, Ajax kept his hands off the weapons because killing is for a courageous man, but stripping a slain enemy of his arms is more for a clothes-stealer.

4   No one would have uttered anything undisciplined or offensive within Ajax's hearing, nor how much they were in disagreement with one another. Instead they rose from their seats out of respect for him and withdrew from his path. Not only did the *hoi polloi* do so, but even those whose lot in life was highly esteemed.

5 He had a friendship with Achilles, and they neither wished to malign each other nor did they stick close together. As for Achilles' sorrows, even if they did not arise on account of trivial matters, he calmed them all, some as if he were a fellow sufferer, others as if he were reproving. Hellas used to pay attention to Achilles and Ajax when they were sitting or walking together, seeing in these men such as had not been since Herakles.

6   They say that Ajax was a foster-child of Herakles, and as an infant he was wrapped in the hero's lion skin. When Herakles dedicated him to Zeus, he asked that the child be invincible like the lion's skin. An eagle came to him as he prayed, bearing a name

7 from Zeus for the child and giving approval to his prayers.[147] It was absolutely clear to anyone who saw him that he did not grow up without divine aid because of the beauty and strength of his physique. Hence, Protesilaos calls him the very picture of war.

8 But when I said, "And certainly this one who was great and godly was always defeated by Odysseus in wrestling," he replied, "If Cyclopes had existed and the story concerning them were true, Odysseus would have wrestled with Polyphemos rather than with Ajax."

9   My guest, I also heard the following about this hero from Protesilaos: how he groomed himself by the river Ilissos in Athens, how the Athenians in Troy cherished him and considered him a

---

[146] Perhaps a reference to the number of Trojan allies (Homer *Il.* 2.824–877).

[147] This story is also found in the epic poem, the *Great Eoiae* (Hesiod frg. 250 [Merkelbach and West]), where it provides an etiology of Ajax's name (*aietos* "eagle"; *Aias* latinized is "Ajax"); see also Pindar *Isthmian* 6.34–54.

leader, and how they did whatever he said.[148] I think he sided with the Athenians because he dwelt in Salamis, which the Athenians made a deme[149] and also because when a child was born to him, whom the Athenians called Eurusakês, he fed him with a strange food that the Athenians recommended. And when the children of Athens were crowned with flowers in the month of Anthestêrion, in the third year of his son's life, he set up *kraters* from there and sacrificed according to Athenian custom. Protesilaos said that he also observed these sacred festivals of Dionysos as established by Theseus.

The account of his death, namely, that he died by killing 10 himself, is true, but perhaps shows pity even for Odysseus. About the things that took place in Hades—

> I wish I had not been the victor in such a contest;
> For the earth has covered such a head for the sake of this ar-
> mor[150]—

he denies that this was said by Odysseus there (according to Protesilaos, Odysseus did not descend to Hades while still alive), but says that it was certainly said somewhere. For it is plausible, I suppose, that even Odysseus suffered somewhat and that he wished away his own victory through pity for this man who died because of it. Although Protesilaos commends these verses 11 of Homer, how much more does he praise the verse in which he says,

> The sons of the Trojans rendered judgment.[151]

[148] In the *Iliad*, the only mention of the Athenians is in the catalogue of ships (Homer *Il.* 2.546–556); this is usually considered a late addition to the catalogue. The prominence of the Athenians here contrasts with their brief mention in the rest of the *Iliad*. Ajax's association with Athens is perhaps suggested by the catalogue of ships in which, immediately after the account of the Athenian forces, Ajax is said to have come from Salamis and placed his twelve ships next to the Athenians (Homer *Il.* 2.557–558).

[149] A territorial district, which during the classical and hellenistic periods constituted the unit of formal subdivision of a *polis*. During the late sixth century B.C.E., Cleisthenes reorganized the 139 demes of Athens and the Attic countryside into ten tribes; one of the eponymous tribes (Aiantis) was named after Ajax. Athens had gained possession of Salamis from Megara in the early sixth century B.C.E., and Salamis was made a *cleruchy*, or a special type of colony.

[150] Homer *Od.* 11.548–549.

[151] Homer *Od.* 11.547.

Indeed, he took away from the Achaeans the unjust decision and appointed judges who were likely to condemn Ajax. Hatred is
12 akin to fear, and after Ajax had gone mad, the Trojans feared him more than they usually did, lest by attacking the wall he break it down. They also prayed to both Poseidon and Apollo, since they labored at the wall, to stand guard before the citadel of the city and to check Ajax in case he seized the battlements. The Hellenes, however, did not cease their fondness for him, but they both publicly mourned Ajax's madness and supplicated the oracles to prophesy how he might turn himself around and
13 come to his senses. When they saw him dead and lying transfixed by his sword, they so wailed aloud all at once that they did not go unheard even in Ilion. The Athenians laid out his body, and Menestheus proclaimed over it the speech by which at Athens they customarily honor those who have died in wars.[152]
14 Protesilaos knows then of a highly esteemed deed of Odysseus: after Odysseus conferred the armor of Achilles upon Ajax as he lay dead and wept, he said, "Be buried with funeral rites in these arms that you loved and have the victory that comes with them, by no means falling into anger." After the Achaeans praised Odysseus, Teukros also commended him, but deprecated this use of the arms, since it is not permitted by divine law for the instruments of
15 death to be interred. They buried him by laying his body in the earth, since Kalkhas prescribed that those who had killed themselves were not permitted by divine law to be honored with a
36 funeral pyre. And consider that Teukros was a young man, but one who had size, a good physique, and might.

The Trojan Heroes (36.2–42.4)

2   PH. Does Protesilaos know stories about the Trojans, vine-

[152] The funeral oration, or *epitaphios*, was a genre and custom peculiar to Athens, beginning most likely in the fifth century B.C.E., and given at the public burial in the Kerameikos of those who died in war. It consisted not only of an exaltation of the excellent deeds of the dead, but also of a summary of Athens' history. The most famous example is the funeral oration of Pericles over those who had died in the first year of the Peloponnesian War (see Thucydides *Peloponnesian War* 2.35–46). For a full discussion of the genre and its setting and function within Athenian democracy, see Nicole Loraux, *The Invention of Athens: The Funeral Oration in the Classical City* (Cambridge, Mass.: Harvard University Press, 1986).

dresser, or does he not think it fit to mention them, lest they appear worthy of great attention?

V. Such is not the case with Protesilaos, my guest. His 3 grudge is gone. In fact, he reports even stories of the Trojans with zealous resolve, for he says that even those men gained for themselves a great account of their excellence. I shall relate these 4 things to you before the story of Achilles, since if they are told afterwards, they will not seem marvelous. So then, by praising **37** Hektor, Protesilaos also praised Homer's report about him. He said that Homer spoke in most excellent terms about his chariotry, battles, councils, and about Troy's dependence upon him and not upon another. However much Hektor boasts in Homer's poem while threatening the Achaeans with fire on the ships, Protesilaos says it certainly befits the bearing of the hero. Protesilaos says that Hektor said many such things in battles, looked most terrifying of all mortals, and shouted loudly. He was smaller than the son 2 of Telamôn, but not at all inferior in fighting, in which he displayed something even of the heat of Achilles. He was filled with 3 resentment against Paris as a coward and as one who gave in to self-adornment. In truth, Hektor thought that to have long hair, even though it is treated with respect by princes and the children of princes, was despicable for himself because of that man. His 4 ears were damaged, not by wrestling (for this sport, as I said, neither he nor the barbarians knew), but he fought against bulls and considered engagement with such beasts warlike. These activities also are a part of wrestling, but when he did them, he was ignorant of this sport, and for military exercise he practiced submitting to bellowing bulls, having no fear of the points of their horns, taming a bull by forcing back its neck, and not giving up, even though he was wounded by it.

The statue in Ilion indeed presents Hektor as young and 5 boyish, but Protesilaos says that he was more pleasant and larger than that statue. He died probably at the age of thirty, and he surely did not flee or let his hands drop idly (for in these matters Hektor is slandered by Homer).[153] Rather he fought mightily, and he alone of the Trojans remained outside the wall of Troy to perish late in the battle. After he died, he was dragged strapped to a chariot, but his body was returned, as is said by Homer.

[153] Compare Homer *Il.* 22.136–231.

38   But Aeneas, although inferior to Hektor as a fighter, surpassed the Trojans in intelligence and was considered worthy of
the same honors as Hektor. He knew well the intentions of the
gods, which had been fated for him once Troy had been captured,
but he was not struck with panic by any fear, for he had intelligence and good judgment, especially in frightening situations.[154]

2 While the Achaeans called Hektor the hand of the Trojans, they
called Aeneas the mind. He presented matters to them more pru-
dently than did the madly raging Hektor. They were both of the

3 same age and height, and although Aeneas's appearance seemed
less radiant, he resembled Hektor more when that man had settled down, and he wore his hair long without offense. He did not
adorn his hair, nor was he enslaved to it. Instead, he made virtue
alone his adornment, and he looked at things so vehemently that
even his glance itself was sufficient against the unruly.

39   Lycia brought forth Sarpêdon, but Troy exalted him. He
was like Aeneas in battle, and he led the whole body of Lycians,

2 along with their two best men, Glaukos and Pandaros. Although
Glaukos, of the two, was famed for being a man at arms, Pandaros claimed that when Lycian Apollo stood near him while still
in his youth, they joined together in archery, and thus he always
prayed to Apollo whenever he grasped his bow for a great cause.

3 Protesilaos says that with the whole army the Trojans met Sarpêdon's arrival, since besides his strength and his appearance, which
was both divine and noble, he attached himself to the Trojans and
to the story of their lineage. For the descendants of Aiakos, Dardanos, and Tantalos are celebrated as springing from Zeus, but to
have been begotten by Zeus himself belonged to that one alone of
all those who came to fight both on behalf of and against Troy.
(By this same divine parentage Herakles was also made greater

4 and more excellent among mortals.) But Sarpêdon died, as has
been told by Homer; he was about forty years old, and there is
a tomb in Lycia to which the Lycians escorted him, showing his
corpse to the peoples through whom he was carried. His body was
prepared with aromatic herbs, and he appeared to be sleeping; for
this reason the poets say that he used Hypnos as an escort.[155]

---

[154] Perhaps a reference to Aeneas's fight with Achilles (Homer
Il. 20.278–352).

[155] Homer *Il.* 16.419–683. See also the depiction of this scene in a vase
painting by Euphronius; MMA 1972.11.10.

Listen also to the deeds of Alexandros, known as Paris, un- **40** less you are exceedingly vexed with him.

PH. I am vexed, but I may as well listen.

V. Protesilaos says that Alexandros was hated by all the **2** Trojans, but that he was not worthless in the business of war; his appearance was most pleasing, and his voice and character were charming inasmuch as he had dealings with the Peloponnesus. He could fight in all ways and, as far as knowledge of bows is concerned, he did not fall short of Pandaros. Protesilaos says **3** that at eighteen he also sailed to Hellas, when he was a guest of Menelaos and seized Helen because of her beauty, and that he was not yet thirty years old when he died. He delighted in his **4** own beauty and was not only admired by others, but also admired himself. For this reason the hero makes sport of him most el- **5** egantly: Once when he saw this peacock (Protesilaos enjoys the brilliance and beauty of this bird) strutting, spreading out its wings, admiring and preening them—that they might appear arranged like necklaces of precious stones—he said, "Behold, Paris, son of Priam, whom we were mentioning just now!" And when I asked him, "How does the peacock resemble Paris?" he said, "By his self-love."[156] For surely that man not only inspected himself **6** all around for the sake of his adornment, but also examined his weapons carefully. He attached panthers' skins to his shoulders, he did not allow dirt to settle on his hair, not even when he was fighting, and he polished his fingernails. He had a rather aquiline nose and white skin, his eyes were painted, and his left eyebrow rose above the eye.

Helenos, Deiphobos, and Polydamas went into the battles **41** together with one another. They attained the same measure of strength and were also highly esteemed at giving counsel, but Helenos also engaged in prophecy equal to that of Kalkhas.

About Euphorbus, son of Panthous, and how a certain Eu- **42** phorbus was in Troy and was killed by Menelaos, you have heard, I suppose, the account of Pythagoras of Samos. For indeed Pythagoras said that he had been Euphorbus and that Euphorbus had changed from a Trojan into an Ionian, from a warrior into a sage, and from one who lived luxuriously into one chastened.

---

[156] On the character of the peacock, see Aristotle *History of the Animals* 1.1 (488b24); Ovid *Metamorphoses* 13.802.

His hair, which the one become a sage adorned with dirt, he
2 dyed golden-yellow in Troy when he was Euphorbus. Protesilaos
thinks that Euphorbus was his own age, pities him, and agrees
that after Patroklos was wounded by Euphorbus, he was handed
over to Hektor.[157] Had Euphorbus come to manhood, Protesilaos
says that he would have been considered no worse than Hektor.
3 He says that his beauty charmed even the Achaeans, for he resembled a statue [of Apollo] whenever Apollo appears his own most
lovely self with unshorn hair and grace.
4   The godly and noble hero narrates so much concerning the
Trojans, my guest. It remains for us, perhaps, to conclude the
story of Achilles, unless you have tired of its length.

V. ON HOMER AND HIS ART (43.1–44.4)

43   PH. If they who in Homer ate the lotus,[158] vinedresser,
were so readily addicted to the meadow as to forget utterly their
own affairs, do not doubt that I also am addicted to the story just
as to the lotus, and I would not even go away from here willingly,
but would be carried off to the ship with difficulty and would be
bound again to it, weeping and lamenting at not getting my fill
2 of the story. For truly, you have so disposed me even toward
Homer's poems that, although I thought they seemed divine and
beyond the capability of a mortal, I am now amazed more not only
at the epic poetry, even if some pleasure pervades Homer's poems, but to a much greater degree at the names of the heroes and
their lineages, and, by Zeus, how each of them obtained the lot of
3 killing a certain person or of dying at the hand of another. For I
do not think it amazing that Protesilaos knows these things, since
he is now a daimon, but from where does knowledge of Euphorbus come to Homer, and of such men as Helenos and Deiphobos,
and, by Zeus, of the many men of the opposing army whom he
4 mentions in the catalogue? Protesilaos testifies that Homer did
not invent these things, but that he made a narrative of deeds that
had happened and were genuine, except for a few of them, which

---

[157] Compare Homer *Il.* 16.808–829.
[158] Homer *Od.* 9.82–104.

he rather seems to transform purposefully so that his poetry appears elaborate and more pleasurable. Hence, that which is said 5 by some, that Apollo, after composing these poems signed the name "Homer" to the work, seems to me to be greatly confirmed, since knowing these stories is more fitting for a god than for a mortal.

V. That the gods are guides to the poets of every song, my 6 guest, the poets themselves, I suppose, confess: some invoke Calliope to be present in their story, others all the Muses, and still others Apollo in addition to the nine Muses. Homer's poems were not uttered without the aid of a god, but surely they were not sung by Apollo or the Muses themselves.

For he existed, my guest, the poet Homer existed and sang 7 twenty-four years after the Trojan War, as some say; but others say one hundred and twenty-seven years afterwards, when they colonized Ionia.[159] Still others say that there were one hundred and sixty years from Troy until the time of Homer and Hesiod, when both of them sang in Chalcis.[160] The former sang the seven epics about the two Ajaxes, how their ranks of battle were joined closely together and strong, and the latter sang songs about the affairs of his own brother, Persês, songs in which he urges Persês to engage in work and to devote himself to farming, so that he will not beg from others or go hungry.[161] The following events 8 of Homer's time, my guest, are quite true since Protesilaos agrees with them. Once, at any rate, after two poets had recited a song 9 in praise of him here and had gone away, the hero came and asked me for which one of them I would cast my vote. When I praised the simpler one (for he happened to have won the contest by far), Protesilaos laughed and said, "Panidês too had the same experience as you did, vinedresser. When that man was king of Chalcis

---

[159] According to Aristarchus, the second-century B.C.E. Alexandrian scholiast of Homer, Homer was an Athenian who lived around 1000 B.C.E. Discussions about the date of Homer characterize later historicizing of the composition of the epic traditions. See Nagy, *Poetry as Performance*, 150–51.

[160] This seems to be a reference to the *certamen* or *agôn*, the contest between Homer and Hesiod, inspired by Hesiod *Works and Days* 650–660.

[161] This is a reference to Hesiod's *Works and Days*.

on the Euripos, he voted for Hesiod over Homer, and this when
his beard was longer than yours."[162]

10   So then, my guest, the poet Homer existed, and these are
11 the poems of a mortal. He used to sing their names and collect
their deeds from the cities that each of them led. Homer went
about Hellas after the time of the Trojan War, when it was not yet
12 long enough for the events at Troy to have faded away. He also
learned these things in another manner as well, a manner both
supernatural and requiring the utmost skill. For they say that
Homer once sailed to Ithaca because he heard that the ghost of
Odysseus still breathed, and they say that Homer summoned him
13 from the dead. When Odysseus came up, Homer began asking
him about the events in Ilion, but Odysseus kept saying that although he knew and remembered them all, he would say nothing
of the things he knew unless there would be a reward for him from
Homer, songs of praise in his poetry and a song for his wisdom
14 and bravery. After Homer agreed to these things and said that in
his poetry he would do whatever he could to favor him, Odysseus
narrated everything truthfully and just as it happened. For you
see, the ghosts of the dead least of all speak falsely in the pres-
15 ence of blood and offering pits.[163] Moreover, just when Homer
was leaving, Odysseus cried out and said, "Palamedes is demand-
ing justice from me for his own murder! I know I did wrong, and I
am completely persuaded of it. Those who issue judgments here
are terrible, Homer, and the punishments of the Poinai are near
at hand! If to mortals above the ground I do not seem to have
done these things to Palamedes, the forces here will destroy me
less. Do not lead Palamedes to Ilion, neither treat him as a soldier
nor say that he was wise! Other poets will say these things, but
because they have not been said by you, they will not seem plausi-
16 ble." This, my guest, was the conversation between Odysseus and
Homer, and in this way Homer learned the truth, but he modified
many things for the expediency of the account that he composed.

---

[162] According to *Certamen* 322 (Allen, p. 237), in the contest between
Homer and Hesiod, the Hellenes recognized Homer's verses as exceeding the
ordinary level, but Panidês crowned Hesiod because his selection was about
peace and farming, rather than war and slaughter.
    [163] On the means of conjuring the dead, see Homer *Odyssey* 11. Pits
(*bothroi*), rather than stone altars, were used for sacrifices to heroes and chthonic
gods.

PH. Vinedresser, did you ever ask Protesilaos about Ho- **44** mer's homeland and from what people he came?

V. Very often, my guest.

PH. What was his answer?

V. Protesilaos says that he knows them. Because Homer **2** omitted them in order that the excellent men of the cities might make him their own citizen, and perhaps also because the decree of the Fates was against Homer, he seems to be without a city. Protesilaos says that he himself would not please either the Fates or the Muses if he disclosed this secret, since it would then come around to praise for Homer. For all cities ally themselves with **3** him, and all peoples, and they would also plead their case about him against one another, when they enter themselves in the public register with Homer as a citizen. Phoenician, let what I have said **4** be proof to you that I would neither keep this story secret from you nor hide it if I knew it. For I think that I have ungrudgingly divulged to you as much as I know.

VI. ACHILLES (44.5–57.17)

Achilles' Life, Appearance, and Character (44.5–52.2)

PH. I believe you, vinedresser. Let us agree with the rea- **5** son why these matters are kept silent. It is time for you to bring Achilles to light, unless he will also strike us with panic, just as he did the Trojans, when he shone forth on them from the trench.

V. Do not be afraid of Achilles, my guest, because you will **45** meet him as a child at the beginning of the story.

PH. You will bestow great gifts if you discuss him in detail from infancy, since after this we shall perhaps meet him armed and fighting.

V. So shall it be, and you will say that you know everything **2** about Achilles. I have heard the following about him. An ap- parition of a daimon of the sea used to visit Peleus. Because she loved him, the daimon had intercourse with Peleus on Mount Pe- lion, although out of shame for the crowd she did not yet speak about herself, not even from where she came. When the sea was **3** calm, she happened to be frolicking seated upon dolphins and sea horses, while he, looking at these things from the summit

of Mount Pelion, became aware of the goddess and feared her approach. But she made Peleus courageous by reminding him how Eos loved Tithônos, how Aphrodite was in love with Anchises, and how Selene habitually visited the sleeping Endymion. "Peleus," she said, "I shall even give to you a child mightier
4 than a mortal." When Achilles was born, they made Kheirôn his foster-father. He fed him honeycombs and the marrow of fawns. When Achilles reached the age at which children need wagons and knucklebones, he did not prohibit such games, but accustomed him to small javelins, darts, and race courses. Achilles also had a small ashen spear hewn by Kheirôn, and he seemed to babble about military affairs.
5   When he became an ephebe, a brightness radiated from his face, and his body was beyond natural size, since he grew more easily than do trees near springs. He was celebrated much at sym-
6 posia[164] and much in serious endeavors. When he appeared to yield to anger, Kheirôn taught him music.[165] Music was enough to tame the readiness and rising of his disposition. Without exertion, he thoroughly learned the musical modes, and he sang to the accompaniment of a lyre. He used to sing of the ancient comrades, Hyacinthus and Narcissus, and something about Adonis. And the lamentations for Hyllas and Abdêros being fresh—since, when both were ephebes, the one was carried into a spring until he disappeared, and upon the other the horses of Diomedes feasted—not without tears did he sing of these matters.
7   I also heard the following things: that he sacrificed to Calliope asking for musical skill and mastery of poetic composition, and that the goddess appeared to him in his sleep and said, "Child, I give you enough musical and poetic skill that you might make banquets more pleasant and lay sufferings to rest. But since it seems both to me and to Athena that you are skilled in war

[164] Symposia, drinking parties held in the evening, were occasions for stories, songs (especially *scolia* or formalized drinking songs), riddles, philosophical discourse, and games.
[165] Homer *Il.* 9.185–191. On music as an important means of education and a preparation for philosophical training, see Plato *Republic* 401e and *Laws* 795d. For a discussion of Plato's views of musical education, see Jaeger, *Paideia*, 2:229; 3:250–51; and Warren D. Anderson, *Ethos and Education in Greek Music* (Cambridge, Mass.: Harvard University Press, 1966). Music was also a central element of sophistic training (Jaeger, *Paideia*, 1:290).

and powerful even in dangerous situations {in army camps}, the Fates command thus: practice those skills and desire them as well. There will be a poet in the future whom I shall send forth to sing your deeds." This was prophesied to him about Homer.

When he became a young lad, he was not, as many say, 8 reared in hiding on Skyros, of all things among young maidens![166] It is not likely that Peleus, who had become the best of heroes, would have sent away his son somewhere secretly, running from battles and dangers. Moreover, when Telamôn sent Ajax forth to war, Achilles would not have put up with being thrown into women's quarters, yielding to others the opportunity to be admired and highly esteemed in Troy. Clearly, the greatest ambition for honor was also found in him.

PH. What then does Protesilaos know about these events, **46** vinedresser?

V. Things more plausible and truthful, my guest. He says 2 that after Theseus had fled from Athens because of the curse against his son, he died in Skyros by the hand of Lykomêdês. Peleus, who had been Theseus's guest-friend and companion in the Calydonian deed, sent Achilles to Skyros to avenge Theseus. And after he set sail together with Phoenix, who by reason of old age knew only the deliberative arts, he overthrew Skyros, which was on high ground away from attack after it had been rebuilt on a rocky hill. He guarded Lykomêdês and indeed did not kill him, but asked him what possessed him to kill a man better than himself. When Lykomêdês said, "Because, Achilles, he 3 came for unjust reasons and made an attempt on my dominion," Achilles released him, since he killed Theseus justly, and said that he would speak in his defense to Peleus. Achilles married 4 Dêidameia, daughter of Lykomêdês, and there was born to them Neoptolemos, who was named this because of Achilles' youth when he rushed forward into war. Thetis appeared to Achilles 5 while he was living there, and she attended to her son just as mortal mothers do. When the army was assembling at Aulis, she carried him over to Phthia because of the fates spun for him when she made Peleus the child's master. It is said that she also made 6

---

[166] This episode appears in Statius's unfinished epic *Achilleid* 207–396. Pausanias (*Description of Greece* 1.22.6) mentions it as an alternative to the tradition that Achilles captured Skyros.

for him weapons such as no one had yet carried. When he arrived at Aulis with these, he filled the army with hope; he was in this way so esteemed as a child of a goddess that they sacrificed to Thetis on the sea and worshipped Achilles when he darted about in his armor.

7   I also asked Protesilaos about the ashen spear—what its wonder was—and he says that the length of this spear was unlike that of any other, that the wooden shaft was straight and strengthened to such an extent that it could not be broken. The point of the spear was of unbreakable metal and could penetrate anything, and the spike on the other end of the shaft had been dipped in mountain copper, so that the whole spear would strike blazing like lightning.

47   PH. And his armor, vinedresser, how does he say it was decorated?

2   V. Not in the way that Homer describes, my guest. He says that the divine armor was also invented by Homer when he depicted cities, stars, wars, fields, weddings, and songs,[167] but the
3 following is what Protesilaos says about it. The armor of Achilles has never been anything other than what he brought to Troy, neither was Achilles' armor ever destroyed, nor did Patroklos put it on because of Achilles' wrath. He says that Patroklos died in his own armor while distinguishing himself in battle and just grasping the wall, and the armor of Achilles remained inviolable and
4 unassailable. Achilles did not even die in his armor, but thinking that he was going to his wedding, he died unarmed and wreathed
5 with a crown just like bridegrooms. Protesilaos says that the armor was fashioned without distinguishing marks and discreetly, and that a variety of material was blended together on it which changed sometimes into one sheen, sometimes into another, like a rainbow. For this reason, the armor is celebrated in song as seeming to be beyond the skill even of Hephaistos.

48   PH. Will you portray Achilles, vinedresser, and describe him from his appearance?

2   V. Why shouldn't I, since I have met you who are so fond of listening? Protesilaos says that Achilles' hair is thick, lovelier than gold, and becoming no matter where and how either the wind or he himself may move it. His nose is not quite aquiline,

---

[167] See Homer's description of the shield in *Il.* 18.478–608.

but almost so; his brow is crescent-shaped. The spirit in his eyes,
which are bluish-gray, casts off a certain eagerness even when he
is still; when he is rushing on, they spring out along with his
purpose, and then he seems more lovely than ever to those who
cherish him. The Achaeans were affected by him as by strong li- 3
ons. For although we greet lions at rest, we are even more pleased
with them whenever, after beginning to be filled with anger, they
rush headlong at a boar, a bull, or one of the bellicose beasts.
Protesilaos says Achilles' courage is evident even from his neck, 4
since it is straight and erect.

By nature and through association with Kheirôn, he be- 5
came the most just of the heroes. I tell you, being filled with
suspicion about possessions accompanied Achilles from then on.
For he was so set against them that, from the twenty-three cities
that he himself captured, although he took the most prisoners
of war, he was able to resist all of them except for a maiden,
whom he did not even give to himself, but asked the Achaeans
for her. When Nestor charged the Achaeans with injustice unless
Achilles should receive the most possessions, Achilles said, "Let
the greater part of the deed be mine, and let whoever wishes be
greedy for possessions."

At that assembly, my guest, Achilles' anger toward Agamem- 6
non on behalf of Palamedes also began. When recalling the cities 7
that the two of them had captured, he said, "Such was the trea-
son of Palamedes, and let whoever wishes condemn me as well
since I have come from the same cities." Agamemnon took these 8
words to be directed against him, and he railed against Achilles.
When Odysseus said that speaking on behalf of a traitor was trea-
son, Achilles drove him out of the assembly because he said things
that were not welcome even to the Achaeans. After attacking
Agamemnon with greater insults, he led a life out of the reach
of missiles of war, neither doing any deed for the common good
nor visiting war councils when supplications for him arrived from
Agamemnon because the Achaeans were already in great distress.
Both Ajax and Nestor acted as ambassadors,[168] the former be- 9
cause of their kinship and because he had already been reconciled

---

[168] This list differs somewhat from that in the *Iliad*, where Nestor proposed the embassy, but the ambassadors were Phoenix, Odysseus, and the
greater Ajax (Homer *Il.* 9.89–713).

with the Achaeans even though he had been angry for the same reasons that Achilles was angry; the latter on account of his sound
10 judgment and age, which all the Achaeans honored. When they discovered from him that Patroklos at least was allied with them, Patroklos, who both did and suffered as many things as Homer says, died fighting at Troy for the sake of the city wall. Achilles neither did anything ignoble toward him nor spoke against him. And after he bewailed him vigorously and buried him both as he himself wished and as he thought would also please Patroklos, he then advanced against Hektor.

11   Indeed, the hyperboles that Homer used about those who perished with their chariots whenever Achilles appeared, about those who were slain in the river, and about the movement of the river, when its own wave rose up against Achilles[169]—these hyperboles even Protesilaos commends as poetic, but he excludes them
12 as gratuitous. He says that neither against Achilles, although he was so great, would the Scamander have been at a loss and weaker than the mighty rivers in this encounter, nor would Achilles have rushed headlong against the river. For even if it had roared violently against him, he would have avoided it by turning away
13 and not moving close to the water. Protesilaos, I believe, recounts those events more plausibly than Homer. He says that the Trojans were driven together into the river, and more of them perished than had in the entire war; surely these deeds were not done by Achilles alone, but since the Hellenes had already been made confident by his presence, they went down against the Trojans and slaughtered them in the river.

14   He says that Achilles was heedless of these things, but contended for a prize in the following contest. There was a man who had come from Paionia, whom Homer also remembered.[170] He calls him Asteropaios, a grandson of the river Axios, and ambidextrous. Although the Paionian was the mightiest of both the Achaeans and the Trojans and rushed into the spears like a
15 wild beast, Homer disregarded this story. Having just arrived at Troy, he led a fresh force, the Paionian horsemen, whom Achilles repulsed by frightening them; they thought that a daimon had fallen upon them because they had not yet encountered such a

[169] Homer *Il.* 21.212–382.
[170] Homer *Il.* 21.136–208.

man. When Asteropaios alone stood his ground, Achilles feared 16
for himself more than when he fought with Hektor, and he did
not go unwounded when he killed the Paionian. For this reason, 17
when the allies forbade him to fight with Hektor on that day, he
did not endure these words, but as he said, "Let him see that I am
even mightier than my wounds," he rushed headlong against Hektor who was stationed before the wall. After he killed him, who 18
was such as I described in the story about him, Achilles dragged
him around the wall in a manner which, while barbarous and un-
pleasant, was pardonable, since he was avenging Patroklos. For 19
Achilles, while possessed with a certain supernatural nature, always did something great for his friends; for this reason he was
angry together with all the Hellenes on account of Palamedes and
avenged Patroklos and Antilokhos. It is especially necessary to 20
know what Achilles is reported to have said to Telamônian Ajax
about his friends, for afterwards, when Ajax asked him what sort
of deeds were most dangerous to him, Achilles said, "Those on
behalf of friends." Again, when asked what sort were both sweeter 21
and less troublesome, he gave the same answer. When Ajax won-
dered how the same deed might be both difficult and easy, he said,
"Because when on behalf of friends I readily take risks that are
great, I cease from grieving for them." "But what sort of wound
hurt you the most, Achilles?" Ajax asked. "The wound that I re- 22
ceived from Hektor." "And yet surely you were not wounded by
him," said Ajax. "By Zeus, he wounded my head and my hands,"
said Achilles, "for I consider you my own head, and Patroklos was
my hands."

My guest, Protesilaos says that Patroklos, although he was **49**
not much older than Achilles, was a divine and sensible man, the
most suitable companion for Achilles. He said that Patroklos rejoiced whenever Achilles also rejoiced, was distressed in the same
manner, was always giving some advice, and listened to Achilles
when he sang. Protesilaos says that even his horses carried Patroklos safe and sound, just as they did Achilles. In size and 2
bravery he was between the two Ajaxes. He fell short of the son
of Telamôn in all things, but he surpassed both the size and bravery of the son of Locris. Patroklos had an olive complexion, black 3
eyes, and sufficiently fine eyebrows, and he commended moder-
ately long hair. His head stood upon his neck as the wrestling

schools cultivate. His nose was straight, and he flared his nostrils as eager horses do.

50   PH. It is good that you have reminded me of Achilles' horses, vinedresser, because I really need to know why, even if they were better than other horses, they were deemed divine.

2   V. I have asked the hero this very question, my guest, and he says that their so-called immortality is a fiction told by Homer.[171] He reports, however, that when Achilles was in the bloom of youth, Thessaly, because it was both famed for its horses and noble, with some divine help nurtured two horses, one white and one chestnut, marvelous in their speed and magnificent in

3   their disposition. And because everyone believed what was spoken by divine providence about Achilles, it immediately seemed that the nature of the horses was divine and appeared to surpass the mortal.

51   Achilles' life came to an end, which Homer also knows. He says that Achilles died at the hands of both Paris and Apollo,[172] knowing, I suppose, what happened in Thymbraion, and how Achilles fell, murdered treacherously while engaged in sacrifices

2   and sacred oaths, of which he made Apollo a witness.[173] The sacrifice of Polyxena on his tomb and Achilles' passion for her,

3   which you hear from the poets, happened like this: Achilles loved Polyxena and was negotiating this marriage for himself with the understanding that he would make the Achaeans withdraw from

4   Ilion. Polyxena also loved Achilles; they had seen one another during the ransom negotiations for Hektor. For when Priam came to Achilles, he made his own child lead him by the hand, since she was the youngest of those Hekabê had borne for him.

5   (Younger children always used to assist their fathers' step.) And thus Achilles so displayed a certain self-control by his sense of justice, even in his amorous desires, that he did not abduct the girl, even though she was under his power, but promised Priam a marriage with her and trusted him when he delayed the wed-

6   ding. After he died unarmed, uttering oaths about these matters, Polyxena is said to have deserted and fled to the Hellenic army, as

[171] Homer *Il.* 16.145–154; see also the Glossary on Balios and Xanthos.
[172] Homer *Il.* 22.358–360.
[173] Protesilaos's story of Achilles' death is similar to the story found in Hyginus *Fabulae* 110 (in contrast to Achilles' death in battle in the *Aithopis*.)

the Trojan women were fleeing from the sanctuary and the Trojan men were scattered (they did not even carry away Achilles' corpse without fear). Polyxena was brought to Agamemnon to live in his excellent and discreet care, just as in the house of her father. But when Achilles' body had already been buried for three days, she ran to the tomb at night and leaned upon a sword while speaking many words of pity and marriage. At this time she also asked Achilles to remain her lover and to take her in marriage lest their marriage be proved false.

Protesilaos says that what is said by Homer in the second 7 weighing of souls,[174] if indeed those verses are by Homer, that after Achilles died the Muses lamented him with songs and the Nereids by beating their breasts, is not too big a boast. Protesilaos says that the Muses neither arrived nor sang, nor did any Nereids appear to the army, although they were known to have come, but that other wondrous events took place and they were not very different from those reported by Homer. From the Black 8 Bay the sea, swelling up, first of all bellowed, and after a short time, having risen up to a great crest, it advanced to Rhoiteion, while the Achaeans were amazed and perplexed by what both they themselves and the earth were about to suffer. When the sea 9 came closer and dashed against the camp, a piercing and incessant lament resounded like that which a throng of women utter in mourning. Because this event seemed godlike and supernatu- 10 ral, and because all agreed that the wave carried the Nereids (for it did not flood the land, but came to rest upon the earth gently and smoothly), the subsequent events seemed far more divine. For 11 when darkness followed next, Thetis's lamentation went through the army, as she shrieked and cried aloud for her son. She made a {greatly} piercing and ringing shout exactly like an echo in the mountains, and then the Achaeans especially understood that Thetis bore Achilles, although they did not believe otherwise.

This hill, my guest, which you see standing in line with the 12

---

[174] The first weighing of souls occurred when Achilles and Hektor were weighed in the scales of Zeus as they fought (Homer *Il.* 22.208–213). The "second weighing" must refer to a similar description of the outcome of Achilles and Paris's conflict. Aeschylus's tragedy *The Weighing of Souls* relates the fight between Achilles and Memnôn.

headland,[175] the Achaeans erected when they came together at the time when Achilles was united with Patroklos in the tomb and bequeathed to himself and that man the loveliest shroud. For this reason they who praise the marks of friendship sing of him.

13 He was buried most spectacularly of mortals with all that Hellas offered to him. The Hellenes no longer considered it proper after Achilles' death to wear their hair long, and they piled up in mass on a funeral pyre their gold and whatever each of them had, whether he had brought it to Troy or had taken it as booty, both right then and when Neoptolemos came to Troy. For Achilles obtained glorious gifts again from both his child and the Achaeans, who were trying to show in return their gratitude to him, and even those who made the voyage from Troy fell upon the tomb and believed that they were embracing Achilles.

52   PH. Does he say, vinedresser, what sort of person Neoptolemos was?

2   V. He was noble, my guest, and, although inferior to his father, was in no way more ordinary than Telamônian Ajax. Protesilaos says the same thing about his appearance as well: he was good-looking and resembled his father, but was inferior to him in the same way that beautiful people are inferior to their statues.

The Cult of Achilles at Troy (52.3–54.1)

3 From Thessaly, of course, Achilles also received hymns, which they sang at night when they visited his tomb every year, mixing something of an initiatory rite with their offerings to the dead, as both the Lemnians and the Peloponnesians descended from Sisyphus practice.

53   PH. Another subject has come up again, vinedresser, which, by Herakles, I would not let go, not even if you should do everything to help it escape.

2   V. But some people, my guest, consider these digressions to be idle talk and nonsense for those not at leisure. I see you, a slave of the ship that you captain and a slave of the winds, of which if even a slight breeze hits the stern, you must unfurl your sails

[175] Akhilleion, a small settlement near Sigeion and the site of the grave of Achilles and Patroklos (Strabo *Geography* 13.1.39, 46).

and be taken out to sea with your ship, since you think that everything takes second place to sailing.

PH. Farewell then to the ship and all that is on board! The 3
soul's cargo is sweeter to me and more profitable. Let's consider
these digressions not as nonsense, but as profit of this trade.

V. You are of sound mind, my guest, thinking in this way, 4
and since you wish, listen. The rites of the Corinthians for
Melikertês[176] (for these people are those whom I called the descendants of Sisyphus) and what the same people do for Medea's
children,[177] whom they killed for the sake of Glaukê, resemble a
lament that is both initiatory and inspired, for they propitiate the
children and sing hymns to Melikertês. And the island of Lemnos 5
is purified every year for the deed once done to the men on Lemnos by their wives at Aphrodite's instigation. The fire on Lemnos
is extinguished for nine days. A sacred ship from Delos, however,
carries the fire, and if it arrives before the offerings for the dead, it
puts in nowhere on Lemnos, but rides at anchor off the headlands
out at sea until sailing into the harbor is permitted by divine law.
For then, while invoking chthonian and ineffable gods, they keep 6
pure, I think, the fire that is out on the sea. Whenever the sacred 7
ship sails in and they distribute the fire both to its new abode and
to the forges of the artisans, from that source is the beginning of
new life.[178]

[176] On the literary and archaeological evidence for rites of Melikertês
at the Corinthian sanctuary at Isthmia and his association with the Isthmian
games, see Helmut Koester, "Melikertes at Isthmia: A Roman Mystery Cult,"
in *Greeks, Romans, and Christians: Essays in Honor of Abraham J. Malherbe*
(ed. David L. Balch, Everett Ferguson, and Wayne A. Meeks; Minneapolis: Fortress, 1990), 355-66; and Corinne Bonnet, "Le culte de Leucothéa et
Mélicerte en Grèce, au Proche-Orient et en Italie," *Studi e Materiali di Storia
della Religione* 10 (1986): 53-71. In the classical period, the use of wild cel-
ery in the victory crown for the Isthmian games indicates a cult for the dead.
Further indications of a mystery cult associated with Melikertês are found in
Pausanias (*Description of Greece* 2.2.1), Plutarch (*Theseus* 25), and Philostratus
(*Imagines* 2.16).

[177] According to Euripides (*Medea* 1378-1383), Medea established a cult
at the temple of Hera on Acrocorinth to atone for the murder of her children.
On the controversy concerning the myth of Medea and the cult in Corinth, see
Emily A. McDermott, *Euripides' Medea: The Incarnation of Disorder* (University Park, Penn.: Pennsylvania University Press, 1989), 9-24.

[178] On this rite, see Burkert, "Jason, Hypsipyle, and New Fire," 1-16.

8   The Thessalian offerings which came regularly to Achilles from Thessaly were decreed for the Thessalians by the oracle at Dodona.[179] For indeed the oracle commanded the Thessalians to sail to Troy each year to sacrifice to Achilles and to slaughter some sacrificial victims as to a god, but to slaughter others as for the
9 dead. At first the following happened: a ship sailed from Thessaly to Troy with black sails raised, bringing twice seven sacred ambassadors, one white bull and one black bull, both tame, and wood from Mount Pelion, so that they would need nothing from the city. They also brought fire from Thessaly, after they had drawn both libations and water from the river Sperkheios. For this reason, the Thessalians first customarily used unfading crowns for mourning, in order that, even if the wind delayed the ship, they
10 would not wear crowns that were wilted or past their season. It was indeed necessary to put into the harbor at night, and before touching land, to sing Thetis a hymn from the ship, a hymn composed as follows:

> Dark Thetis, Pelian Thetis,
> you who bore the great son Achilles:
> Troy gained a share of him
> to the extent that his mortal nature held sway,
> but to the extent that the child derives from your immortal
>   lineage,
> the Pontus possesses him.
> Come to this lofty hill
> in quest of the burnt offerings with Achilles.
> Come without tears, come with Thessaly:
> Dark Thetis, Pelian Thetis.

11 When they approached the tomb after this hymn, a shield was struck heavily as in battle, and together they cried aloud with rhythmic rapid delivery, calling repeatedly upon Achilles. When they had wreathed the summit of the hill and dug offering pits on
12 it, they slaughtered the black bull as to one who is dead. They also summoned Patroklos to the feast, in the belief that they were do-
13 ing this to please Achilles. After they slit the victim's throat[180]

[179] For a discussion of these rituals, see Radet, "Notes sur l'histoire d'Alexandre," 81–96.
[180] *entemnô* designates the act of slitting the victim's throat in the sacrifice; see P. Stengel, *Opferbräuche der Griechen* (Leipzig: Teubner, 1910), 103.

and made this sacrifice, they immediately went down to the ship, and after sacrificing the other bull on the beach again to Achilles and having begun the offering by taking from the basket[181] and by partaking of the entrails for that sacrifice (for they made this sacrifice as to a god),[182] they sailed away toward dawn, taking the sacrificed animal so as not to feast in the enemy's country.

My guest, these rites, so holy and ancient, they say were 14 both abolished by the tyrants, who are said to have ruled the Thessalians after the Aiakidai, and were neglected by Thessaly. Some cities sent their offerings, others did not consider them worthwhile, others said they would send them next year, and still others rejected the matter. When the land was hard pressed 15 by drought and the oracle gave the order to honor Achilles "as was meet and right,"[183] they removed from the rites what they customarily observed for a god, interpreting "as was meet and right" in this way. They used to sacrifice to him as to one who is dead, and they would cut up as a sacrifice the first animals they encountered. Thus it was until Xerxes' expedition into Greece occurred. During this expedition, the Thessalians, who sided with the Medes,[184] once again abandoned the prescribed customs for Achilles, seeing that a ship sailed to Salamis from Aegina carrying the house of the Aiakidai to support the Hellenic alliance.[185] When in later times Alexander, the son of Philip, subjugated 16

---

[181] The basket contained grains or cakes of barley for the sacrifice, along with the sacrificial knife, hidden under the cakes. At the beginning of the sacrifice, the barley was customarily thrown on the altar and the sacrificial victim, after which the knife was taken from the basket. After the victim was slaughtered, its entrails (heart and liver) were roasted on the fire. See Burkert, *Greek Religion*, 56–57.

[182] The terminology here for the beginning acts of a sacrifice and the participants' tasting of the raw entrails marks this sacrifice as one "to a god" in distinction to a holocaust offering appropriate for "one who is dead" (Burkert, *Greek Religion*, 56–57, 63, 199–200).

[183] A formulaic reference to behavior that is expected by virtue of the established custom of a city.

[184] The Alôadai, the ruling family of Thessaly in Larissa, supported the Persians when they invaded Greece, although a minority of the Thessalian states opposed this policy.

[185] Herodotus (*Hist.* 8.64) records that during the discussion whether to defend Salamis or retreat to the Peloponnesus, the Greeks called upon Aiakos (Achilles' grandfather) and his descendants to fight against the Persians with them. A ship was sent to Aegina and as Herodotus says, "Aiakos himself and his

the other part of Thessaly and dedicated Phthia to Achilles, he made Achilles his ally in Troy while marching against Darius. The Thessalians returned to Achilles and, in addition, they rode the cavalry, which Alexander brought from Thessaly, around his tomb and fell upon one another as though they were fighting on horseback. And after praying and sacrificing they departed; they invoked Achilles against Darius, and along with him Balios and
17 Xanthos, as they shouted these prayers from their horses. But after Darius was captured and Alexander was in India, the Thessalians reduced the sacrifices and sent black lambs. Because the sacrifices did not even reach Troy, and if each arrived in broad daylight, they were not done in proper order, Achilles became angry. And if I should relate how much harm he hurled upon
18 Thessaly, the tale would be tedious. Protesilaos said that he had come from the Pontus about four years before meeting me here. When he had procured a ship, he sailed like a guest-friend to
19 Achilles, and this he did often. When I said that he was devoted and gracious in his friendship for Achilles, he said, "But now, because I have quarreled with him, I have come here. When I perceived that he was angry with the Thessalians over the offerings to the dead, I said, 'For my sake, Achilles, disregard this.' But he was not persuaded and said that he would give them some misfortune from the sea. I certainly feared that this dread and cruel
20 hero would find something from Thetis to use against them." As for me, my guest, after I heard these things from Protesilaos, I believed that red blights and fogs had been hurled by Achilles upon the grainfields of Thessaly for destruction of their agricultural produce, since these misfortunes from the sea seemed somehow
21 to settle upon their fruitful lands. I also thought that some of the cities in Thessaly would be flooded, in the way that Boura and Helikê, as well as Atalantê near Locris, had suffered; they say that the former two sank, and the latter one broke apart.
22   Other actions seemed good instead to Achilles and Thetis, by whom the Thessalians were destroyed. Because the prices for the shellfish from which people skillfully extract the purple dye[186]

---

other sons," were brought to Salamis. It is not clear if Herodotus is referring to their cult statues or their bones.

[186] Latin *murex*, a source of purple dye in the ancient world.

were quite great, the Thessalians were somewhat guilty of trans-
gressing the law in order to obtain this dye. If these things are 23
true, I do not know. Stones then hung over them,[187] because of
which some people gave up their fields and others their homes.
Some of their slaves ran away from them, others were sold. And
the common folk did not even offer sacrifice to their ancestors,
for they even sold the tombs. And so this we believe, my guest,
was the evil that Achilles had threatened to give to the Thessalians
from the sea.

PH. You speak of an anger that is "ruinous"[188] and impla- **54**
cable, vinedresser. But tell me what marvel Protesilaos knows
about the island in the Pontus, since it was there, I suppose, that
he was with Achilles.

On Leukê (54.2–57.17) —
  The Songs of Achilles and Helen (54.2–55.6)

V. It was there, my guest, and he tells the following sorts 2
of stories about it. He says that it is one of the islands in the
Pontus more toward its inhospitable side, which those sailing into
the mouth of the Pontus put on their left. It is about thirty
stades long, but not more than four stades wide; the trees growing on it are poplars and elms, some stand without order, but
others already stand in good order around the sanctuary. The 3
sanctuary is situated near the Sea of Maiôtis (which, equal in

---

[187] Perhaps an allusion to one of the punishments of Tantalos, over
whom Zeus suspended a huge stone that constantly threatened him. The vinedresser may be suggesting that the constant fear that their crime would be
discovered and punished hung over them. See, however, the discussion in Paul
Huvelin's appendix "ΛΙΘΟΙ ΕΠΙΚΡΕΜΑΝΤΑΙ," in Radet, "Notes sur l'histoire d'Alexandre," 94–96. Radet argues that the Thessalians engaged in the
purple trade illegally, namely, by not paying taxes to Rome on their profits and
that the punishment may consist of a lien imposed on their real estate, creating
severe economic hardship and a general panic. According to Huvelin, moreover,
the phrase "the stones hung over them" refers either to the practice of *skopelismos* whereby boundary stones were set up to prevent a farmer tilling the land or
to the interdict marked by the rite of *jactus lapilli* ("the throwing of a stone");
both of these practices are attested in the legal works of Ulpian who was active
in the Severan period, 202–223 C.E. Huvelin suggests that the phrase is more
likely to be a reference to the practice of *jactus lapilli*, since *skopelismos* is only
known as an Arabian rite.

[188] Homer *Il.* 1.2.

size to the Pontus, flows into it), and the statues in it, fash-
4 ioned by the Fates, are Achilles and Helen. Indeed, although
the act of desire lies in the eyes and poets in song celebrate desire as originating from this, Achilles and Helen, because they
had not even been seen by one another, since she was in Egypt
and he in Ilion, were the first who started to desire one another
by finding their ears to be the origin of their longing for the
5 body. Because no land under the sun had been fated for them
as an abode for the immortal part of their life—although the
Ekhinades downstream from Oiniadai and Acarnania were immediately defiled at the very time when Alkmaiôn killed his mother,
he settled at the estuary of the Akhelôos on land formed more
recently than his deed—Thetis beseeched Poseidon to send up
6 from the sea an island where they could dwell. After Poseidon
had pondered the length of the Pontus and that, because no island lay in it, it was sailed uninhabited,[189] he made Leukê appear,
of the size I have described, for Achilles and Helen to inhabit,
7 but also for sailors to stay and set their anchor in the sea. As
ruler over everything that is by nature wet, after he also conceived of the rivers Thermôdôn, Borysthênes, and Istros so that
they were carried off into the Pontus by irresistible and continually flowing currents, Poseidon heaped together the sediment
from the rivers, which they sweep into the sea starting at their
sources in Scythia. He then neatly fashioned an island of just
the size I mentioned and set its foundation on the bottom of
8 the Pontus. There Achilles and Helen first saw and embraced
one another, and Poseidon himself and Amphitritê hosted their
wedding feast, along with all the Nereids and as many rivers
and water-spirits as flow into the Sea of Maiôtis and the Pontus.
9   They say that white birds live on the island and that these
marine birds smell of the sea. Achilles made them his servants,
since they furnish the grove for him with the breeze and rain
drops from their wings. They do this by fluttering on the ground
10 and lifting themselves off a little bit above the earth. For mortals
who sail the broad expanse of the sea, it is permitted by divine
law to enter the island, for it is situated like a welcoming hearth
for ships. But it is forbidden to all those who sail the sea and for

---

[189] In other words, without encountering any settlement.

the Hellenes and barbarians from around the Pontus to make it a
place of habitation. Those who anchor near the island and sacri- 11
fice must go onboard when the sun sets, so that they do not sleep
on its land. If the wind should follow them, they must sail, and if
it does not, they must wait in the bay after mooring their ship.

Then Achilles and Helen are said to drink together and to 12
be engaged in singing. They celebrate in song their desire for one
another, Homer's epics on the Trojan War, and Homer himself.
Achilles still praises the gift of poetry which came to him from
Calliope, and he pursues it more seriously, since he has ceased
from military activities. At any rate, my guest, his song about 13
Homer was composed with divine inspiration and the art of poetry. Indeed, Protesilaos knows and sings that song.

PH. May I hear the song, vinedresser, or is it not proper to **55**
disclose it?

V. Why, of course you may, my guest! Many of those 2
who approach the island say that they hear Achilles singing other
things as well, but only last year, I believe, did he compose this
song, which is most graceful in thought and intentions. It goes 3
like this:

> Echo, dwelling round about the vast waters
> beyond great Pontus,
> my lyre serenades you by my hand.
> And you, sing to me divine Homer,
> glory of men,
> glory of our labors,
> through whom I did not die,
> through whom Patroklos is mine,
> through whom my Ajax is
> equal to the immortals,
> through whom Troy, celebrated by the skilled as won
>   by the spear,
> gained glory and did not fall.

PH. Vinedresser, Achilles sings at any rate by divine in- 4
spiration and in a manner worthy of both himself and Homer.
Besides, it is sensible not to lengthen these matters in lyric songs
or to perform them in an extended fashion. From of old, poetry
was thus both esteemed and cleverly devised.

V. It has been practiced thus from of old, my guest, for 5

they say that after Herakles impaled the body of Asbolos the centaur, he inscribed the following epigram for him:

> I, Asbolos, trembling at the vengeance of neither gods nor
> mortals,
> as I hang from a prickly, resin-filled pine tree,
> I am offered as a great feast for the immensely long-lived
> ravens.

6   PH. Herakles, it seems, became a champion even of these skills when he commends elevated speech, vinedresser, with which the poet doubtless must speak. But let us return to the island, since the stream that moves greatly to and fro about the Pontus has seized us and is leading us astray from the story.

On Leukê (54.2–57.17) —
The Vengeance of Achilles (56.1–57.17)

56   V. Yes, my guest, let us return. There are such songs on the island, and the voice with which they sing sounds both divine and excellent. At any rate, such a great voice reaches to the high seas
2 that a chill comes over sailors because of their terror. Those who have cast their anchor there say that they hear both the trampling of horses and the clash of weapons, as well as a shout like men call
3 out in battle. If, after they have anchored at the north or south end of the island, a wind is about to blow against their anchorage, Achilles announces this at their stern and orders them to stay
4 out of the wind by shifting their anchor. Many of those who also travel out of the Pontus sail to me and report these matters. By Zeus, they tell me that when they have caught sight of the island, I suppose since they are being carried on the boundless sea, they embrace one another and come to tears because of their delight. After they have put into harbor and welcomed the land, they go to the sanctuary to pray to Achilles and offer sacrifices. The sacred victim of its own will stands near the altar opposite the ship and the sailors.
5   My guest, the story concerning the golden pitcher that once appeared in the island of Chios has been told by skilled men, and what might someone grasp anew of tales told plainly?
6   Achilles himself is said to have appeared to a merchant who once visited the island often, related what took place in Troy, entertained him with drink as well, and ordered him after sailing to

Ilion to bring him a Trojan maiden, saying that this particular
woman was a slave to a certain man in Ilion. When the guest was 7
astonished at the command and because of his new-found bold-
ness asked Achilles why he needed a Trojan slave, Achilles said,
"Because, my guest, she was born of the lineage from which Hektor and those living before him came and is what remains of the
blood of the descendants of Priam and Dardanos." Of course, the 8
merchant thought that Achilles was in love, and after he bought
the maiden, he sailed back to the island. When he came, Achilles
praised the merchant and ordered him to guard the maiden for
him on the ship, because, I suppose, the island was inaccessible
for women. He ordered the merchant to come to the sanctuary at
evening and to be entertained sumptuously with him and Helen.
When he arrived Achilles gave him many things that merchants 9
are unable to resist; he said that he considered him a guest-friend
and granted him lucrative trade and safe passage for his ship.
When day came, he said, "Sail away with these things, but leave 10
the girl on the shore for me." They had not yet gone a stade
away from the land when the girl's wailing struck them, because
Achilles was pulling her apart and tearing her limb from limb.

In Troy, however, Achilles did not kill the Amazons, whom 11
some of the poets say came to Troy to fight Achilles.[190] I do not
know how it is plausible that, after Priam had fought against them
on the side of the Phrygians during the reign of Mugdôn,[191] the
Amazons later would have come to Ilion as allies. But I think that
at the time of the Olympic games in which Leonidas of Rhodes
first won the *stadion*,[192] Achilles destroyed the most warlike group
of them, they say, on the island itself.

PH. You have touched upon a great story, vinedresser, and 57
aroused my ears, which otherwise were attentive to your words. It
is likely that these matters have come to you as well from Protesilaos.

V. From this gracious teacher they have come, my guest, 2
but these things are also evident to many of those who sail into the

---

[190] According to the *Aithiopis*, the Amazons came to Priam's aid after
Hektor's death.

[191] Homer *Il.* 3.184–189.

[192] The *stadion* was a short race in which the competitors sprinted down
the straight length of the stadium, about 200 yards.

3 Pontus. Near the inhospitable side of the Pontus, along which the
Taurus Mountains extend, there, on the firm land around which
the rivers Thermôdôn and Phasis flow as they come out of the
mountains, are said to dwell some Amazons, whom both their father and nurturer, Ares, taught to be engaged in affairs of war and
to live a life armed and on horseback. For them a troop of horses
4 enough for the army is tended in marshy meadows. They do not
permit men to live in their own country, but, whenever they need
children, they go down to the river Halys to do business in the
marketplace and to have intercourse with men in any old place.
After they return to their haunts and homes, they carry to the borders of the country whatever male children they bear so that those
who have begotten them can claim them; those men claim what-
5 ever child each happens to find and make them slaves. But the
females to whom they give birth they are said to love immediately,
to regard as belonging to their own race, and to care for them as is
the nature of mothers, except for withholding their milk. They do
this because of their battles, so that the children do not become ef-
6 feminate and their breasts do not hang down. Let us believe that
the Amazons' name comes from not being reared at the breast.[193]
They nurse the infants with the milk of grazing horses and with
honeycombs full of the dew that settles on the reeds of the river
like honey.
7   Let us leave out of our account the things said by both poets
and compilers of myths about these Amazons, since they would
not be profitable for the present endeavor. Rather, let their deed
concerning the island be told, what sort of thing was done by
them, and to what end it was accomplished, since this is part
8 of Protesilaos's accounts. When ships were once more numerous, some sailors and shipbuilders, from among those people who
brought merchandise to the Hellespont from the Pontus, were
carried off course down toward the left shore of the sea, round
9 about which the women are said to live. After they were captured
by the women, for a period of time they were kept locked up, being
fed at mangers, so that the women, taking them across the river,
10 could sell them to the Scythian cannibals. But when one of the

[193] The name "Amazon" was understood as formed from *a* privative
("not") + *mazos* ("breast"). The vinedresser offers one interpretation of the etymology; see also "Amazons" in the Glossary.

Amazons took pity on a lad who had been captured along with them because of his youth, and when some erotic attraction resulted, she asked the chief Amazon, who was her sister, not to sell the strangers. After the men were released and had formed close 11 friendships with the women, they now began to speak in their idiom. While they were recounting their tale about the winter storm and their experiences on the sea, they passed on to their recollection of the sanctuary, since they had sailed to the island not long before, and they told about the wealth in it.

Since the strangers were both sailors and shipbuilders, and 12 since that area was also suitable to them for shipbuilding, the Amazons who had come upon them had them make a ship for transporting horses in the hope that they would possess Achilles along with his mares (for once the Amazons dismount from their horses, they are female in gender and women in every respect). Indeed, first the Amazons engaged in rowing and practiced sail- 13 ing, and so they gathered knowledge of sailing. Getting underway from the outlets of the Thermôdôn at about springtime, they went forth on fifty ships, I think, to the sanctuary, about two thousand stades away. When they anchored at the island, they first ordered their Hellespontian guests to cut down the trees with which the sanctuary was adorned round about. But when their axes, driven 14 back against them, went into the head of some, into the neck of others, and all fell near the trees, the Amazons streamed to the sanctuary, crying aloud and driving on their mares.

And Achilles, on seeing the heat and terror in them and leap- 15 ing as he had at the Scamander and in Ilion, inflicted on their mares a terror mightier than a bit, at which they reared up, regarding the women as an unnatural and superfluous burden. The horses took on the habits of wild beasts, and as they fell upon the Amazons, who lay on the ground, the horses thrust their hooves, bristled their manes, and pricked up their ears against them, just like savage lions. They ate the naked forearms of the supine women, and after they had broken open their chests, they devoted themselves to the entrails and gulped them down. Stuffed with human flesh, they stamped around the island and raged, sated with gore. Then, standing on the promontories and seeing the wide surface of the sea, they thought that they had encountered a wide plain and hurled themselves down toward the sea. The 16 Amazons' ships also perished, when a violent wind blew upon them; because they lay at anchor empty and in disarray, they struck against one another and were dashed into pieces, I suppose. Ship sank ship and broke up just as in a naval battle, and just as many rammings of ship against ship, both athwart and prow-to-prow, as helmsmen make while fighting at sea, these all fell upon the ships, which were empty and floating without direc-

17 tion. Because many pieces of wreckage were carried back to the sanctuary and because humans were lying in it still breathing and half-eaten—both scattered human limbs and the pieces of flesh that the mares had spat upon—Achilles easily purified the island, for by drawing in a wave of the sea he both washed these things clean and rinsed them.

VII. EVENING FALLS (58.1–6)

58   PH. Vinedresser, whoever does not consider you exceedingly beloved of the gods is himself hated by the gods. I think that the knowledge of such divine stories has thus come to you from those who have also made you an intimate and a close friend

2 of Protesilaos. But after you have filled us with heroic stories, I would no longer ask how he himself returned to life, since you

3 say that he treats that story as inviolable and secret.[194] On those who dwell by the Kôkytos and the Pyriphlegethôn, and about the Akherousias, and such names of rivers and seas, and, by Zeus, the Aiakidai and their courts of justice and places of punishments, you yourself will perhaps report and he will agree to set forth the details.

4   V. He agrees, but it is already evening and the herds must go to their rest. You see, at any rate, the small teams of oxen because the time for unyoking them has come. I must attend to

5 them, and the story is longer than time allows. Now, go to your ship rejoicing with all that the garden bears, and, my guest, if the wind is yours, set sail once you have poured a libation to Protesilaos from the ship. It is customary for those leaving here to do so.

---

[194] From the beginning of the dialogue, according to the vinedresser, Protesilaos refuses to speak of his death and return to life (see *Her.* 2.9–11), despite the Phoenician's skepticism about Protesilaos's return to life (see *Her.* 3.1; 5.2).

If the wind should be against you, come here at sunrise and you will obtain what you wish.

Ph.   I am persuaded by you, vinedresser, and so shall it be.   6
May I not sail, by Poseidon, before I listen to this story as well.

Maps

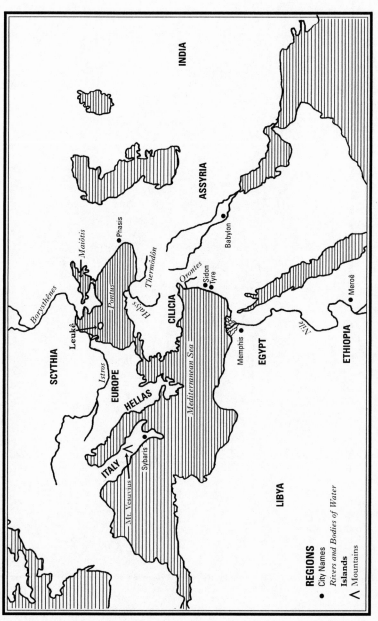

REGIONS
• City Names
Rivers and Bodies of Water
Islands
∧ Mountains

GENERAL VIEW OF THE MEDITERRANEAN

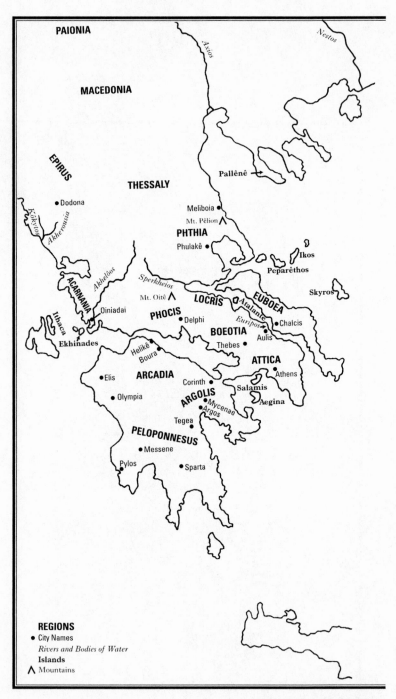

PAIONIA

MACEDONIA

EPIRUS

THESSALY

• Dodona

Pallênê

Meliboia •

Mt. Pêlion ∧

PHTHIA

Phulakê •

Ikos

Peparêthos

Skyros

Sperkheios

Mt. Oitê ∧

LOCRIS

Atalante

EUBOEA

ACARNANIA

Akhelóos

PHOCIS

• Delphi

Euripos

BOEOTIA

Chalcis

Oiniadai

Aulis

Ithaca

Thebes •

Ekhinades

Helikê •

Boura

ATTICA

Athens

• Elis

ARCADIA

Corinth •

Salamis

• Olympia

ARGOLIS

Aegina

Mycenae •

Argos

Tegea •

PELOPONNESUS

• Messene

Pylos •

• Sparta

Kókytos

Akherousia

Axiós

Nestos

REGIONS
• City Names
Rivers and Bodies of Water
Islands
∧ Mountains

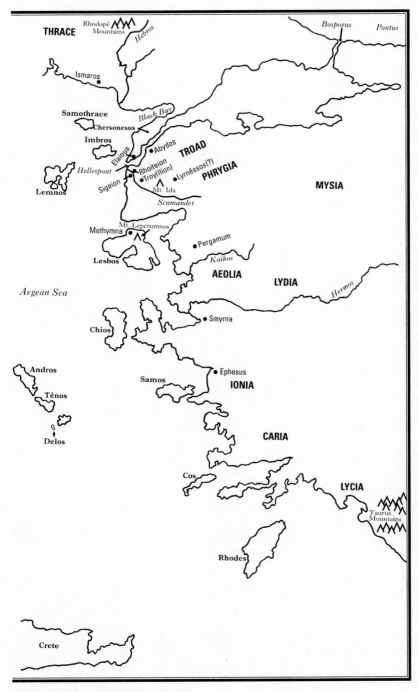

AND WESTERN ASIA MINOR

Glossary

Abdêros: Son of Hermes or Poseidon, lover and page of Herakles, who was devoured by the man-eating mares of Diomedes. Herakles founded the Thracian city of Abdera in his lover's memory.

Abians: Legendary Scythian people, usually located in the far north, said to be among the most just people on earth (Homer *Il.* 13.6).

Abydos: City on the eastern shore of the narrowest point of the Dardanelles (modern Avido), it was a Milesian colony since ca. 600 B.C.E. and was later controlled by the Persians. Xerxes reviewed his troops here in 480 B.C.E. before building the bridge across the Dardanelles and invading Macedonia and Greece.

Acarnania: Westernmost area of central Greece between the Ionian Sea, the Ambracian Gulf, and the Gulf of Patras, along the lower course of the river Akhelôos.

Achaeans: In Homer this term refers to the followers of Achilles and Agamemnon. The Achaeans were the paleolithic inhabitants of Achaea, the region in the northeast Peloponnesus and southeast Thessaly. In Hittite and Egyptian texts from 1400–1200 B.C.E., the terms "Aḫḫijawa" and "Ekwesh," respectively, may refer to the Achaeans.

Achilles: Son of Peleus and Thetis, leader of the Myrmidons and a principal hero of the *Iliad*, the plot of which revolves around Achilles' anger at the Achaeans and his refusal to join the battle against the Trojans until after the death of Patroklos. He was known for his episodes of uncontrollable rage as, for example, when he dragged Hektor's corpse around the walls of Troy to avenge Patroklos's death. Achilles' death at the hands of Paris and Apollo is foretold in the *Iliad* (22.358–360); according to the lost *Aithiopis*, Achilles died in battle attempting to avenge the death of Antilokhos at the hands of Memnôn. He was educated by Kheirôn on Mount Pelion and is usually depicted in art as a young man, often beard-less. Various traditions exist about his love for Patroklos and Trôilos, as well as about his marriage to Polyxena and to Helen. His cult was strong in the region of the Black Sea, particularly in association with the White Island (Leukê; see also Pausanias *Description of Greece* 3.19.13), and to a lesser extent in Asia Minor, Epirus, Thessaly, and Elis. According to Strabo (*Geography* 13.1.32), there was a sanctuary of Achilles in Sigeion on the Troad.

Admêtos: King of Pherai in Thessaly and one of the Argonauts. He was offered the gift of immortality if another human being would die in his stead. When even his aged parents re-fused to die for him, his wife Alcestis offered herself (Homer *Il.* 2.713–715; see also Euripides *Alcestis*).

Adonis: Greek hero of Syrian origin. Known for his great beauty, he was fought over by Aphrodite and Persephone. The dispute between the goddesses was settled by Calliope on Zeus's behalf: Adonis was to spend one-third of each year with each goddess and the remaining third wherever he chose. He always chose to be with Aphrodite. Adonis was killed at an early age by a wild boar.

Aegean: The sea between Greece and Asia Minor.

Aegina: Island in the Saronic Gulf located about 20 km south of Salamis. A prominent naval power throughout the archaic period, Aegina was often at war with Samos. Extended hos-tilities with Athens began in 506 B.C.E., but at the battle of Salamis, Aegina sided with Greece against the Persians. War erupted between Athens and Aegina in 459; Aegina was defeated and forced to join the Delian League, but later helped to provoke the Peloponnesian War. The Athenians thereupon expelled the inhabitants of Aegina from the is-land; it was occupied by Athens until 405 when it came under Spartan governance. Associated with Aiakos and his descendants, the island contains a *heroon*, that is, a shrine or temple dedicated to a hero, associated with the hero's grave, to Aiakos, and its inhabitants celebrated a festival in his honor.

Aeneas: Son of Anchises and Aphrodite, Trojan hero, whose descendants founded Rome. His escape from Troy and his journey to Italy are the subject of Virgil's *Aeneid*.

Aeolia: According to ancient geography, the west coast of Asia Minor between Lekton and the river Hermos. Later it also included the region of Troy.

Agamemnon: One of the sons of Atreus, grandson of Pelops, and king of Mycenae. Homer characterized Agamemnon as "ruler of men" (*anax andrôn*), "shepherd of the people" (*poimên laôn*), and of divine descent (*dios*) (see, e.g., *Il.* 1.30, 79, 186, 278; 2.8, 82, 100, 108, 197, 477, 569, 576, 610). The abduction of his brother Menelaos's wife Helen is the occasion for the Trojan War, and Agamemnon became the supreme commander of the Achaeans in this war against Troy. Agamemnon antagonized Achilles by taking his war prize Briseis. Homer's *Iliad* describes the conflict between Agamemnon and Achilles, Achilles' withdrawal from fighting, and Agamemnon's attempts at appeasement. Both Homer and Aeschylus recount Agamemnon's death after his return from the war: According to Aeschylus, Agamemnon was murdered by his wife Clytemnestra; in Homer the murder is performed by her lover, Aigisthos.

Aiaia: Island of Circe, the divine enchantress, under whose spell Odysseus's companions were changed into pigs (Homer *Od.* 9.32; 10.135; 11.70; 12.268, 273).

Aiakidai: Literally the descendants of Aiakos, but the term generally refers to Achilles and the greater Ajax (Homer *Il.* 16.15; 18.433; 21.189).

Aiakos: The son of Zeus, father of Peleus and Telamôn, and grandfather of Achilles. Celebrated for his piety, Aiakos became a judge of the dead (Plato *Apology* 41a; *Gorgias* 523e).

Aidôneus: See Hades.

Ajax the Greater: Ajax the son of Telamôn was from Salamis and, next to Achilles, the mightiest in battle among the Achaeans (Homer *Il.* 2.768; 7.199). Achilles' weapons, after his death, were destined by his mother Thetis for the one who had inspired most fear in the Trojans. The Trojan prisoners were questioned, and they named Odysseus, rather than Ajax.

During the night Ajax went mad and slaughtered flocks of sheep, whom he mistook for his enemies; he killed himself when he realized the state of madness into which he had fallen (*Little Iliad*). Ajax was not cremated but placed in a coffin and buried (see *Little Iliad* 4, whose story denies Ajax the customary burial for a hero). Ajax refused to speak with Odysseus in the Underworld because of their previous rivalry (Homer *Od.* 11.543–564). Sophocles expanded the story of his demise in his tragedy *Ajax*, but gave Ajax an honorable burial. For an alternative tradition about Ajax's death, see Pindar *Isthmian* 6.

Ajax the Lesser: Son of the Locrian king Oileus (Homer *Il.* 13.712). He dragged Cassandra away from Athena's statue after the fall of Troy and was thus persecuted by Athena on his return journey. When he found safety on a rocky outcrop in the sea (the Gyrian rock), he blasphemed the gods; he was then killed by Poseidon, who split the rock so that he drowned (Homer *Od.* 4.499–511).

Akesa: According to Philostratus, the name given by Philoktêtês to a portion of Lemnos. Akesa is derived from the Greek word *akesis*, which means "healing" or "cure."

Akhelôos: The longest Greek river, which originates in central Epirus, runs for 150 miles and empties into the Corinthian Gulf. The Aetolian river god Akhelô[i]os then became the representation of all rivers and flowing waters; he was held to be the father of the nymphs and received cultic veneration in many places. He is mentioned twice in Homer (*Il.* 21.194; 24.616, though this latter reference is to a river in Phrygia).

Akherousias: More commonly known as Akheron, a river of Thesprôtia in southern Epirus, which breaks through a gorge into the plain of Akheron where a lake lay in ancient times. The entrance to Hades was reputed to be at the junction of Akheron with the Kôkytos and the Pyriphlegethôn (Homer *Od.* 10.513–514). The setting of Odysseus's evocation of the dead in the *Odyssey* draws on the scenery of the plain of Akheron. The name became applied to the lower world in general.

Aktaios: See Heloros and Aktaios.

Alcestis: Wife of Admêtos and the most beautiful and pious of women (Homer *Il.* 2.715). According to Euripides' *Alcestis*, her marriage to Admêtos was a model of connubial devotion to the extent that Alcestis agreed to die in her husband's place. After her death, Herakles descended into Hades and brought her back to earth, more beautiful and younger than ever.

Alexander the Great: (356–323 B.C.E.) Son of Philip II and Olympias, and king of Macedon (336–323 B.C.E.). Alexander and his armies crossed the Hellespont in 334 B.C.E. in order to "liberate" the Greek cities in Asia Minor from Persian control. According to Arrian (*Anabasis* 1.12.1–2), Alexander placed a wreath on Achilles' tomb. Plutarch (*Alexander* 15.4–5 [Perrin, LCL]) records that Alexander sacrificed to heroes at Troy and honored Achilles' grave by anointing the grave stone with oil, running a race naked with his companions around the grave, and "pronouncing the hero happy in having, while he lived, a faithful friend, and after death, a great herald of his fame."

Alexandros: Another name for Paris (see entry), used more frequently in the *Iliad*.

Alkmaiôn: Argive hero, son of Amphiaraos and Eriphylê, and one of the Epigonoi. Alkmaiôn killed his mother, who had been bribed to convince her husband to join the expedition against Thebes in return for Harmonia's necklace (Pausanias *Description of Greece* 9.41.2; Aristotle *Poetics* 1453b). In some versions, this heinous murder was commanded by Alkmaiôn's father, in others by the oracle of Apollo (cf. Apollodorus *Library* 3.6.2 and 3.7.5). Pursued by a Fury and driven insane, Alkmaiôn was released from his madness only after receiving purification for the murder and, according to Pausanias, settling on the "youngest of countries," that is, the alluvial deposits at the mouth of the Akhelôos river (Apollodorus *Library* 3.7.5; Pausanias *Description of Greece* 8.24.7–10; Thucydides *Peloponnesian War* 2.102.5).

Alkmênê: Daughter of Êlektruôn, king of Mycenae (or Tiryns). Loved by Zeus and in the same night by her husband Amphitryon, she bore twins, the divine Herakles and the human

Iphiklês.   Her husband accused her of adultery and sentenced her to be burned alive, but a heavy rain extinguished the flames (Euripides *Heraclidae*). Persecuted later by Eurystheus of Tiryns, she was protected by the Athenians, and then moved to Thebes, where she died. Hermes brought her to the fields of the blessed dead where she was married to Rhadamanthys (Homer *Il.* 14.323; 19.99, 119).

Alkyoneus: Perhaps originally the legendary hero of the Argolid and the Isthmus, then one of the giants. He was killed by Herakles, who buried him under a huge rock, which in antiquity was believed to be on the Thracian isthmus. On the Great Altar of Pergamum, Athena drags the winged Alkyoneus by his hair. Alkyoneus cannot be killed as long as he stands on the soil of his own country. See Pindar *Isthmian* 6.31–35; *Nemean* 4.25–30; Apollodorus *Library* 1.6.1.

Alôadai: Ôtos and Ephialtês, mythological sons of Iphidameia and her lover Poseidon (Iphidameia's husband was Alôeus). At the age of nine, they reached a height of nine fathoms and a width of nine cubits. After various misdeeds—they bound Ares for thirteen months, tried to marry Hera and Artemis, and threatened the Olympian gods—they were killed by Apollo (Homer *Od.* 11.305–320). In some local traditions they appear as founders of cities. Some accounts claim that their tombs were on Crete, but according to others (*IG* 12.5.56; Diodorus Siculus *Library* 5.51.1–3) they were buried on Naxos, where they had a hero cult. Philostratus (*Her.* 8.14) says that they were buried in Thessaly.

Amaltheia: She-goat nurse of Zeus whose horn flowed with nectar and ambrosia or, alternatively, a nymph who received the goat's horn from Zeus. Colloquially, the "horn of Amaltheia" is the horn of plenty or cornucopia.

Amazons: A mythical race of female warriors thought to inhabit the region near the Thermôdôn river (Diodorus Siculus *Library* 2.45; cf. 3.53–54) and who claimed Ares as their ancestor; they lived apart from men, and their sons were either killed, made lame, or returned to their fathers. On the basis of the presumed etymology "without breast," many ancient writers believed that they had only a single breast, which allowed them to throw the javelin and draw the bow better

(Apollodorus *Library* 2.5.9; Strabo *Geography* 11.5.1); the vinedresser offers an alternative etymology focusing on the Amazons' refusal to breast-feed their female children. In sculpture they are usually depicted with two breasts. The Amazons were said to have frequently encountered male warriors (the Phrygians, the Achaean forces at Troy, Herakles, Theseus), by whom the women are defeated; the epic *Aithiopis* features Achilles' simultaneous slaying and falling in love with the Amazon queen Penthesileia.

Amphiaraos: Son of Oiklês and Hypermnêstra, a seer, who took part in the expedition of the seven princes against Thebes (see entry); he was spared from death by Zeus, who opened up the ground beneath him before he was struck by a spear. In the classical period, a large sanctuary in Ôrôpos (north of Athens), replete with temple, stoas, and theater, made him famous as a healing deity. Other shrines of Amphiaraos were located at Sparta, Corinth, and Mallos in Cilicia (Pausanias *Description of Greece* 1.34.2).

Amphilokhos: Son of Amphiaraos and Eriphylê, a seer like his father, joined the subsequent attack on Thebes; he also appeared among the heroes before they set forth for Troy (Apollodorus *Library* 3.10.8). With the seer Mopsos he went to Cilicia, where together they founded Mallos. He was also the founder of Amphilokhian Argos in Acarnania and its famous oracle. There were cults of Amphilokhos in Ôrôpos, Athens, Sparta, and Aetolia.

Amphitritê: Goddess of the sea, married to Poseidon and mother of the Nereids. She was worshipped together with Poseidon, especially on the Cyclades.

Anchises: Trojan prince, cousin of Priam, king of Dardanos on Mount Ida. He fell in love with Aphrodite, who bore him a son, Aeneas. Because he did not keep this love affair a secret, Zeus made him lame. Aeneas carried his father out of the burning Troy and took him on his journey west. He died on Sicily and was honored with funeral games and a *heroon*, that is, a sanctuary dedicated to him as a hero (Homer *Il.* 2.819; 5.247, 313; 13.428; 20.239; 23.296; *Homeric Hymn to Aphrodite*; Virgil *Aeneid* 3–6).

Andros: Northernmost and second-largest island of the Cyclades.

Anthestêrion: The "month of the flowers" in Athens (February/March). Tradition maintains that the month was so named because young children were crowned with flowers. The eleventh, twelfth, and thirteenth days of this month were dedicated to the festival of Dionysos Limnaios, which culminated in the festive entry of the god on a boat-shaped chariot and his sacred marriage with the wife of the royal archon.

Antilokhos: Son of Nestor, king of Pylos, and a good friend of Achilles (Homer *Il.* 23.556). His close association with Achilles and Patroklos in death and cult is a theme of the *Heroikos* (cf. Homer *Od.* 11.466–470; and the *Aithiopis*).

Antiphatês: King of the mythical Laestrygonians (Homer *Od.* 10.107).

Aphrodite: Goddess of love, beauty, and fertility; daughter of Zeus and Diônê; lover of the Trojan Anchises by whom she bore Aeneas. She was the protector and advocate for Helen and fought on the side of the Trojans. According to Homer (*Il.* 5.334–554) she was wounded by Diomedes when she tried to participate in the battle. Hesiod makes the suggestion (*Theogony* 188–206) that her name comes from *aphros* ("foam"), that is, from the white foam produced when Kronos castrated his father Ouranos and threw his genitals into the sea.

Apollo: God of music, archery, prophecy, and medicine, with particular care for flocks and herds. Born with his twin sister Artemis on Delos, he was son of Zeus and Leto, and was worshipped at Troy as guardian of the Trojans. Often portrayed as the ideal of young manly beauty, usually without a beard. His oracles at Delphi, Klaros, and Branchidae were considered especially authoritative. *Lykios* (generally meaning "Lycian") and *Lykeios* (probably meaning "wolf-killer" or "belonging to the wolf") are used as epithets for Apollo, apparently interchangeably. Here *Lykios* still indicates a connection with wolves and with Apollo's role as the guardian of the herds. The epithet *Phyxios*, "putting to flight," is usually associated with Zeus, but here is linked to Apollo's skill in medicine for averting plagues.

Arcadia: The central mountainous area of the Peloponnesus (Homer *Il.* 2.603–611).

Ares: God of war, son of Zeus and Hera, and the lover of Aphrodite; he fought on the Trojan side in the Trojan War. He was the father of Penthesileia, the queen of the Amazons; together with Artemis he was said to be worshipped by the Amazons. His cult was especially prominent in Thebes and to a lesser extent in Aetolia and Thessaly.

Argos: City on the Inakhos river in the Argolid on the Peloponnesus. In the *Iliad*, the city belongs to the realm of Diomedes (2.559; 4.52; 14.119) but also appears as a designation of Agamemnon's kingdom (2.108, 115) or of the realm of Achilles (2.681; 6.456). In other instances "Argos" is used as a name for all of Greece (see, e.g., 12.70). The term "Argive" is used in Homer to designate both Helen and the followers of Agamemnon and Menelaos. Homer also refers (*Il.* 4.8; 5.908) to "Argive Hera," and there was an important sanctuary (the Argive Heraion) dedicated to Hera outside Argos and shared with Mycenae from the seventh century B.C.E.

Aryadês: One of the race of giants.

Asbolos: One of the Centaurs' leaders in their battle against the Lapiths. According to the *Shield of Herakles*, possibly composed by Hesiod, Asbolos was a diviner, and the Centaurs fought the Lapiths using gold pine trees for weapons (188–189; see also Ovid *Metamorphoses* 12.308).

Asclepiades: Literally, the sons of Asclepius, the term refers to Podaleirios and Makhaôn (Homer *Il.* 4.204; 11.614; 14.2). In the plural, it also designates a guild of physicians.

Asclepius: The Greek god of healing, son of Apollo and Korônis. He is said to have been killed by the thunderbolt of Zeus when he tried to make human beings immortal. His oldest sanctuaries are Trikka in Thessaly and Epidaurus on the Peloponnesus. Later Cos and Pergamum were important sites of Asclepius sanctuaries.

Assyria: An ancient kingdom centered on the upper Tigris valley that at its height of power (911–612 B.C.E.) extended as far north as the Caucasus Mountains and as far west as the

Mediterranean Sea. During the eighth century B.C.E., Assyria conquered numerous cities of Syria (Damascus in 732 B.C.E.), Phoenicia (Byblos, Tyre, and Gaza in 734 B.C.E.), and Palestine (Samaria in 722/721 B.C.E.). Assyria may also have been the name of a short-lived province formed by Trajan from the kingdom of Adiabene, but later made independent by Hadrian (Millar, *The Roman Near East*, 100–101).

Asteropaios: Comrade of Sarpêdon, involved in the battle over the body of Patroklos (Homer *Il.* 17.35–741) and in the battle of Achilles with the Scamander River (*Il.* 21.200–341). Asteropaios was the son of Periboia, the eldest daughter of Akessamenos, and Pêlegôn, son of the wide-flowing Axios. In Homer's account of his fight with Achilles, he holds two spears and hits Achilles' shield with one, wounding Achilles' right forearm with the other. His sword and bracelet are among the prizes at the funeral games for Patroklos.

Atalantê: An island off the coast of Opuntian Locris. In 431 B.C.E., during the Peloponnesian War, the Athenians established a fortification on this previously uninhabited island. In 426 B.C.E. an earthquake and the resulting tidal wave washed away part of the Athenian fort on Atalantê, and one of the two Athenian ships there was destroyed (Thucydides *Peloponnesian War* 2.32; 3.89.3).

Athena: Goddess of wisdom, skill, and stagecraft, she was the daughter of Zeus. According to Hesiod (*Theogony* 886), her mother was Mêtis, but other versions of her origin, including Pindar *Olympian* 7.35, say that she was born fully adult from Zeus's forehead. A virgin goddess, she is described as expert in battles and often depicted with the aegis and helmet. In the *Iliad*, Athena is protector of the Achaeans, particularly Achilles, Diomedes, and Odysseus. She oversees Odysseus's homecoming, according to the *Odyssey*. Her most prominent cult was on the Acropolis at Athens, where she was regarded as the guardian and patron of the city. She nurtured both Erekhtheus and Erikhthonios (who are sometimes identified with each other), first kings of Athens.

Athens: Chief city of Attica in mainland Greece, sacred to Athena; by legend it was founded by Theseus. In the archaic period, it was a monarchy, then an aristocracy, until after the reforms of Kleisthenes in the sixth century, when it became a democracy. Prominent at that time as a cultural center, it remained so in the Roman period, although its military strength was lost after it sided with Mithridates against Rome.

Atreidai: Agamemnon and Menelaos, the sons of Atreus.

Aulis: Located on the coast of Boeotia, opposite Euboea. Here the Greeks assembled before sailing to Troy (Homer *Il.* 2.303).

Axios: Major river of Macedonia (modern Vardar), which flows into the Thermaic Gulf. It was known already to Homer and praised for its beauty (*Il.* 2.849–850; 21.141).

Babylon: City in southern Mesopotamia, located on the Euphrates river. After Nabopolassar's defeat of the Assyrian empire (626–606 B.C.E.), Babylon flourished as the capital of the neo-Babylonian empire (605–539 B.C.E.), which eventually extended from Palestine to modern Iran. The infamous neo-Babylonian king Nebuchadnezzar II captured the city of Jerusalem in 587/586 B.C.E. and destroyed the temple erected by King Solomon. Babylon itself remained an important city for the Persian and Seleucid empires. For the military exploits of the Persian Empire, see the entry for Cyrus.

Bacchic: Relating to Dionysos and his cult; the term is derived from "Bacchus," a common cult name for Dionysos, e.g., in the *Bacchae* of Euripides.

Balios and Xanthos: Literally, "Dappled" and "Golden-haired," the horses of Achilles. According to Homer, they were the immortal offspring of one of the Harpies and the West Wind and possessed great speed (*Il.* 16.145–154). As Achilles rode into battle to avenge Patroklos, Hera gave speech to Xanthos, who predicted Achilles' death at the hands of a god and a mortal (*Il.* 19.404–417).

Black Bay: The modern Saronic Gulf, that is, the bay between the Thracian Chersonesus and the Greek mainland (Herodotus *Hist.* 6.41; Strabo *Geography* 2.5.21).

Boeotia: A region in central Greece, bordering on Attica in the south. Its heartland consisted of the plains of Orkhomenos

and Thebes. Boeotia possessed many famous oracles, including an oracle of the nymphs in Plataia, a polylingual
oracle of Apollo near Akraiphnion, and the oracle of Tro-
phônios in Lebadeia (Pausanias *Description of Greece* 9.11.1;
9.37.4–6; 9.39.4–40.2).

Borysthênes: A river located in Scythia (the modern Dnieper).
Only the Nile and Istros were larger, according to Herodotus (*Hist.* 4.53). The Borysthênes was the chief Greek trade
route into Scythia.

Boura: An Achaean city on the Corinthian gulf, destroyed by the
same earthquake that devastated Helikê in 373 B.C.E. According to Pausanias (*Description of Greece* 7.25.8–9), Boura
was not inundated with water as was Helikê.

C: see also K

Calliope: One of the nine Muses and mother of Orpheus. She was
the Muse of epic poetry.

Calydonian affair: The hunt for the Calydonian boar, who ravaged
Aetolia (located on mainland Greece) as punishment because the king, Oineus, neglected to sacrifice the first fruits
to Athena. Many ancient heroes were said to have participated in the hunt.

Caria: A region in southwest Asia Minor.

Cassandra: Most beautiful daughter of Priam (Homer *Il.* 13.366;
24.699). While Homer does not tell of her mantic abil-
ity, later epic and tragedy report the story of the Locrian
Ajax's sacrilege and how she was given to Agamemnon who
took her back to Mycenae, where she was murdered by
Clytemnestra (Aeschylus *Agamemnon*).

Chalcis: A city in Euboea where a poetic contest between Homer
and Hesiod is said to have taken place (*Certamen* 315).

Chersonesus: The long and narrow peninsula of Thrace that runs
along the western side of the Hellespont. At the southern
end of the peninsula lay Elaious (see entry), the site of Protesilaos's sanctuary and the setting for this dialogue.

Chios: A long island in the Aegean lying off the Erythraean peninsula of Asia Minor. It was renowned for its wine, grain, and
figs. In antiquity it had a distinguished literary tradition and
claimed to be Homer's birthplace (*Certamen* 13–15).

Cilicia: District of southern Asia Minor, settled by Greeks, possibly from the Troad. The seer Mopsos bested Kalkhas in a context (Apollodorus *Epitome* 6.2–4) and along with Amphilokhos founded the oracle at Mallos (Strabo *Geography* 14.5.16).

Circe: This daughter of Helios and Persêis (or, in some accounts, Hekatê) lived on the island of Aiaia. Odysseus arrived at Aiaia on his way home from Troy. After Circe had bewitched half of his forces, turning them into animals, Odysseus was able to remove the enchantment with the aid of Hermes. Afterwards Circe and Odysseus became lovers, and Odysseus remained with Circe for a year (Homer *Odyssey* 10).

Corinth: A city located on the isthmus between mainland Greece and the Peloponnesus.

Cos: One of the twelve islands of the Dodecanesus, it was famous as the birthplace of Hippocrates, among others. A sanctuary of Asclepius and a renowned medical school were located there.

Crete: Large island south of the Aegean. It was the domain of King Idomeneus, a suitor of Helen and a commander at Troy.

Cyclopes: One-eyed beings who, according to Homer, live in a remote part of the earth. They are without government or laws, and are savage, pastoral beings. The most famous Cyclops in Homer (*Odyssey* 9) is Polyphemos, the son of Poseidon, who traps Odysseus and his men in his cave with the intent of eating them. Odysseus outwits him by getting him drunk with the wine from Marôn and then blinds his single eye. A separate tradition about the Cyclops is known to Hesiod (*Theogony* 139–141), who says that there were three Cyclopes, named Brontês, Steropês, and Argês, all excellent craftsmen and the makers of the divine thunderbolts. According to Callimachus (*Hymn* 3.46–97), they are associated with Hephaistos and are the builders of the ancient fortifications of Tiryns and other cities of the Argolid (hence "Cyclopean walls").

Cyrus: (d. 529 B.C.E.) King of the Persian Empire. Croesus of Lydia, Nabonidos of Babylon, and Amasis II of Egypt tried to build a strong alliance against him, but to no avail. He defeated and captured Croesus (546 B.C.E.), and Lydia became a satrapy under the Persian government. Cyrus demanded the surrender of the Greek cities under Lydian rule, and they also became satrapies of Persia. Cyrus never conquered Egypt, but the Chaldaean Empire of Babylon fell to him in 538 B.C.E.

Danaans: The subjects of Danaos, the mythological king of Argos. In the *Iliad* the name Danaans usually appears to be synonymous with Achaeans and Argives as a general designation of the Hellenic forces.

Dardanos: This son of Zeus and Electra migrated from Samothrace to the coast of Asia, where King Teukros gave him part of his kingdom, together with his daughter Batieia. Dardanos built the city that carried his name, and on Teukros's death he called the whole country Dardania. Dardanos's son Erikhthonios was an ancestor of the Trojan kings, and thus in the *Iliad* (2.819) the term "Dardanians" is used of the Trojans under Aeneas. The patronymic "Dardanides" appears in the *Heroikos*.

Darius: (ca. 380–330 B.C.E.) Darius III ascended to the Persian throne in 336 B.C.E. Darius was defeated by Alexander the Great and was captured in 330 B.C.E.

Dêidameia: Daughter of king Lykomêdês of Skyros. She was wife of Achilles and mother of their son Neoptolemos.

Deiphobos: Trojan hero, son of Priam and Hekabê (see, e.g., Homer *Il.* 12.94; 13.156, 527).

Delos: A small Aegean island sacred to Apollo.

Delphi: A sanctuary in Phocis that was the seat of the oracle of the Pythian Apollo and the site of the Pythian Games, athletic competitions similar to those held at Olympia.

Demeter: Goddess of the fruits of the earth, especially grain, and hence of the fertility of the earth; mother of Persephone (Korê) whose abduction by Hades and return to earth are told in the *Homeric Hymn to Demeter*. Demeter is worshipped in the Eleusinian mysteries. In art, she is depicted with a scepter, ears of grain, or torches.

Dêmodokos: The blind bard of King Alkinoos of the Phaeacians, to whom Odysseus tells all his adventures. Dêmodokos's songs treat the fight between Achilles and Odysseus, the adultery of Aphrodite and Ares, and the story of the wooden horse (Homer *Od.* 8.62–82, 266–369, 482–522).

Deucalion: Son of Prometheus. The great destruction that took place in his time was the flood that Zeus unleashed to destroy the entire world. Zeus's anger was instigated by the crimes of Lykaôn's sons, who killed their brother and served him to Zeus in a soup. Only Deucalion and his wife Pyrrha were spared from the flood, since they built the ark. After the waters receded, they repopulated the earth at Zeus's instruction by bringing rocks to life.

Diomedes: Son of Tydeus and leader of the men from Argos and Tiryns in the Trojan expedition. He was an impetuous and fiery captain. Many of his exploits are recounted by Homer (*Il.* 2.567; 4.406, 421; 5.15, 142, 412; etc.). Diomedes was also one of the Epigonoi, who successfully conquered Thebes in retaliation for their fathers' earlier defeat (for more on the saga of the Seven Against Thebes, see the entry for Thebes).

Diomedes: Son of Ares and king of the Bistonians in Thrace, who fed his horses the flesh of strangers. Herakles threw Diomedes to his own horses and took the horses to Mycenae.

Dionysos: According to Hesiod (*Theogony* 940–942), he was the son of Zeus and Semelê, daughter of Kadmos. By tradition, he came from Thrace. He can be characterized as the god of ecstatic religion, of wine and viticulture, and (in association with Apollo and the Muses) of poets and musicians. His cult was important particularly in Boeotia, Attica, and Thrace, and often associated with frenzied, ecstatic worship. His association with the theater derives from festivals in his honor at which poets and musicians competed. Among these festivals was the Greater Dionysia at Athens, which became the occasion for performances of tragic and comic drama.

Dodona: Ancient and famous oracle of Zeus in Epirus, where Zeus was worshipped together with his consort Diônê. The oracle was given through a dove and an oak tree.

Echo: A nymph vainly loved by Pan; she drove the shepherds mad and they tore her to pieces. Earth hid the fragments, which continued to sing and imitate other sounds.

Egypt: An ancient kingdom extending from the southeastern Mediterranean along the Nile valley; in the archaic and classical period it maintained trading relations with Greece. In the fifth century it came under Persian rule until 405 B.C.E., when it again became independent. Captured again by the Persians in 343, Egypt passed to Alexander the Great in 333. After Alexander's death, it became the center of Ptolemaic administration, until it came under Roman control in the second century B.C.E. Egypt was an imperial province, coming directly under the administration of the emperor rather than the Roman senate. In antiquity, Egypt had considerable wealth, derived from a strong agricultural economy and its export of grain and papyrus through the Mediterranean. Its chief cities were Naukratis, Memphis, and the hellenistic city, Alexandria, founded by Alexander upon his conquest of Egypt.

Ekhinades: The islands in front of the coast of Acarnania and the estuary of the Akhelôos, today called the Dragonara Islands. It was already noted in antiquity that more and more of these islands were joined to the land because of the silt deposited by the Akhelôos (Herodotus *Hist.* 2.10).

Elaious: Port city at the southern end of the Thracian Chersonesus and site of the tomb and sanctuary of Protesilaos (Pausanias *Description of Greece* 1.34.2; Thucydides *Peloponnesian War* 8.102.3; Herodotus *Hist.* 7.33.1; Strabo *Geography* 7.frg. 51; 13.1.31). Lucian knows of the oracle of Protesilaos there (*Parliament of the Gods* 12).

Elis: City in the Peloponnesus that controlled the Olympian games.

Endymion: A beautiful young man, perhaps a king of Elis or a Carian. Selene, the moon, loved him. In one version, she bore him fifty daughters, supposedly symbolic of the fifty months of an Olympiad (Pausanias *Description of Greece* 5.1.3–5). He keeps his beauty in unceasing slumber (Apollodorus *Library* 1.7.5).

Enkelados: One of the giants, the sons of Earth, who were born where the blood of Ouranos's genitals fell on the ground, after they had been severed by Kronos. During the battle that the giants fought against the Olympian gods (the "Gigantomachy"), Enkelados fled, but Athena threw the island of Sicily at him and buried him under it; since this did not kill him, his fiery breath still issues forth from the volcano Etna.

Eos: The dawn goddess. She asked Zeus to make her mortal consort, Tithônos, immortal, but forgot to ask for his eternal youth as well (Homer *Od.* 5.1; *Homeric Hymn to Aphrodite*).

Epeios: Son of Panopeus and builder of the Trojan horse (Homer *Il.* 23.665).

Erytheia: The island beyond the Mediterranean Sea in the far west where Geryon lived. Both Pausanias (*Description of Greece* 1.35.8) and Strabo (*Geography* 3.5.3–4) identify Erytheia as Gades (modern Cadiz), located on the coast of Spain just outside of the Pillars of Herakles (modern Gibraltar).

Ethiopia: This term was usually used to denote any distant, southern region, but since the time of Herodotus, the term referred to the area south of Egypt. Ethiopia was often confused with India, another region located, to the Greek mind, at the furthermost reaches of civilization. The Ethiopian city Meroê, located on the Nile, was influenced by hellenistic culture under the Ptolemies.

Euadnê: Devoted wife of Kapaneus, who threw herself on his funeral pyre.

Euanthês: Father of Marôn.

Euboea: An island extending off the coast of Phocis, Boeotia, and Attica, from the Gulf of Pagasae to the island of Andros.

Eudaimôn: An otherwise unknown athlete, but Eudaimôn may be a pseudonym or nickname for Hermeias the Egyptian (see entry); see P. Lond. 3.1159.48, 82, which mentions "Eudaimôn who is also called Hermaios" and (perhaps his son) "Eudaimôn who is also called Phamon, the son of Hermaios."

Euneôs: One of the twin sons of Jason and Hypsipylê, whom Jason met and married at Lemnos. According to Homer, Euneôs aided both the Trojans and Achaeans during the war. He sent a large cargo of wine to the Achaeans (*Il.* 7.467–475), and redeemed the captured Lykaôn, Priam's son, from Patroklos (*Il.* 23.746–747).

Euphorbus: Trojan hero, son of Panthous (Homer *Il.* 16.808, 850; 17.59, 81). A descendant of Dardanos of Samothrace, he was the first to wound Patroklos and was then killed by Menelaos (Homer *Il.* 16.806–815; 17.1–81), who dedicated his shield in the Heraion of Argos. Pythagoras claimed to be a reincarnation of Euphorbus.

Euripides: (ca. 485–406 B.C.E.) One of the three great Attic tragedians. The titles of eighty-one of his plays are known, although only nineteen are extant. *Oineus*, the king of Calydon who was deposed by nephews, is the title of a lost play by Euripides (Aristophanes *Acharnians* 418–419).

Euripos: The strait that separates Euboea from Boeotia.

Europe: Originally a name for central Greece (*Homeric Hymn to Apollo* 251, 291). This term soon was applied to the entire Greek mainland.

Eurusakês: Son of Ajax the Greater and Tekmêssa. Eurusakês moved from Salamis to Attica and founded an important Athenian family (Sophocles *Ajax* 575; Plutarch *Solon* 10). Pausanias (*Description of Greece* 1.35.3) notes that there was an altar of Eurusakês in Athens.

Fates: Known in Greek as the Moirai and in Latin as the Parcae, these divinities were characterized as spinners, in accordance with the image found in epic depicting human life as a thread spun by the gods, who wrap it around the person as though around a spindle. According to Hesiod (*Theogony* 904–906), there are three Fates: Klôthô ("the spinner"), Lakhesis ("the one who assigns the lot"), and Atropos ("the unchanging one"); they are the children of Zeus and Themis. The Fates are often associated with birth and marriage, key periods for the destiny of a person, and are included, for example, in depictions of the wedding of Peleus and Thetis.

Geryon: A three-headed or three-bodied monster, who had many cattle and lived on an island in the stream Okeanos with his herdsman Eurytiôn and his formidable double-headed dog Orthos. The tenth labor of Herakles was his abduction of the cattle; Herakles brought the cattle to Mycenae and dedicated them to Hera. According to Philostratus, Neleus and eleven of his twelve sons (only Nestor did not participate in the act) stole these cattle from Herakles.

Giants: A mythological race, which according to Hesiod were offspring of Gê (Earth) and Ouranos, but according to Homer were savage warriors. The Gigantomachy, the war between the Olympian gods and the giants, was only won by the Olympians with the help of the mortal Herakles (Apollodorus *Library* 1.6.1–2; Pindar *Pythian* 8.12–20). The giants (or "Titans," as they are sometimes called) were thought to have been buried beneath volcanoes. According to Pausanias (*Description of Greece* 8.29.3–4) the giant Orontes had "a human body in every detail," and early depictions of the giants on vase paintings show them as human-like warriors. Apollodorus (*Library* 1.6.1–3), however, described the serpentine aspects of the giants, a portrayal confirmed by later artistic renderings of the giants with a human torso and serpent-like legs (e.g., on the Great Altar of Pergamum).

Glaukê: The daughter of Creon, king of Corinth, she became engaged to Jason. According to Euripides' *Medea*, after Glaukê became engaged to Jason, she was killed by a poisoned robe given to her by Medea, Jason's spurned wife.

Glaukos: With his companion Sarpêdon, he commanded the Lycian contingent at Troy (Homer *Il.* 2.876–877). In the fight around the city he found himself facing Diomedes in battle, but both recalled their familial ties of friendship. Diomedes gave Glaukos his own weapons, which were bronze, and Glaukos gave him his own, which were gold (Homer *Il.* 6.119–236). Glaukos died at Ajax's hands during the battle to recover Achilles' body (Apollodorus *Epitome* 5.3–4). According to the fourth-century C.E. epic poet Quintus of Smyrna (*Fall of Troy* 4.1–12), the winds, at the behest of Apollo, seized Glaukos's corpse from the funeral pyre and carried it to Lycia for burial, where the nymphs caused the river "Glaukos" to flow around his grave.

Gorgons: Female monsters with a round face, wings, snakes for hair, and whose gaze could change human beings into stone. The most famous Gorgon, Medusa, was killed by Perseus who avoided her deadly glare by looking at her reflection in his shield (Hesiod *Theogony* 270–280; *Shield of Herakles* 223–237; Apollodorus *Library* 2.4.2). Her figure is a common apotropaic symbol.

Graces: The three goddesses—or two depending on the tradition—were daughters of Zeus, who personify grace, charm, and beauty. Their gifts are physical, intellectual, artistic, and moral (see Hesiod *Theogony* 907–911).

Gyges: Founder of the Lydian dynasty of the Mermnads (ca. 685 B.C.E.). He was the first Lydian king to make war on the Asiatic Greeks. According to Plato (*Republic* 359d), when Gyges was a shepherd, he descended into a chasm in the earth and there found a hollow bronze horse containing a corpse, from the finger of which he took a gold ring. When he wore this ring, it made him invisible. With its help, he committed adultery with the queen, murdered her husband, and usurped the throne.

Gyrian rock: The site of the death of Ajax the Lesser. Poseidon drove Ajax onto this rock; when Ajax boasted that he had saved himself from the gods' wrath, Poseidon split the rock apart and Ajax perished (Homer *Od.* 4.499–511).

Hades: Properly, the name Hades denotes the god of the dead, the lord of the Underworld. By classical times, however, it also came to stand for the House of Hades, that is, the Underworld where the dead go. The god is presented as a judge of wrongful acts, not as a tormentor. The famous journey of Odysseus to Hades appears in Book 11 (the Nekyia) of the *Odyssey*.

Hadrian: 76–138 C.E. Born in Spain and adopted son of Trajan, Hadrian became emperor of Rome in 117 C.E. Much of his reign was spent touring the provinces (he visited Troy in 123 C.E.), during which time he funded the building of cities, temples, and sanctuaries.

Haimos: According to Protesilaos, Haimos was the son of Ares and a participant in the battle at Mysia prior to the Trojan

War. He was a formidable warrior, who was only killed by the combined force of Palamedes, Diomedes, and Sthenelos. Protesilaos does not clearly identify Haimos's city of origin. Haimos is not mentioned by Homer and thus should be considered another of Protesilaos's examples of great heroes overlooked by Homer.

Halter: An otherwise unknown athlete.

Halys: Longest river of Anatolia, forming the border between Cappadocia and Phrygia, and issuing into the Black Sea or Pontus.

Hekabê: Daughter of Dymas. She was Priam's wife and queen in Troy; Hektor and Paris were two of their sons.

Hektor: Son of Priam and Hekabê and husband of Andromache, the most excellent and distinguished of Trojan heroes, feared by the Greeks more than anyone else among the defenders of Troy. He was killed by Achilles (Homer *Il*. 22.326). His body was delivered to Priam, and the Trojans gave him a proper burial (Homer *Il*. 24.486–804).

Helen: Daughter of Zeus and Leda, although another version of her birth says that she hatched from an egg laid by her mother Nemesis and was cared for by Leda (Apollodorus *Library* 3.10.7). Helen was the wife of Menelaos; according to Homer, she was abducted to Troy by Paris and became his wife there, thus provoking the Trojan War (see, e.g., *Il*. 2.160, 356; 3.173–175, 426). Competing stories of this event exist: Hesiod (frg. 176.7 [Merkelbach and West]) says that Helen went with Paris as far as Egypt but that she remained there while he brought her image (*eidôlon*) to Troy. The lyric poet Stesichorus is said to have been blinded by the gods for telling a version of her abduction to Troy that was parallel to Homer's account and which blamed Helen. Stesichorus then composed two recantations, rejecting the stories of both Homer and Hesiod and affirming that Helen did not go to Troy; Helen thereupon restored his sight (PMG 192, 193; Plato *Phaedrus* 243a; Isocrates *Helen* 64–66). Herodotus likewise denies that Helen was in Troy; she spent the war in the court of Prôteus in Memphis, and after the war Menelaos retrieved both her and the property stolen by Paris (*Hist*. 2.112–120). Dio Chrysostom offers a more radical solution to the apparent problem of Helen's presence in Troy: Helen was lawfully married to Paris, not Menelaos (*Troikos* 53), and the war resulted from Agamemnon's fear of Paris's further influence among the Hellenes (*Troikos* 61–64). Furthermore, it was Helen herself who blinded the offending Stesichorus (*Troikos* 40). Pausanias reports a tradition that after the Trojan War Helen married Achilles and lived with him on the White Island (*Description of Greece* 3.19.11–13). In the *Odyssey*, however, Helen is pictured as living happily with Menelaos in Lacedaemonia in Sparta. A hero cult for Helen is attested in Sparta and elsewhere.

Helenos: Trojan hero, a seer and warrior, he was the son of Priam, (Homer *Il.* 7.44; 12.94; 13.576). After the fall of Troy, he was carried off by Neoptolemos, who gave Andromache to him as wife. They settled in Epirus, which they made a "little Troy." When Aeneas encountered them in Epirus, Helenos prophesied to Aeneas his future wanderings, his arrival in Italy, and the sign by which he would know where to establish a city (Virgil *Aeneid* 3.294–505).

Helikê: An Achaean city on the Corinthian gulf destroyed by an earthquake and tidal wave in 373 B.C.E. The city, it was said, sank into the sea. According to Pausanias (*Description of Greece* 7.24.5–13), this devastation was a punishment from Poseidon because the inhabitants of Helikê had expelled suppliants from his sanctuary.

Helios: The sun god. Helios is usually depicted as a charioteer, driving westward across the sky. "Helios" is the Greek word for "sun."

Helix: Aurelius Helix, a Phoenician athlete of considerable talent and renown (see also Philostratus *On Gymnastics* 46). In addition to his Olympic victories (209/213 and 213/217 C.E.), he also won both the wrestling and the pancratium at the Capitoline Games of 219 C.E. Dio Cassius offers an alternative version of Helix's troubles at Olympia: The officials at Elis feared that Helix would be the eighth athlete to achieve Herakles' feat of winning the pancratium and wrestling on the same day (Pausanias *Description of Greece* 5.8.4;

5.21.10); not wishing to award him this honor, they conspired so that Helix would miss the wrestling competition (Dio Cassius *Roman History* 80.10; see also Rachel Sargent Robinson, *Sources for the History of Greek Athletics in English Translation* [Cincinnati: n.p., 1955], 171, 267–68). For the most recent compilation of references to Olympic victories and their dates, see Moretti, *Olympionikai* and its supplements, "Supplemento al catalogo degli Olympionikai," *Klio* 52 (1970): 295–303; and "Nuovo Supplemento al catalogo degli Olympionikai," *Miscellanea greca e romana* 12 (1987): 67–91. It is likely that this Helix is pictured as a pancratist on a mosaic at Ostia found in the so-called Caupona of Alexander; see C. P. Jones, "The Pancratists Helix and Alexander on an Ostian Mosaic," *JRA* 11 (1998): 293–98.

Hellas: Originally the name of a town or district in Thessaly. It later came to mean the country or land of the ancient Greeks.

Hellenes/Hellenic: Originally the name of a tribe in southern Thessaly (Homer *Il.* 2.683–685), eventually the term referred to the Greek people in general.

Hellespont: The strait between the Troad and Thrace, now called the Dardanelles.

Heloros and Aktaios: In Pergamene legend, sons of the river god Istros (Danube) and allies of Têlephos, who were killed by the greater Ajax. They are portrayed on the Têlephos frieze of the Great Altar of Pergamum.

Hephaistos: Son of Hera, husband of Aphrodite, and often associated with volcanoes, he is the god of fire and known as the smith of the gods. Born lame and ugly, he was thrown out of Olympus into the sea by Hera, whereupon he was rescued by Thetis and Eurynomê and cared for by the Nereids. He was later cast out of Olympus again, this time by Zeus. On this occasion, he landed on Lemnos. Because of their welcome, he established a forge on the island and staffed it with Cyclopes. As the divine artisan, he crafted many famous articles, notably, Achilles' armor. He also defended Achilles against the river Scamander by drying up the river with his fire.

Herakles: Son of Alkmênê and Zeus and widely worshipped Greek
hero. Associated with Herakles are the stories of various
"labors" or trials, told variously but usually as a cycle of
twelve episodes. They were as follows: capture of the hide of
the Nemean lion, killing of the many-headed Hydra, capture
of the Erymanthian boar—a task that involved a battle with
the Centaurs and Herakles' accidental wounding and death
of his friend Kheirôn—capture of the golden-horned hind,
driving off the bronze-beaked birds of Ares, cleaning the
stables of Augeas, capture of the Cretan bull, capture of the
man-eating mares of Diomedes, procuring the girdle of the
Amazon queen Hippolytê, capture of the cattle of Geryon,
acquisition of the golden apples of Hesperides, and capture
of Cerberus from Hades. Theban versions of the labors include Herakles' conquest of Orkhomenos, killing the lion of
Mount Kithairôn, and bedding the fifty daughters of Thes-
pius. After his labors were completed, Herakles went with
Telamôn to attack Troy in order to avenge injustices done to
him during his labors. His death on Mount Oitê, assisted by
Poias, was tragic, but he attained deification on Olympus.

Hermeias the Egyptian: An Olympic boxer. A papyrus from 194
C.E. (P. Lond. 3.1178) records the membership in an athletic guild of a boxer from Hermopolis named Herminus
(also known as Môros or Môron). Herminus's family had
been important in the Hermopolis gymnasium for three
generations (P. Lond. 3.935). Perhaps Hermeias the Egyptian is to be identified with this Herminus; this identification
is problematic, however, if one follows Moretti's dating of
his opponent Ploutarkhos's Olympic victory to 205 C.E.,
since in 194 C.E. Herminus was already twenty-seven years
old.

Hermes: Son of Zeus and Maia, a daughter of Atlas, Hermes
was the divine messenger and guide, often represented as
a herald with hat, sandals, and caduceus or herald's staff.
He is particularly associated with Arcadia (see entry) and
was said to have been born on Mount Cyllene. He is
the trickster god, protector of travelers, and guide of the
dead. Apollodorus (*Epitome* 3.30) relates the story that Hermes brought Protesilaos out of Hades. Hermes also has a

connection with fertility, and phallic statues set up along roadways are known as "herms." According to various traditions, in addition to inventing sandals and the lyre, the infant Hermes stole fifty of Apollo's cattle, hid them in a cave at Pylos (see entry), and offered two of them as the first sacrifices to the gods. With his lyre, however, he enchanted Apollo and was forgiven. The reference in *Her.* 25.9 to contending with Leto probably refers to this story.

Hesiod: Poet of the late eighth century B.C.E. and author of the *Theogony*, *Works and Days*, and perhaps the *Shield*, a poem about Herakles' fight with Kyknos.

Hiera: Wife of Têlephos, king of Mysia. According to the *Heroikos*, during the Trojan War she led the Mysian women against the Greeks. She was famous for her beauty, which is said to have surpassed Helen's. She has been identified with the female warrior depicted on the Têlephos frieze of the Great Altar of Pergamum.

Homer: The supposed author of the *Iliad* and *Odyssey*. Tradition holds that he was a blind epic singer. Many cities claimed to be his birthplace, most notably Smyrna and Chios, where the Homeridai, who claimed descent from him, lived. Hadrian consulted the Delphic oracle as to Homer's birthplace and received an answer that coheres with Protesilaos's claim of Homer's special relationship with Odysseus: Homer hailed from Ithaca and his father was Telemachus, Odysseus's son (*Certamen* 314). Professional itinerant singers recited Homer's poems throughout Asia Minor and Greece, though his poems were first written down only in the sixth century B.C.E. On the criticism of Homer's poems, see the Introduction.

Hyacinthus: One of a number of semidivine heroes known for his beauty. Apollo was among those smitten by his beauty. When Hyacinthus was killed while throwing a discus, Apollo made his friend's name immortal by transforming the blood from Hyacinthus's wound into a new flower, the hyacinth.

Hyllas: The young son of Theiodamas who participated with Herakles in the expedition of the Argonauts. During a landing in Mysia, Herakles went to cut a tree to make an oar,

while Hyllas (usually written Hylas) left to draw water from
a nearby spring. At the edge of the spring he encountered
nymphs who, seeing his great beauty, lured him into the
spring where he drowned.

Hyllos: Two sons of Herakles bear the name Hyllos. Hyllos, the
son of Herakles and Dêianeira, killed his kinsman Eurystheus, who had imposed on Herakles the twelve labors. Hyllos later misinterpreted the Delphic oracle's advice about
when to conquer Eurystheus' kingdom and died during the
ill-fated invasion (Apollodorus *Library* 2.8.2; cf. Herodotus
Hist. 9.26; Pausanias *Description of Greece* 8.5.1). The other
Hyllos, the son of Herakles and Melitê, is less well known
(Apollonius of Rhodes *Argonautica* 4.537–551) and is associated with Dalmatia, Illyria, or Thrace. Hyllos has no direct
connection with Phrygia. Perhaps the tradition known to
Philostratus has conflated Hyllos with Hyllas (see entry),
with Hyllos the son of Gê, or with the Phrygian river Hyllos (see Pausanias *Description of Greece* 1.35.8).

Hymnaios of Peparêthos: An acquaintance of the vinedresser,
whom the vinedresser claims to be a contemporary and reliable witness of the recent discovery of the huge skeletons of
ancient heroes and giants.

Hypnos: The personification of sleep, he was the son of Nyx
(Night) and Erebos and the twin of Thanatos (Death).

Ida: Wooded mountain range south and east of Troy. Zeus and
Cybele were worshipped on its highest peak, Gargaron.

Idomeneus: Leader of the Cretan forces (Homer *Il.* 2.645) and one
of Helen's suitors.

Ikos: Island of the northern Sporades just east of Peparêthos and
today officially called Alonnisos. In antiquity, the tomb of
Peleus was believed to be on the island (*Anthologia Palatina*
7.2.9).

Ilion: Another name for the city of Troy. The name "Ilion"
derives from its eponymous founder Ilos, the son of Trôs.
After Ilos traveled from Dardania to Phrygia and won an
athletic contest there, an oracle instructed the local king to
award Ilos a spotted cow; Ilos was commanded to follow the

cow and found a city where she came to rest (Apollodorus *Library* 3.12.3).

Ilissos: A river in Attica, which flows near the southeast walls of Athens.

Imbros: An island in the Thracian Sea off the coast of Troy (Homer *Il.* 13.33).

India: Believed by the Greeks to lie in the farthest reaches of the East, Indians were often confused with Ethiopians, another people believed to inhabit the edges of the world. Little was known about India until Alexander's conquests (327–325 B.C.E.).

Ionia: The central part of the west coast of Asia Minor. Named for Ion, the legendary father of the Ionians, whose name is twice used here (1.1; 42.1) to designate one who comes from Ionia.

Iphis: Slave girl of Patroklos, given to him by Achilles (Homer *Il.* 9.667).

Ismaros: Capital of the Thracian tribe of the Kikones, according to Strabo (*Geography* 7.frg. 44), located on the Aegean coast of Thrace near Maroneia and opposite Samothrace. The area is known for its excellent wine. According to Homer (*Od.* 9.40), the town was destroyed by Odysseus.

Issêdonians: Scythian tribe located southeast of the Aral Sea. They are often named together with the Massagetai. Their primary area of residence was Chinese East-Turkestan in central Asia, and they controlled important parts of the silk road.

Istros: The Greeks gave this name to the lower Danube, although the identification with the Danube was not made until the first century B.C.E. The Istros flowed through Thrace and into the Pontus along its northwestern shore; in the Roman period the Danube was the northern limit of the empire. The highly revered river god Istros was considered the son of Okeanos.

Italy: Originally the name for the southern "toe" of modern Italy. By the third century B.C.E. it included the entire region south of Cisalpine Gaul.

Ithaca: An island off the northwest coast of Greece in the Ionian Sea. It was the home of Odysseus.

Jason: Father of Euneôs and leader of the Argonauts. On Jason's betrayal of Medea, see Medea and Glaukê.

Kaikos: A river in Mysia (northwestern Asia Minor; Strabo *Geography* 12.8.2; Herodotus *Hist*. 7.42).

Kalkhas: Seer of the Achaean army who guided the fleet to Troy. According to Homer he "knew all things that were, the things to come and the things past" (Homer *Il*. 1.70 [Lattimore]). He told the future by observing birds and made many prophecies concerning the Trojan War, for example, the crucial role of Achilles and Philoktêtês, the length of the war, and the return of Khryséis (Homer *Il*. 1.69–72; 2.300).

Kapaneus: Son of Hipponoos, father of Sthenelos, and one of the seven leaders to attack Thebes on behalf of Polyneikês (for more on the saga of the Seven Against Thebes, see the entry for Thebes). In this first attack upon Thebes Kapaneus was killed by Zeus's thunderbolt just as he was about to scale the Theban walls, boasting that not even Zeus could keep him out of the city. The vinedresser here relies upon the story in which the Athenian king Theseus attacked Thebes and buried the dead heroes in Eleusis, where Euadnê, the wife of Kapaneus, threw herself on his funeral pyre. The sons of the seven leaders, the Epigonoi, mounted a successful attack against Thebes ten years later.

Kheirôn: Among the violent and sexually uncontrollable Centaurs, Kheirôn stands out as civilized and wise. Born an immortal, he lived in a cave on Mount Pelion in Thessaly. He was judicious and kind to humans. His knowledge covered music, martial arts, hunting, ethics, and medicine (Homer *Il*. 4.219; 11.832; 16.143; Apollodorus *Library* 3.4.4; 3.10.3). He helped Peleus to win Thetis; when she deserted Peleus, Peleus gave their son Achilles to Kheirôn to raise (Euripides *Iphigeneia at Aulis* 206–209, 1058–1079; Apollodorus *Library* 3.13.5–6). Kheirôn relinquished his immortality to Prometheus in order to escape the unbearable pain caused by his accidental wounding by Herakles (Apollodorus *Library* 2.5.4, 11; Pausanias *Description of Greece* 5.5.10).

Khrysês: A priest of Apollo and the father of Khrysêis, a woman held as captive spoil by Agamemnon. Homer (*Il.* 1.11) recounts that Khrysês came to ransom his daughter, but Agamemnon refused and so dishonored him, thus causing offense to Apollo. Apollo then sent a plague on the Achaeans. The return of Khrysêis to her father so as to appease Apollo and Agamemnon's seizure of Achilles' slave woman Briseis as compensation caused the wrath of Achilles and his withdrawal from the fighting (Homer *Il.* 1.318–356).

Kikones: A Thracian tribe living between the rivers Nestos and Hebros, near the Aegean coast. They supported Troy in the Trojan War (Homer *Il.* 2.846). After his departure from Troy, Odysseus sacked Ismaros and destroyed them in battle (Homer *Od.* 9.39–61).

Kôkytos: A stream in southern Epirus and one of the rivers of Hades, running parallel to the river Styx. The souls of the dead had to cross it before they could reach the kingdom of Hades.

Kyknos: Son of Ares and robber of those bringing gifts to Apollo at Delphi. According to one legend, Herakles killed him at the precinct of Apollo and took his armor. Philostratus here attributes a work describing the shield of Kyknos to Hesiod. The poem *Shield of Herakles*, which describes the shield that Herakles used in his fight against Kyknos, is usually now attributed to Hesiod.

Lacedaemonians: The people who inhabited the kingdom of Lacedaemon, son of Zeus and Taygetê. Lacedaemon married Sparta, the daughter of Emotas, and Sparta gave her name to the capital of the kingdom inhabited by the Lacedaemonians.

Laestrygonians: Man-eating giants who destroyed all of Odysseus's ships except his own by throwing rocks at them, spearing like fish all the men in the ships, and then eating them (Homer *Od.* 10.80–132).

Laodameia: Daughter of Akastos and Astydameia, and wife of Protesilaos. Her extreme love for Protesilaos is mentioned by Homer (*Il.* 2.694–702) and is the subject of a poem of Catullus (68) and Ovid (*Heroides* 13), in which Laodameia embraces a wax image of Protesilaos. Later versions say that after Protesilaos's death, Hermes guided him back from the Underworld to see his wife for three hours; upon his parting she either died from grief or stabbed herself to death, and thus went with him as he returned to Hades (Apollodorus *Epitome* 3.30; Hyginus *Fabulae* 103). Hyginus records another story in which Laodameia threw herself into a fire when her father ordered the wax image burned (*Fabulae* 104).

Laomedôn: King of Troy and father of Priam. Herakles offered to kill a sea monster that threatened Laomedôn's daughter. (The monster was Poseidon's punishment for Laomedôn's refusal to pay Poseidon and Apollo for their construction of the city's walls.) Laomedôn agreed to give Herakles Zeus's magic horses, which had been given to Troy in exchange for Ganymede, a Trojan youth whom the gods wanted for their cup–bearer, but once again Laomedôn's promise proved empty. Herakles attacked Troy and slew Laomedôn and his sons, except for Priam.

Lemnos: Island in the northern Aegean southwest of Imbros and directly opposite Troy. Lemnos was colonized by the Athenians as early as the sixth century B.C.E., and except for a few brief periods, the Athenians retained control of Lemnos through the Roman period. According to Homer, Hephaistos landed on Lemnos when Zeus threw him out of Olympus (*Il.* 1.590–594), and Hephaestia (modern Palaiopolis) on the northeastern peninsula of Lemnos was perhaps Hephaistos's most important cult site. The nearby site of Mosykhlos, whose soil was high in silica content, was famous through the Middle Ages for its healing effects. One of the island's most famous legends concerns Aphrodite's curse upon the Lemnian women for neglecting her worship: Their resulting foul smell alienated them from their husbands, who turned instead to Thracian slave-girls. The Lemnian women murdered all the men of the island, although Hypsipylê allowed her father Thoas the king to escape (according to Herodotus Thoas was murdered; *Hist.* 6.138). The island remained entirely female until the arrival of Jason, who fathered Euneôs and Thoas by

Hypsipylê. The term "Lemnian deed" for a shocking crime has its origin in this legend and a later atrocity on Lemnos, namely, the slaughter of captured Athenian women and their children (Herodotus *Hist.* 6.138). The vinedresser's reference to the mixing of an initiation rite with offerings to the dead seems to refer not to a cult of Achilles, but to the initiatory cult of the Kabeiroi, who were also worshipped on Imbros and Samothrace; the foundations of an *anaktoron* and *telesterion*, as well as numerous inscriptions, have been discovered on Lemnos.

Leonidas of Rhodes: The most famous Olympic runner, Leonidas competed in four successive Olympiads (164–152 B.C.E.) and gained twelve victories (Pausanias *Description of Greece* 6.13.4; Philostratus *On Gymnastics* 33; Sextus Julius Africanus *Chronographies* Olympiad 154–57 [Moretti, *Olympionikai*, 618–20, 622–24, 626–28, 633–35]).

Lepetumnos: Mountain on the north side of the island of Lesbos and site of the sanctuary of the hero Lepetumnos. Other ancient commentators on Homer place Palamedes' sanctuary on this mountain.

Lesbos: An island and city opposite the region of Mysia on the coast of Asia Minor, south of Troy.

Leto: The mother of Apollo and Artemis by Zeus. Pursued by the relentless and jealous Hera, Leto had to give birth to the divine twins on a small island, subsequently called Delos. Leto was beloved to her children, who made every effort to defend her. They slaughtered the sons and daughters of Niobê for the sake of Leto's reputation, they killed Tityos because he tried to mimic her, and because the Python had threatened her, Apollo killed it at Delphi.

Leukê: An island sacred to Achilles (Pindar *Nemean* 4.49; Euripides *Iphigeneia in Tauris* 436–438). According to Pausanias (*Description of Greece* 3.19.11), this island was located in the Black Sea at the mouth of the Istros. Pausanias relates the experience of the island's first visitor, Leonymos of Croton, who claimed to have seen not only Achilles on the island, but also both Ajaxes, Patroklos, Antilokhos, and Helen (*Description of Greece* 3.19.11–13). Strabo locates the island near the mouth of the Dnieper (*Geography* 7.3.16) and Herodotus mentions the existence of a cult of Achilles in Olbia in the Crimea (*Hist.* 4.55). For the archaeological evidence of a cult of Achilles in the area of Olbia and on a small island southeast of the Istros delta, see Guy Hedreen, "The Cult of Achilles in the Euxine," *Hesperia* 60 (1991): 313–30.

Libya: Greek name for the African continent.

Locris: A district in east-central Greece, the domain of Ajax the Lesser.

Lycia: A district on the southern coast of Asia Minor, the domain of Sarpêdon and Glaukos. Apollo is said to have had a palace there.

Lydia: A territory in western Asia Minor, north of Caria and south of Mysia; its capital was Sardis. King Croesus (mid-sixth century B.C.E.) was its most famous ruler.

Lykomêdês: King of the Dolopians on the island of Skyros. He killed Theseus by throwing him from a high rock, because he feared him as a rival. Achilles married Lykomêdês' daughter Dêidameia.

Lyrnêssos: A city on the Troad, the home of Briseis, who was the dearly loved slave of Achilles.

Maiôtis: The present-day Sea of Azov, north of the Black Sea and connected with it through the Cimmerian Bosporus. In antiquity its size was usually overestimated.

Marôn: A priest of Apollo in Thracian Ismaros, who gave Odysseus the wine that made the Cyclops Polyphemos drunk (Homer *Od.* 9.197). His cult was established in Thracian Maroneia, which he is said to have founded.

Massagetai: General term for the people living east of the Caspian Sea. The term is often used synonymously with the designations Scythians and Eastern Scythians. The Massagetai defeated and killed the Persian king Cyrus in 529 B.C.E. (Herodotus *Hist.* 1.204–216; Strabo *Geography* 11.8.2–8).

Medea: Daughter of the king of Colchis, commonly known as a witch. Medea fell in love with Jason, betrayed her father, and fled with Jason. According to Euripides' *Medea*, after Medea and Jason settled in Corinth, King Creon offered Jason his daughter Glaukê as his wife. Outraged by this betrayal, Medea killed Glaukê, Creon, and her own two sons.

In an earlier version of the myth, Medea was the rightful queen of Corinth and her children, although promised immortality by Hera, died in her sanctuary (Eumelus *Corinthiaca*; see also Pausanias *Description of Greece* 2.3.6–8). In any case they later became the object of cultic worship in Corinth (Euripides *Medea* 1378–1383).

Median/Mede(s): The Medes, an Indo-European people closely related to the Persians, defeated the Assyrians in 612 B.C.E. and gained control of Iran and Cappadocia until their defeat by Cyrus in 549 B.C.E. The term "Median" continued to be used to refer to Persian affairs. The Persian expansion to the west resulted in multiple conflicts with the Greeks in the fifth century B.C.E. Under Darius I, Mardonius captured Thrace and Macedonia. In 492 Darius's attempt to control the mainland was prevented by the Greek victory at Marathon. In 480 Darius's son Xerxes launched a campaign against Greece and, despite the alliance between Athens and Sparta, quickly gained control of central Greece: the oracle at Delphi and even Athens itself fell to the Persians. The Greek naval victory at Salamis forced Xerxes to return to Asia, and in 479 the Greeks defeated the Persians at Plataia. The Persian threat and their ultimate defeat gave the Greeks a sense of unity and increased their conviction of the superiority of their language, religion, and way of life.

Meliboia: A Thessalian city and the home of Philoktêtês, one of Helen's suitors, who joined the Trojan expedition but failed to reach Troy immediately because he was bitten by a snake during a sacrifice at Tenedos.

Melikertês: The younger son of Inô, who drowned along with his mother. Inô was fleeing Athamas, the father of her children, who had been driven mad by the gods. Zeus transformed Inô into the goddess Leukothea. At the place where Inô cast herself into the sea, the body of Melikertês was retrieved by a dolphin who hung the body on a pine tree. Sisyphus instituted the worship of Melikertês under the name Palaimôn and founded the Isthmian Games in his honor.

Memnôn: Legendary king of Ethiopia; son of the goddess Eos and Tithônos; nephew of Priam. The lost archaic epic *Aithiopis* treated the events of the Trojan War after those in *Iliad*, including the arrival of the Amazons, Memnôn's killing of Antilokhos, the slaying of Memnôn by Achilles, the death of Achilles at the hands of Aeneas and Apollo, and the fight of Odysseus and Ajax over Achilles' weapons. In this account Memnôn wore armor fashioned by Hephaistos; after his death, his mother obtained immortality for him from Zeus. Homer's *Odyssey* (4.188) mentions the death of Antilokhos by the son of Eos, presumably Memnôn. Philostratus assigns the slaying of Antilokhos to "another Memnôn," a young Trojan hero, whom he distinguishes from the Ethiopian Memnôn. Philostratus elsewhere denies that the Ethiopian Memnôn ever came to Troy (*Life of Apollonius* 6.4). The legendary Ethiopian king Memnôn had already been conflated with the Egyptian Pharaoh Amenophis III (14th century B.C.E.), whose name was understood by the Greeks to be a reference to the well-known Memnôn. The so-called Colossi of Memnôn were seated figures, twenty meters high, in front of the Temple of Amenophis III, located on the Nile near the Valley of the Kings. When one of the statues was broken in the earthquake of 27 B.C.E., small fragments of it flew off with a singing sound as the rays of the rising sun heated the stone (Strabo *Geography* 17.1.46; Philostratus *Imagines* 1.7; *Life of Apollonius* 6.4). This phenomenon was a tourist attraction during the Roman period until Septimius Severus repaired the statues (199/200 C.E.), which put an end to the miracle. The phenomenon of the singing statue was remembered, however, even in the fourth century C.E. (see Himerius *Orations* 8.5).

Memphis: The daughter of the Nile, she was married to Epaphos and gave birth to Libya. The Egyptian city of Memphis was named in her honor.

Menekratês of Steiria: An acquaintance of the vinedresser, whom the vinedresser uses as a contemporary and reliable witness of the recent discovery of the huge skeletons of ancient heroes and giants. This Menekratês may be the same prominent Athenian mentioned in an inscription from Myrina; see Simone Follet, "Inscription inédite de Myrina," *Annuario della Scuola Archaeologica Italiana di Atene* 36/37 (1974): 309–12.

Menelaos: The brother of Agamemnon and the husband of Helen. Menelaos and Helen lived peacefully as king and queen of Sparta until Paris arrived, while Menelaos was in Crete, and abducted Helen. On Helen's whereabouts during the Trojan War, see Helen.

Menestheus: He became king of Athens with the help of Helen's brothers, the Dioscuri. According to Homer (*Il.* 2.552–556), during the Trojan War he was the leader of the Athenian contingent; he was also one of the warriors inside the Trojan horse.

Meroê: A city located near the junction of the Nile and the Astaboras (modern Atbara). Meroê became hellenized under the Ptolemies.

Merops: Eponymous ancestor of the inhabitants of Meropis, a legendary land, which stretches beyond the ocean surrounding the inhabited land. Its people have twice the height of human beings and live twice as long. Meropis also appears as a surname of the island of Cos.

Messene: City in the southwestern Peloponnesus, west of Sparta. Because Nestor was the only one among his brothers and father to accept Herakles when he came to Messene seeking purification from murder, Herakles allowed Nestor to live.

Methymna: A city located in the far north of the island of Lesbos.

Minos: King of Crete who possessed great military power and influence. Meeting with him in a cave, Zeus gave him laws which were then established in Crete. Crete's early naval supremacy is also attributed to Minos. Attic legends portray Minos as a cruel tyrant, who in retaliation for his son's murder forced the Athenians to send fourteen youths every nine years as an offering to the Minotaur.

Mousaios: Legendary sage who, according to Aristophanes (*Frogs* 1032–1033), taught oracles and cures for diseases.

Mugdôn: Leader of Phrygia and the eponymous hero of the tribe of the Mugdônes (Pausanias *Description of Greece* 10.27.1). Homer relates Priam's alliance with Mugdôn and Otreus against the Amazons (Homer *Il.* 3.181–190).

Muses: Daughters of Zeus and Mnêmosunê, divine inspirers of poetry, music, dance, art, and (later) other cultural and intellectual activities. Hesiod (*Theogony* 74–79) names nine Muses: Calliope, Clio, Euterpê, Terpsichore, Eratô, Melpomenê, Thaleia, Polyhymnia, and Ouraniê; these names and the number nine became canonical.

Myrmidons: Thessalian tribe in the Trojan War, they fought under the command of Achilles. According to another legend, they came to Thessaly from the island of Aegina, where Zeus had created them out of ants (*murmêkes*).

Mysia: Region of northwest Anatolia, north of Ionia and south of the Troad, including Pergamum. Its inhabitants are said to have come from the area of the lower Istros (Homer *Il.* 13.5), thus connecting them with the Moesians of the Roman period. Têlephos was king of Mysia and was wounded by Achilles when the Greeks sacked Mysia.

Narcissus: Narcissus was the handsome son of the Boeotian river Kêphisos and the nymph Liriopê. He was so handsome that when he bent over a spring and saw his own reflection, he was entranced. Unable to tear himself away from this vision, he eventually died. At the spot where he died, there later grew a flower which was given his name (Pausanias *Description of Greece* 9.31.7–8; Ovid *Metamorphoses* 3.339–508).

Naulokhos: Literally, "giving safe anchorage," this name was also given to a city on the northeast coast of Sicily, in addition to this harbor on Imbros.

Nauplios: Father of Palamedes and descendant of Nauplios, a son of Poseidon. In order to avenge Palamedes' death, Nauplios destroyed the Greek fleet when it returned from Troy by setting up signal lights on Euboea's cliffs thus luring the fleet to destruction (Euripides *Helen* 767; 1122–1131).

Nausicaa: Daughter of Alkinoos and Arêtê, the king and queen of the Phaeacians. Prompted by a dream sent from Athena, she and her servants went to the mouth of the river to do the family washing. There she encountered Odysseus, who had washed up on the shore the previous evening, and led him back to the city. The Phaeacians eventually gave Odysseus safe passage back to Ithaca (Homer *Odyssey* 6).

Neapolis: A coastal Greek city in southern Italy (modern Naples).

Neleus: Father of Nestor and king of Pylos, who along with eleven of his sons was slain by Herakles (Homer *Il.* 11.688–692). According to Hesiod (as preserved in a fragment from Stephanus of Byzantium, s.v. Gerania = frg.34 [Merkelbach and West]), after Herakles murdered Iphitos, he sought purification from Neleus, who refused it. Thereupon, Herakles killed him and all his sons except Nestor. Philostratus transmits a different tradition, namely, that Herakles killed Neleus and his sons because they stole the cattle of Geryon.

Neoptolemos: Literally "young warrior," the son of Achilles and Dêidameia. After Achilles' death Neoptolemos was summoned to Troy, where he distinguished himself as both warrior and counselor (*Little Iliad*).

Nereids: Daughters of the sea god Nêreus (Homer *Il.* 18.39–64). Achilles' mother Thetis was one of the Nereids.

Nestor: King of Pylos, oldest and wisest of the Greek leaders in the Trojan War (see, e.g., Homer *Il.* 1.252; 2.77, 370, 555) and the father of Antilokhos. Concerning the death of Nestor's father Neleus and his eleven brothers at the hand of Herakles, see the entry on Neleus.

Nile: The river that runs north-south through Egypt from its sources in modern Uganda and Ethiopia to its outlet into the Mediterranean. The yearly flooding of the Nile created a fertile strip of land on both banks, to which Egypt's rulers were indebted for their wealth and power. The Nile owes its name to its river god Nilos.

Nireus: The leader of the Hellenic contingent from Symê. Although he was handsome, Homer labeled him a weakling (*Il.* 2.671–675).

Odrysai: Powerful tribe of Thracians who lived along the river Hebros and founded the most important league of the Thracian tribes in the fifth century B.C.E.

Odysseus: The hero of Homer's *Odyssey*, he was the son of Laertes and Antikleia, and the king of Ithaca. In the *Iliad* Homer portrays Odysseus as courageous and skillful in war and diplomacy. His reputation as a trickster stems from his exploits in the *Odyssey*, where he outwits, often through

cunning deception and with divine help (especially from his
patron Athena), all those who try to prevent his safe return
to Ithaca (e.g., the Cyclops Polyphemos, the Sirens, Circe,
Scylla and Charybdis). In the *Odyssey* (11.134–136), Teire-
sias prophesies that he will live to an old age and experience
a peaceful death "from the sea." An alternative account,
followed by both Philostratus (*Her.* 25.15) and Apollodorus
(*Epitome* 7.36–37), is found in the epic the *Telegonia*, where
Odysseus was unwittingly killed by Têlegonos (his son by
Circe), whose spear-point was a poisonous sting-ray given to
him by Circe. Representations of Odysseus in other epics
and in tragedy are not quite so uniformly complimentary of
Odysseus' character. The story of Odysseus' feigned madness to avoid going to Troy and his exposure by Palamedes
(by threatening Odysseus' infant son Telemachus) appeared
first in the *Cypria* (see also Apollodorus *Epitome* 3.7 and
Hyginus *Fabulae* 95.2), as well as his collaboration with
Diomedes in the retaliatory drowning of Palamedes (see
Pausanias *Description of Greece* 10.31.2). A more noble portrait of Odysseus is found in Sophocles *Ajax*, where he and
Teukros convince Agamemnon to give Ajax a proper burial
(see also Homer *Od.* 11.541–562).

Ôgugia: Island of Kalypso, a nymph who saved Odysseus from
drowning and held him there in bonds of love for seven years
(Homer *Od.* 6.172).

Oiax: Son of Nauplios and brother of Palamedes. He is not mentioned by Homer. He notified their father of Palamedes'
death by writing the report on boards from a ship and
throwing them into the sea (Hyginus *Fabulae* 117, perhaps
drawn from Euripides' *Palamedes*).

Oineus: Legendary king of Calydon in Aetolia; among his children
are Meleagros, Dêianeira, and Tydeus (who was the father
of Diomedes). He was driven out of his kingdom by his
brother Agrios, avenged later by Diomedes, and buried in
Oinoê. A number of fragments of Euripides' tragedy about
him are preserved.

Oiniadai: City in Acarnania on a rocky outcrop in the plain of the
mouth of the Akhelôos.

Oitê: The mountain site of Herakles' self-immolation to escape the effects of the poisoned robe given to him by Dêianeira, his wife who was deceived into believing that the poison was a love potion. In some versions of the myth, Poias, the father of Philoktêtês, lights the pyre.

Okeanos: The oldest of the Titans, the sons of Gê and Ouranos. He lived with his wife Têthys in the far west and was identified as a river that encircles the world. Mythological monsters and the most remote and foreign tribes of people are said to live by Okeanos.

Olympia: The famous sanctuary of Zeus located on the river Alpheios in the northwestern Peloponnesus. This district belonged to the Eleans, who controlled the sanctuary and its festivals. Local legend attributed the sanctuary's origin to the hero Pelops; Pindar, however, says the athletic festival held there every four years was founded by Herakles. The sacred precinct (called the Altis) contained numerous statues of victorious athletes. (The first Olympiad is dated to 776 B.C.E.)

Olympic Games: Competitors traveled from Greece, Ionia, Italy, as well as from eastern cities to participate in these athletic competitions held at Olympia. The games were presided over by judges elected from and by the Eleans; these judges insured that all contestants followed the strict regulations of each contest. Violations resulted in fines or loss of one's prize. A list of Olympic victors is preserved by Eusebius in his *Chronicles*.

Orestes: The son of Agamemnon and Clytemnestra who avenged his father's murder. According to Homer, after returning from exile in Athens, he killed both Clytemnestra and her lover Aigisthos, who had killed Agamemnon (*Od.* 3.303–312; 11.395–434). In contrast, Aeschylus portrayed Clytemnestra as Agamemnon's murderer; after Orestes slew her, he was pursued by the Furies to Delphi and then to Athens, where Orestes was declared innocent by a trial presided over by Athena herself. Orestes regained his father's dominion and also became Menelaos's heir to Sparta after murdering Neoptolemos and marrying his wife Hermionê, the daughter of Menelaos and Helen (Pausanias *Description of Greece* 2.18.5–6; Euripides *Andromache*). The story of finding Orestes' corpse in Tegea and the transfer of his body to Sparta is narrated in Herodotus (*Hist.* 1.67–68).

Orontes: The primary river of Syria, which begins near Heliopolis (northeast of modern Beirut) and winds through Antioch and to the Mediterranean.

Orpheus: A Thracian hero, famous for singing and playing the lyre, Orpheus was son of Oiagros, king of Thrace, and Calliope, although according to some traditions he is a child of Apollo or the Muses. A well-known story about him relates his journey into the Underworld in search of his wife, Eurydice, who was killed by a snakebite. Orpheus charmed Hades with his lyre playing, and Hades released Eurydice provided that, as she followed Orpheus into the upper world, he must never look back upon her—a condition that Orpheus did not fulfill. According to many traditions, Orpheus died by dismemberment by a group of ecstatic Thracian women or maenads. His head and lyre were thrown into the Hebros River; the lyre played a lamentation and the head sang in accompaniment as they floated to the shores of Lesbos. His head became a famous oracle on Lesbos, after it was placed in a cave at Antissa. It prophesied continually, until Apollo, fearing competition for his oracle at Delphi, stopped it. The Muses gathered his other limbs and buried them at the foot of Mount Olympus. His lyre is said to have been placed in the temple of Apollo on Lesbos; this tradition is associated with the origin of the Lesbian tradition of lyric poetry.

Paionia: Northern district, along the Axios river, of what became the Macedonian empire. The Paionians were a number of individual tribes, whose migrations led to settlements along the Strymon and Nestos rivers as well. According to Homer, the Paionians were allies of Troy and were led by Pyraikhmês (*Il.* 2.848–850).

Palamedes: Grandson of Poseidon and hero from Nauplia (modern Nauplion) in the Argolid, a region in the Peloponnesus south-east of Achaea, near Corinth (the fortress of Nauplion is still called "Palamidi"). In wisdom and power of invention, he rivals Prometheus, Orpheus, and Kadmos.

According to the lost *Cypria*, the rivalry of Odysseus and
Palamedes began when Palamedes saw through Odysseus's
feigned madness, by which the latter had tried to avoid service in the Trojan War; Palamedes was ultimately drowned
by Odysseus and Diomedes in this version of the story
(*Cypria* frg. 21 = Pausanias *Description of Greece* 10.31.2).
The story of Palamedes' death found in Dictys of Crete is
closer to that found in the *Heroikos*. After luring Palamedes
down a well by claiming that they had found gold there,
Diomedes and Odysseus stoned Palamedes (*Journal of the
Trojan War* 2.15). Palamedes was also the subject of an
tragedy by Euripides, but the traditions about Palamedes
were passed over by Homer.

Pallênê: Also called Phlegra, it is the westernmost peninsula of the
Macedonian Chalcidice.

Pamphôs: According to Pausanias (*Description of Greece* 8.37.9), a
pre-Homeric poet, although the extant fragments indicate a
later date.

Pandaros: Ally of the Trojans from Lycia. Beloved by Apollo, he
was known for his archery with a bow that he himself had
made (Homer *Il.* 4.86, 105; 5.166).

Panidês: A king of Chalcis, who presided over the competition between Homer and Hesiod (*Certamen* 315, 321–322).

Panthous: Father of Euphorbus and a Trojan elder. Later sources
(Servius *Commentary on Virgil's Aeneid* 2.318) identify him
as a priest of Apollo in Delphi, who was taken back to Troy
by an Trojan envoy.

Paris: A Trojan prince, the second son of Priam and Hekabê. Although the name Paris is prominently used in this text (but
see *Her.* 40.1–2), the Greek name Alexandros appears more
frequently in the *Iliad*. Paris's birth was accompanied by
divine warnings. Hekabê dreamed that she gave birth to
a torch which set alight the citadel of Troy, and prior to
his birth a seer warned that he would cause the destruction
of Troy. According to the lost *Cypria*, Paris was to judge
which of the three goddesses Athena, Hera, and Aphrodite
was the most beautiful. The victorious goddess was to possess the golden apple of Eris (the goddess of discord), which

was inscribed "to the fairest." Having awarded the apple to Aphrodite, Paris received the right to possess the most beautiful woman on earth, Helen. Paris seized Helen from her home in Sparta, thus causing the Trojan War. The *Iliad* sometimes depicts Paris as wearing heavy armor; he is usually said, however, to be an archer, and as an archer he killed Achilles. Paris himself was killed by one of Philoktêtês' arrows, which pierced his groin. He is often depicted as cowardly, especially in comparison to his brother Hektor.

Patroklos: Son of Menoitios and Stenelê, from Opus; long-time friend of Achilles. News of Patroklos's death brought Achilles back into the battle, swearing vengeance upon the Trojans. After Achilles was killed, he and Patroklos were entombed together (Homer *Iliad* 23).

Peleus: King of the Myrmidons, husband of the sea goddess Thetis, and father of Achilles.

Pelion: Mountain in Thessalian Magnesia, just northeast of modern Volos. It was the home of the centaur Kheirôn, and where Achilles and Jason were raised in Kheirôn's care. It was also the region where Peleus lived and married Thetis.

Peloponnesus: The large Greek peninsula connected to the mainland by the Isthmus of Corinth.

Peparêthos: An island in the northern Sporades known today as Skopelos.

Persês: The brother of Hesiod and ostensibly the target of Hesiod's *Works and Days*, which advises honest work and denounces dishonesty and laziness. Persês, it appears, had bribed the local village elders and defrauded Hesiod of his rightful inheritance (*Works and Days* 37–39).

Phaeacians: The inhabitants of Skheria, a peaceful and seafaring people (Homer *Od.* 6.262–274). Odysseus encountered them toward the end of his wanderings when he was shipwrecked on their shore. Taken into the court of their king, Alkinoos, Odysseus did not reveal his identity until the epic song of the bard Dêmodokos about Odysseus's deeds at Troy caused him to weep so much that Alkinoos began to guess who he was. The Phaeacians equipped Odysseus with a ship to carry him and many gifts home to Ithaca. This action so enraged Poseidon—because Odysseus had blinded his son Polyphemos—that as the ship returned to Phaeacia, he turned it to stone outside the harbor. Much of the story of Odysseus's wanderings in Homer's *Odyssey* is told in the court of the Phaeacians by Odysseus.

Phaethôn: Son of Helios. He was given the sun chariot for one day, but half of the earth burned when the horses ran wild and he crashed to earth with his father's chariot (Ovid *Metamorphoses* 1.749–2.328; Euripides *Hippolytus* 740; Plato *Timaeus* 22c).

Phasis: In Colchis, a river flowing from the Caucasus Mountains to the Black Sea. Its modern name is Rion.

Phêmios: A bard of Odysseus at his home in Ithaca (Homer *Od.* 1.153–154, 337–344; 17.261–263; 22.331–356).

Philip: Philip II was the king of Macedon from 359–336 B.C.E. and father of Alexander the Great. Philip unified Macedonia and transformed it into a tremendous economic and military power.

Philoktêtês: Son of Poias (Homer *Od.* 3.190) and leader of the seven ships from Methonê and other towns of the southwestern part of the Peloponnesus, he is the subject of Sophocles' tragedies *Philoctetes* and *Philoctetes at Troy*. On the way to the Trojan War, he was left behind in Lemnos, suffering from a snake bite (see the *Cypria*). In contrast to Protesilaos's story, the lost epic *Little Iliad* presents Philoktêtês as healed in Troy by Makhaôn, the son of Asclepius. Philoktêtês was in possession of the bow and arrows of Herakles, given to him by his father Poias. Because an oracle had ordained that Troy could not be taken without the bow and arrows of Herakles, Philoktêtês' presence in Troy was necessary. For a survey of the various versions of Philoktêtês' story and its gradual conformity to Roman ideas of masculinity and suffering, see Bowersock, *Fiction as History*, 55–76.

Phlegra: Originally a mythical place where the Gigantomachy ended in defeat of the giants (Pindar *Nemean* 1.67; Euripides *Ion* 988), later identified with Pallênê (Herodotus *Hist.* 7.123.1). Campi Phlegraei is a region of Campania near Puteoli, rich in sulfur, where Herakles is said to have killed the giants.

Phocis: A region of central Greece, comprising the valleys of the middle Kêphisos and of Krisa, which are linked loosely by the passes over the southern spurs of Mount Parnassos. The oracles of Phocis included the oracles of Apollo at Delphi and at Abae, and an oracle of Dionysos at Amphikleia (Pausanias *Description of Greece* 10.5.5–8; 10.35.1; 10.33.11).

Phoenician(s): An ancient people, whose territory lying along the eastern Mediterranean coast was more or less coextensive with modern Lebanon. Before 1000 B.C.E. the Phoenicians had invented the alphabet; around the same time they emerged as traders and seafarers. Their products included gemstones, metals, glass items, and textiles, such as their famous purple robes. They were also skilled architects. In 64 B.C.E. Phoenicia was annexed to the Roman province of Syria.

Phoenix: Teacher and adviser of Achilles. In Homer (*Il.* 9.168, 427–622), he appears first among those chosen for the embassy to Achilles to persuade him to return to the fighting at Troy. Elsewhere in the *Iliad*, he appears only as one of the older leaders of the Myrmidons (16.196; 17.555; 19.311). Phoenix was son of Amyntôr, and was befriended by Peleus and made a companion and mentor for his son Achilles (Homer *Il.* 9.430–495).

Phrygia: A country in central Asia Minor; its inhabitants probably came from Europe.

Phthia: District in Thessaly that was home to Achilles and the Myrmidons, as well as Protesilaos and those under his command (Strabo *Geography* 9.5.14).

Phulakê: A Thessalian city. According to Homer (*Il.* 2.695), Protesilaos was the ruler of this city.

Ploutarkhos: An otherwise unknown Olympic boxer, whose Olympic victory Moretti (*Olympionikai*, 904) tentatively dates to 205 C.E.

Poias: Father of Philoktêtês. When Herakles clothed himself with the poisoned robe on Mount Oitê, Poias was the only one who helped him to end his sufferings in death. After being transported to Olympus by Athena and gaining immortality, Herakles gave his bow and arrow to Poias as a reward for his help. His son Philoktêtês inherited these weapons.

Poinai: Goddesses of vengeance.

Polydamas: Trojan hero, son of Panthous and brother of Euphorbus. In Troy, Polydamas was second only to Hektor; he was a good fighter and a thoughtful advisor (Homer *Il.* 11.57; 14.425; 15.339, 520; 17.597).

Polyphemos: Son of Poseidon and the nymph Thoôsa, he was the Cyclops who held Odysseus prisoner in his cave and ate several of his companions until the hero made him drunk and blinded him (Homer *Odyssey* 9). Poseidon punished Odysseus with a difficult homecoming.

Polyxena: This daughter of Priam and Hekabê is not mentioned in the *Iliad*, but appears in later epics. Early traditions report that Polyxena was sacrificed on the tomb of Achilles (*Destruction of Ilion*). This version is followed by Euripides in the tragedy *Hecuba*, where Achilles' ghost demands the sacrifice of Polyxena (*Hecuba* 35–44, 220–224, 534–540; see also *Trojan Women* 39–40). Hyginus's alternative story (*Fabulae* 110) bears many similarities to Philostratus's version: Polyxena is said to have come with Priam and Andromache to reclaim Hektor's body from Achilles. Although Achilles was unmoved by the entreaties of Hektor's father and widow, Polyxena managed to sway him, since he had fallen in love with her. The story of Achilles' betrayal is also connected with this tradition: in order to win the hand of Polyxena, Achilles suggested to Priam that he would abandon the Greeks. The negotiations were to be concluded in the temple of the Thymbrian Apollo, but Paris, hidden behind the statue of the god, killed Achilles with an arrow.

Pontus: The region of north-central Asia Minor between the Halys River and Colchis, and including the coast of the Black Sea to the north and extending to Cappadocia in the south. "Pontus" also refers to the part of the Black Sea adjacent to this region.

Poseidon: The god of the ocean and of earthquakes, with the epithet Earth-shaker, Poseidon was the son of Kronos and

Rheia, brother of Zeus and Hades, father of the Cyclopes, and an ancestor of Palamedes. Although he was a protector of the Achaeans, he was antagonistic to Odysseus (variously for the blinding of the Cyclops Polyphemos or for the death of Palamedes) and long delayed Odysseus's homecoming. With Apollo, he built the walls of Troy for the first ruler of the city, Laomedôn, but after the Achaeans built a wall around their ships at Troy, he feared that it would surpass the walls of Troy. After the war, he diverted rivers in order to destroy the Achaean wall. His attribute is the trident, or fisher's spear, which he used to split rocks to bring forth streams and springs, as well as to stir up storms at sea.

Priam: King of Troy during the Trojan War, son of Laomedôn, and father of fifty sons, among whom were Hektor and Paris. After ransoming Hektor's corpse from Achilles, he was killed by Neoptolemos during the sack of Troy.

Protesilaos: According to the *Iliad*, the son of Iphiklês and commander of a contingent from Phulakê in Thessaly. He was the first to be killed at Troy, dying as he jumped from his ship onto the shore (Homer *Il.* 2.695–709; 13.681; 15.705; 16.286). While the *Iliad* does not identify his killer, Hektor is frequently blamed in later versions of the story (e.g., the *Cypria*, Apollodorus *Epitome* 3.30; Ovid *Metamorphoses* 12.66–68); later scholia also name Aeneas, Akhatês, or Euphorbus as his killer. Protesilaos greatly loved his wife Laodameia, and his return from Hades to see her was taken up by Lucian (*Dialogues of the Dead* 23). Protesilaos was the object of cult in Phulakê and at his tomb at Elaious on the Thracian Chersonesus (see entries); according to Pausanias, Protesilaos was one of the few mortals to receive divine honors after his death (*Description of Greece* 1.34.2).

Pylos: The home of Nestor and Antilokhos. Most ancient authors locate Pylos in Messene in the southwestern Peloponnesus at the bay of Navarino, although some place Pylos in Triphylia, further to the north on the western coast of the Peloponnesus, south of the Alpheios. Homer's description of Pylos as "sandy" (*Il.* 2.77) fits the Triphylian Pylos.

Pyriphlegethôn: A stream in Epirus. See also Akherousias.

Pythagoras: Philosopher and founder of a religious community. Originally an inhabitant of Samos, Pythagoras emigrated to Croton, an Athenian colony in Italy, in ca. 531 B.C.E. One of his central tenets was metempsychosis, the reincarnation of the soul, a process that can only be terminated through strict asceticism and the Pythagorean way of life. He believed that he was the reincarnation of the Trojan warrior Euphorbus (Ovid *Metamorphoses* 15.160–161). Pythagoras is also famed for his discovery of the numerical ratios of musical scales and for the belief that numbers are the basis of the world.

Pythian oracle: The oracle of Apollo at Delphi, which during the classical period was the most important Greek oracle. Oracular responses were given by the Pythia, an ecstatic prophetess, and were interpreted and written in verse by the temple priests. The oracle's reputation suffered after it discouraged the Greeks from resisting the Persian invasion.

Rhêsos: A Thracian king, son of Êioneus, who was known for his snow-white horses. He came to Troy in the tenth year of the war and devastated the Greek camp for one day. At the end of the day he was killed by Odysseus and Diomedes, who took away his horses (Homer *Il.* 10.435, 474, 519). Rhêsos's exploits at Troy were also recounted in the *Rhesus*, attributed to Euripides; the play concludes with his mother (in this version a Muse) declaring over her son's body that he will become a demigod (970–973). Rhêsos's bones were also renowned in connection with the founding of Amphipolis (Polyaenus *Strategica* 6.53).

Rhodes: An island off the coast of western Asia Minor colonized by Greeks who formed three separate city states, which eventually united. Due to its access to eastern ports, especially in Egypt, Phoenicia, and Cyprus, Rhodes became extremely wealthy and prosperous as a trading center.

Rhodopê: Large mountainous massif in Thrace, stretching from the headwaters of the Nestos and Hebros rivers to the outlet of the Hebros.

Rhoiteion: A small town near Troy and a nearby promontory; on the promontory was the tomb of the greater Ajax; Ajax's statue was brought to Egypt by Mark Antony, but returned by order of Augustus (Strabo *Geography* 13.1.30).

Salamis: An island in the Saronic Gulf, just to the west of Athens/
Piraeus and east of Megara. According to Pausanias (*De-scription of Greece* 1.35.3), Salamis was colonized by Aegina,
along with Telamôn, the father of Ajax the Greater, and a
temple and ebony statue of Ajax could still be seen there.
Salamis had been associated with Athens since the sixth
century B.C.E. and was the site of the Persian naval defeat
in 480 B.C.E. Athens' claim on the island during the pro-tracted war with Megara was supported by references to
her prominence and control of much of Attica in Homer
(*Il.* 2.546–556; *Od.* 3.278, but note that these verses may
well have been composed for Athenian propagandistic pur-poses); Pausanias (*Description of Greece* 1.35.2) relates that
Philaios, the son of Eurusakês and grandson of Ajax, gave
Salamis to Athens in return for Athenian citizenship.

Samos: An island off the western coast of Asia Minor settled by
Ionians. In the sixth century B.C.E. Samos was known for
its architects, sculptors, poets, and moralists, but its most fa-mous inhabitant was the philosopher Pythagoras.

Sarpêdon: According to Homer (*Il.* 2.876; 5.629–662; 6.198–199;
16.462–507), Sarpêdon was leader of a Lycian contingent
which fought alongside the Trojans. He was said to be son of
Zeus and Laodameia, the daughter of Bellerophon. Sarpê-don played a major role in the attack on the Achaean camp
and the assault on the walls. Patroklos killed him, and a great
battle was fought around his body.

Scamander: River southwest of Troy, called Xanthos among the
gods. It derives from a warm and a cold spring on Mount
Ida and flows into the Hellespont (Homer *Il.* 11.499; 14.343).
Scamander is also the name of the river god whom Achilles
fought during the Trojan War (Homer *Il.* 21.211–382).

Scylla: A sea monster who dwelt near the deadly whirlpool Cha-rybdis, she was encountered by Odysseus (Homer *Od.*
12.85–110, 245–259). This fantastic creature had six heads,
and any ship that approached would be attacked and its men
devoured. Ovid identified Scylla as a particularly dangerous
rock (Ovid *Metamorphoses* 14.73).

Scythia: The territory between the Carpathian Mountains and
the river Don was so named by the Greeks, although the

term Scythian is often used for those central Asian tribes
that by 650 B.C.E. governed northwestern Iran and eastern Turkey, as far as the river Halys. The Scythians were
expelled from the Turkish-Iranian region by the Medes
ca. 622, after which they founded a kingdom on the lower
reaches of the river Dnieper. Expelled from this area by
the Sarmatae in the second century B.C.E., they moved to
the Crimea. They engaged in considerable trade with the
Greeks on the Black Sea, even though to the Greeks they
were barbarians par excellence. Mostly likely a nomadic
people, their military strength was as mounted archers.

Selene: Goddess of the moon and daughter of Titans (her parents'
names are variously given). Selene fell in love with a mortal,
Endymion, whom Zeus punished with eternal sleep.

Sidon: Hellenized city on the coast of Phoenicia; its two important commercial industries were purple-dyeing and glass-
blowing.

Sigeion: Promontory in the Troad (modern Kumkale), opposite
the Thracian Chersonesus, and city south of the promontory of the same name. The city of Sigeion was originally an
Aeolian settlement, but in the seventh century was acquired
by Athens; the city was destroyed by Ilion (third–second
century B.C.E.?). According to Strabo (*Geography* 13.1.32),
Sigeion was the site of a temple of Achilles and monuments
to both Patroklos and Antilokhos.

Sirens: Mythical singing creatures that inhabited an island near
Scylla and Charybdis. The Sirens lured sailors onto the island and caused them to forget their journey and to lose their
desire for home. Odysseus sailed past their island safely
(Homer *Od.* 12.37–54, 153–200) by stopping his men's ears
with wax while he had himself lashed to the mast of the ship
and listened to their songs. These creatures' physical appearance was not described by Homer, but they were often
depicted as half-women and half-birds.

Sisyphus: The son of Aiolos, who according to Homer (*Od.*
11.593–600) was perpetually tormented in Hades; he continually pushed a stone up a hill, but it always rolled down
before he could reach the top. A sanctuary of Sisyphus

was located on the acropolis in Corinth (Strabo *Geography* 8.6.21), and his grave is said to be on the Isthmus (Pausanias *Description of Greece* 2.2.2).

Skyros: Island in the northern Sporades in the Aegean Sea. Lykomêdês murdered Theseus on Skyros, and Achilles traveled there to avenge his death (Homer *Il.* 9.668). According to Statius (*Achilleid* 207–396), Thetis disguised Achilles as a young girl and hid him on Skyros to prevent him going to fight at Troy. Pausanias (*Description of Greece* 1.22.6) presents these two stories as competing traditions. Skyros was also known as the realm of Achilles' son, Neoptolemos (Sophocles *Philoctetes* 239).

Smyrna: A city on the west coast of Asia Minor at the outlet of the Hermos River, north of Ephesus and south of Pergamum. In the Roman period, Smyrna was known for its interest in science and medicine.

Sparta: A Lacedaemonian city in the southeast of Greece that was the home of Menelaos.

Sperkheios: A river in the domain of Peleus and Achilles in Thessaly. Homer (*Il.* 16.174) recounts that Sperkheios was the father of the fighter Menesthios, whose mother was Polydorê, a daughter of Peleus.

Steiria: An Athenian deme that belonged to the tribe Pandionis. The legendary ancestor of the tribe was the mythical king Pandiôn.

Sthenelos: Son of Kapaneus; leader of the Argives, along with Diomedes and Euryalos; close companion of Diomedes (Homer *Il.* 2.564; 4.367); father of Eurystheus, the taskmaster of Herakles (*Il.* 19.119–123). As one of the Epigonoi, Sthenelos participated in Thebes' capture (*Il.* 4.401–410; for more on the saga of the Seven Against Thebes, see the entry for Thebes). Reputed to have been a suitor of Helen before the Trojan War, he was inside the Trojan horse (Virgil *Aeneid* 2.261; Hyginus *Fabulae* 257). According to Homer (*Il.* 4.367–371), Sthenelos was insulted by Agamemnon as inferior to his father, Kapaneus. Pausanias (*Description of Greece* 2.22.9) locates his grave in Argos; other traditions (Lycophron frg. 433) report that he was buried together with Idomeneus and Kalkhas in Colophon.

Sybaris: Greek city in Lucania in southern Italy, founded by Achaea and Trozen ca. 720 C.E. Sybaris was famous for its wealth and the luxurious life-style of its inhabitants. It was destroyed in 510 B.C.E. by Croton, at the instigation of exiled Sybarites; the Sybarites joined the new Athenian colony at nearby Thurii, but later the new city of Sybaris was founded on the river Traeis.

Tantalos: A son of Zeus, he reigned on Mount Sipylos in Lydia. He was extremely rich and beloved by the gods, but also one of the archetypal law breakers of Greek legends. Tantalos was welcomed at divine feasts and according to various accounts he either revealed the gods' secrets to humans (Euripides *Orestes* 4–11), stole the divine drinks of nectar and ambrosia and gave them to mortals (Pindar *Olympian* 1.60–64), or cooked and served his son Pelops to the gods in order to test them (Pindar *Olympian* 1.25–53). His punishment was that he was plunged into water up to his neck, but the water withdrew whenever he tried to drink from it. Similarly, a branch laden with fruit hung just above his head, but if he raised his arm the branch would spring out of reach (Homer *Od.* 11.582–592). According to another version a rock hung precariously over his head, threatening imminent doom (Pindar *Olympian* 1.55–58; Euripides *Orestes* 4–11; Archilochus 53; Pausanias *Description of Greece* 10.31.12).

Taurus Mountains: These mountains are probably the well-forested range that begins in southwestern Asia Minor and continues along the Lycian coast through Pisidia and Isauria to the borders of Cilicia and Lykaonia. Ancient cartographers and geographers regarded these mountains, which rise over seven thousand feet, as the backbone of Asia.

Tegea: City in the Peloponnesus, north of Sparta. According to Greek legend, Orestes' tomb was located there (Pausanias *Description of Greece* 3.3.5; 8.54.4). Roman tradition, however, asserted that Orestes died at Aricia and that his bones were transferred to Rome and buried under the Temple of Saturn.

Tekmêssa: Slave girl, perhaps mentioned in Homer (*Il.* 1.138) without name, given as booty to Ajax the Greater by Agamemnon. In Sophocles' *Ajax* she is daughter of the Phrygian king Teleutas and became the rightful wife of Ajax, with whom he bore the son Eurusakês.

Telamôn: Father of Ajax the Greater and associate of Herakles in his revenge against Troy.

Telemachus: The son of Odysseus and Penelope. According to the *Cypria*, when Telemachus was a baby, Odysseus feigned madness in order to avoid helping in the Trojan War; Palamedes threatened the child's life and thus tricked Odysseus into saving his son and proving his sanity. Telemachus thus grew up in Ithaca during his father's absence due to the Trojan War and his long delayed attempts to return home. The first four books of Homer's *Odyssey* are especially concerned with Telemachus's anger at his mother's suitors and his quest for news of Odysseus.

Têlephos: Son of Herakles and Augê, and the king of Mysia. Têlephos was wounded by Achilles, but eventually healed by filings from his spear (Apollodorus *Epitome* 3.20). Mistaking Mysia for Troy and the wounding of Têlephos, not mentioned in Homer, are found in the extant fragments of the *Cypria*. The story explains that, by order of an oracle, Têlephos was healed by Achilles and then served as a guide to Troy for the Greek forces.

Tênos: An island in the Aegean, north of Mykonos and Andros.

Teukros: The son of Telamôn and half-brother of the greater Ajax. Teukros was an Achaean archer and spearfighter (Homer *Il.* 8.266–334).

Thasian: Of or pertaining to Thasos, an island in the Thracian Sea, rich in natural resources and also well known for its export of wine.

Thebes: A city in Boeotia and the site of the famous battle of the Seven kings against Thebes. The sons of Oedipus, Polyneikês and Eteoklês, were to reign in Thebes in alternate years. When Eteoklês would not relinquish the throne, Polyneikês gathered six leaders to help him gain his rightful place. Their attempt to take Thebes was disastrous, and only one of the seven leaders survived. The saga of the Seven Against Thebes was the subject of a number of dramas, including Aeschylus's *Seven Against Thebes*, Euripides' *Phoenician Women*, Seneca's *Phoenician Women*, and Statius's epic *Thebaid*.

Thermôdôn: A river in Pontus (modern Terme Çayi) that forms the eastern border of the central plain of Themiskyra. Tradition places the Amazons' home at the mouth of this river.

Theseus: Athenian hero, son of Aigeus or Poseidon and eventually a king of Athens. The legends surrounding Theseus include numerous labors in Attica, partly influenced by the myths of Herakles, and the slaying of the Minotaur in Crete. The story alluded to in this text seems to connect the death of Theseus's son Hippolytos with Theseus's flight from Athens. Hippolytos had been falsely accused by his stepmother Phaedra of adulterous advances toward her, whereupon Theseus cursed him. Upon hearing the curse, Poseidon sent a bull from the sea, which frightened Hippolytos's horses and resulted in his being fatally thrown from his chariot.

Thessaly: District of northern Greece. Thessaly is surrounded by mountains, with access to the sea only at the Bay of Volo. It has two large, fertile plains, separated by hills; these plains made Thessaly rich in grain, horses, and cattle. Mountains notable in legend include Mount Pelion, home of the centaur Kheirôn, and Mount Oitê, site of Herakles' funeral pyre. Phthia in Thessaly was the home of both Achilles and Protesilaos. In the sixth century, Thessaly was particularly strong and dominated northern Greece under the rule of a few aristocratic families. Thessaly later declined after the prominent family of the Alôadai supported the Persian cause. In the time of Philip of Macedon and Alexander the Great, Thessaly was technically independent, but under Macedonian influence. Thessaly was part of the province of Macedonia, under the Roman empire.

Thetis: Daughter of the sea god Nêreus and one of the Nereids. Different myths explain why she was given in marriage to a mortal, Peleus, king of Phthia, with whom she bore Achilles. In the *Iliad*, especially in books 1, 18, and 19, she intercedes for Achilles before Zeus, provides armor for him, and mourns the death of Patroklos and Achilles' impending doom.

Thrace: A region in northeastern Greece bounded, in Roman times, by the Black Sea, the Nestos River, and the Hellespont.

Thrasymedes: One of Nestor's sons. According to Homer, Thrasymedes accompanied his father Nestor to Troy (*Il*. 9.81; 10.255; 14.10); other legends say that he was a chief of the Greek sentries at Troy.

Thymbraion: A temple of Apollo located at the confluence of the Thymbrian River and the Scamander in Troy (Strabo *Geography* 13.1.35). According to some legends, this was the location of Achilles' death at the hands of Paris and of Polyxena's suicide.

Tithônos: The lover of Eos, goddess of the dawn. According to the *Homeric Hymn to Aphrodite*, Tithônos was a Trojan with whom Eos fell in love. She asked Zeus to grant him immortality, but neglected to ask for agelessness. As a beautiful young man he lived with Eos on the banks of Okeanos, but as he grew older, Eos shut him up in a room where he could be heard babbling but not seen.

Tlêpolemos: Son of Herakles and of Astyokhê or Astydameia, king of Rhodes, and ally of the Trojans (Homer *Il*. 2.653–670).

Troy: Troy was a city (modern Hisarlik) in northwest Asia Minor, close to the Aegean and the Hellespont, under the rule of Priam during the Trojan War. By the seventh century B.C.E., the city was also called Ilion. The surrounding region is known as the Troad.

Tydeus: Son of Oineus and father of Diomedes (Homer *Il*. 14.113–125), and one of the seven leaders to attack Thebes on behalf of Polyneikês (for more on the saga of the Seven Against Thebes, see the entry for Thebes). Tydeus was fatally wounded by Melanippos (who was in turn slain by Amphiaraos), but lost Athena's gift of immortality when she saw him consume the brains of the dead Melanippos (Apollodorus *Library* 3.6.8).

Tyre: Merchant city on the coast of Phoenicia.

Vesuvius: Volcano located south of Naples in Italy. Although the ancients thought it was extinct (see Diodorus Siculus *Library* 4.21.5), it erupted on 24 August 79 C.E., destroying the nearby cities of Pompeii, Herculaneum, and Stabiae.

Xanthos: See Balios and Xanthos.

Xeinis the Chersonesian: The former owner of Protesilaos's sanctuary.

Xerxes: (486–465 B.C.E.) King of Persia and son of Darius and Atossa. His third campaign was an invasion of Greece, which ended in his great defeat at Plataia. His campaigns in Egypt and then in Babylon preceded his invasion of Greece.

Zeus: Chief of the gods, lordly head of the family of the gods, he is the son of Kronos, whom he overthrew, and the brother and husband of Hera. He is usually described as enthroned on mountain peaks, principally Mount Olympus, and as the upholder of law, morals, and civic justice.

Topical Bibliographies

The following bibliographies indicate key works on a number of topics central to reading *On Heroes*. The works included are intended as starting points for further reading and research, and are thus selective rather than exhaustive. English language works are emphasized, although many other fine works are available on these topics in other languages. For a full bibliography on editions of and works related to Philostratus's *On Heroes*, the reader is advised to consult the Select Bibliography in Jennifer K. Berenson Maclean and Ellen Bradshaw Aitken, trans., *Flavius Philostratus: Heroikos* (SBLWGRW 1; Atlanta: Society of Biblical Literature, 2001).

ATHLETES AND ATHLETIC CONTESTS

Gardiner, E. Norman. *Athletics of the Ancient World*. Oxford: Clarendon, 1930.

Jones, Christopher P. "The Pancratists Helix and Alexander on an Ostian Mosaic." *JRA* 11 (1998): 293–98.

Matz, David. *Greek and Roman Sport: A Dictionary of Athletes and Events From the Eighth Century B.C. to the Third Century A.D.* Jefferson, N.C.: McFarland, 1991.

Robinson, Rachel Sargent. *Sources for the History of Greek Athletics in English Translation*. Cincinnati: n. p., 1955.

Sansone, David. *Greek Athletics and the Genesis of Sport*. Berkeley: University of California Press, 1988.

Scanlon, Thomas F. *Eros and Greek Athletics*. New York: Oxford University Press, 2002.

CULTURAL IDENTITY IN THE ROMAN WORLD

Alcock, Susan E. *Graecia Capta: The Landscapes of Roman Greece*. New York: Cambridge University Press, 1993.

Bowie, Ewen L. "Greeks and Their Past in the Second Sophistic." *Past and Present* 46 (1970): 3–41. Rev. ed. in *Studies in Ancient Society*. Edited by M. I. Finley. London: Routledge, 1974.

Clarke, Katherine. *Between Geography and History: Hellenistic Constructions of the Roman World.* Oxford: Clarendon, 1999.

Erskine, Andrew. *Troy Between Greece and Rome: Local Tradition and Imperial Power.* New York: Oxford University Press, 2001.

Goldhill, Simon, ed. *Being Greek under Rome: Cultural Identity, the Second Sophistic, and the Development of Empire.* New York: Cambridge University Press, 2001.

Jaeger, Werner. *Paideia: The Ideals of Greek Culture.* 3 vols. 2d ed. New York: Oxford University Press, 1943–1945.

Swain, Simon. *Hellenism and Empire: Language, Classicism, and Power in the Greek World AD 50–250.* Oxford: Clarendon, 1996.

Whitmarsh, Timothy. *Greek Literature and the Roman Empire: The Politics of Imitation.* New York: Oxford, 2001.

DEATH, RESURRECTION, AND IMMORTALITY

Davies, Jon. *Death, Burial, and Rebirth in the Religions of Antiquity.* New York: Routledge, 1999.

Nickelsburg, George W. E. *Resurrection, Immortality, and Eternal Life in Intertestamental Judaism.* Cambridge, Mass.: Harvard University Press, 1972.

Riley, Gregory J. *Resurrection Reconsidered: Thomas and John in Controversy.* Minneapolis: Fortress Press, 1995.

EARLY CHRISTIANITY

Balch, David L., Everett Ferguson, and Wayne A. Meeks, eds. *Greeks, Romans, and Christians: Essays in Honor of Abraham J. Malherbe.* Minneapolis: Fortress, 1990.

Betz, Hans Dieter. "Heroenverehrung und Christusglaube: Religionsgeschichtliche Beobachtungen zu Philostrats *Heroicus.*" Pages 119–39 in *Griechische und römische Religion.* Edited by Hubert Cancik. Vol. 2 of *Geschichte—Tradition—Reflexion: Festschrift für Martin Hengel zum 70. Geburtstag.* Edited by Hubert Cancik, Hermann Lichtenberger, and Peter Schäfer. Tübingen: Mohr/Siebeck, 1996. English Translation in *Philostratus's* Heroikos: *Religion and Cultural Identity in the Third Century* C.E. Edited by Ellen Bradshaw Aitken and Jennifer K. Berenson Maclean. SBLWGRW 4. Atlanta: Society of Biblical Literature. Forthcoming.

Campenhausen, Hans von. *The Formation of the Christian Bible*. Philadelphia: Fortress, 1972.
Clark, Elizabeth A. *Reading Renunciation: Asceticism and Scripture in Early Christianity*. Princeton: Princeton University Press, 1999.
Frend, W. H. C. *The Rise of Christianity*. Philadelphia: Fortress Press, 1984.
Hengel, Martin. *The Atonement: The Origins of the Doctrine in the New Testament*. Philadelphia: Fortress, 1981.
Koester, Helmut. "Apocryphal and Canonical Gospels." *HTR* 73 (1980): 105–30.
———. *Introduction to the New Testament*. 2 vols. 2d ed. New York: de Gruyter, 1995–2000.
Riley, Gregory J. *One Jesus, Many Christs*. San Francisco: HarperSanFrancisco, 1997.

GIANTS AND GIANT BONES

Boedeker, Deborah. "Hero Cult and Politics in Herodotus: The Bones of Orestes." Pages 164–77 in *Cultural Poetics in Archaic Greece*. Edited by Carol Dougherty and Leslie Kurke. Cambridge: Cambridge University Press, 1993.
Dreyfus, Renée and Ellen Schraudolph, eds. *Pergamon: The Telephos Frieze from the Great Altar*. San Francisco: Fine Arts Museums of San Francisco, 1996–1997.
Farkas, Ann E., Prudence O. Harper, and Evelyn B. Harrison, eds. *Monsters and Demons in the Ancient and Medieval Worlds: Papers Presented in Honor of Edith Porada*. Mainz on Rhine: Zabern, 1987.
Mayor, Adrienne. *The First Fossil Hunters: Paleontology in Greek and Roman Times*. Princeton: Princeton University Press, 2000.

HEROES (SEE ALSO POETRY AND PERFORMANCE)

Antonaccio, Carla M. *An Archaeology of Ancestors: Tomb Cult and Hero Cult in Early Greece*. Lanham, Md.: Rowman & Littlefield, 1995.
Boedeker, Deborah. "Protesilaos and the End of Herodotus' *Histories*." *Classical Antiquity* 7/1 (1988): 30–48.
Brelich, A. *Gli eroi greci: Un problema storico-religioso*. Rome: Edizioni dell'Ateneo, 1958.
Dué, Casey. "Achilles' Golden Amphora and the Afterlife of Oral Tradition in Aeschines' *Against Timarchus*." *CP* 96 (2001): 33–47.

Farnell, Lewis Richard. *Greek Hero Cults and Ideas of Immortality.* Oxford: Clarendon, 1921.

Hadas, Moses and Morton Smith. *Heroes and Gods: Spiritual Biographies in Antiquity.* New York: Harper & Row, 1965.

Hedreen, Guy. "The Cult of Achilles in the Euxine." *Hesperia* 60/3 (1991): 313–30.

Henrichs, Albert. "The Tomb of Aias and the Prospect of Hero Cult in Sophokles." *Classical Antiquity* 12 (1993): 165–80.

Nagy, Gregory. *The Best of the Achaeans: Concepts of the Hero in Archaic Greek Poetry.* 2d rev. ed. Baltimore: Johns Hopkins University Press, 1999.

———. "The Sign of Protesilaos." *ΜΗΤΙΣ: Revue d'anthropologie du monde grec ancien* 2/2 (1987): 207–13.

Pfister, Friedrich. *Der Reliquienkult im Altertum.* 2 vols. Giessen: A. Topelmann, 1909–1912.

Pucci, Pietro. *Odysseus Polutropos: Intertextual Readings in the* Odyssey *and the* Iliad. Ithaca: Cornell University Press, 1987.

West, M. L. *Immortal Helen.* London: Bedford College, 1975.

HOMER

Carter, Jane B. and Sarah P. Morris. *The Ages of Homer: A Tribute to Emily Townsend Vermeule.* Austin: University of Texas Press, 1995.

Lamberton, Robert. *Homer the Theologian: Neoplatonist Allegorical Reading and the Growth of the Epic Tradition.* Berkeley: University of California Press, 1986.

Lamberton, Robert and John J. Keaney, eds. *Homer's Ancient Readers: The Hermeneutics of Greek Epic's Earliest Exegetes.* Princeton: Princeton University Press, 1992.

Lord, Albert Bates. *The Singer of Tales.* 2d ed. Cambridge, Mass.: Harvard University Press, 2000.

Martin, Richard P. *The Language of Heroes: Speech and Performance in the* Iliad. Myth and Poetics. Ithaca: Cornell University Press, 1989.

Nagy, Gregory. *Homeric Questions.* Austin: University of Texas Press, 1996.

———. *Pindar's Homer: The Lyric Possession of an Epic Past.* Baltimore: Johns Hopkins University Press, 1990.

IMPERIAL ROME

Ball, Warwick. *Rome in the East: The Transformation of an Empire*. New York: Routledge, 2000.

Birley, Anthony R. *Hadrian: The Restless Emperor*. New York: Routledge, 1997.

———. *Septimius Severus: The African Emperor*. London: Eyre & Spottiswoode, 1971.

Bowersock, Glen Warren. *Fiction as History: Nero to Julian*. Berkeley: University of California Press, 1994.

———. *Roman Arabia*. Cambridge, Mass.: Harvard University Press, 1983.

Mattern, Susan P. *Rome and the Enemy: Imperial Strategy in the Principate*. Berkeley: University of California, 1999.

Millar, Fergus. *The Emperor in the Roman World (31 BC–AD 337)*. Ithaca: Cornell University Press, 1992.

———. *The Roman Near East 31 BC–AD 337*. Cambridge, Mass.: Harvard University Press, 1993.

Wells, Colin M. *The Roman Empire*. 2d ed. Cambridge, Mass.: Harvard University Press, 1995.

ORACLES

Curnow, Trevor. *The Oracles of the Ancient World*. London: Duckworth. Forthcoming.

Nilsson, Martin P. *Cults, Myths, Oracles and Politics in Ancient Greece*. Lund: Gleerup, 1951.

Parke, H. W. *Greek Oracles*. London: Hutchinson, 1967.

———. *The Oracles of Apollo in Asia Minor*. Dover, N.H.: Croom Helm, 1985.

PARTHIA

Colledge, Malcolm A.R. *The Parthian Period*. Leiden: Brill, 1986.

Debevoise, Neilson Carel. *A Political History of Parthia*. New York: Greenwood, 1938.

Ward-Perkins, J. B. *The Roman West and the Parthian East*. London: Oxford University Press, 1965.

PHILOSTRATUS (SEE ALSO SECOND SOPHISTIC AND ITS
LITERARY TECHNIQUES)

Aitken, Ellen Bradshaw and Jennifer K. Berenson Maclean, eds. *Philostratus's* Heroikos: *Religion and Cultural Identity in the Third Century* C.E. SBLWGRW 4. Atlanta: Society of Biblical Literature. Forthcoming.

Anderson, Graham. *Philostratus: Biography and Belles Lettres in the Third Century A.D.* London: Croom Helm, 1986.

Bowie, Ewen L. "Philostratus: Writer of Fiction." Pages 181–99 in *Greek Fiction: The Greek Novel in Context.* Edited by J. R. Morgan and Richard Stoneman. New York: Routledge, 1994.

Eitrem, Samson. "Zu Philostrats Heroikos." *Symbolae Osloenses* 8 (1929): 1–56.

Flinterman, Jaap-Jan. *Power,* Paideia *& Pythagoreanism: Greek Identity, Conceptions of the Relationship Between Philosophers and Monarchs and Political Ideas in Philostratus' Life of Apollonius.* Amsterdam: Gieben, 1995.

Jones, C. P. "Time and Place in Philostratus' *Heroikos.*" *JHS* 121 (2001): 141–48.

Mantero, Teresa. *Ricerche sull' Heroikos di Filostrato.* Genoa: University of Genoa, Istituto di Filologia Classica e Medioevale, 1966.

Solmsen, Friedrich. "Some Works of Philostratus the Elder." *TAPA* 71 (1940): 556–72.

POETRY AND PERFORMANCE (SEE ALSO HOMER)

Alexiou, M. *Ritual Lament in the Greek Tradition.* 2d ed. Lanham, Md.: Rowman & Littlefield, 2002.

Allen, Thomas W., ed. *Homeri Opera V: Hymnos, Cyclum Fragmenta, Margiten, Batrachomyomachiam, Vitas Continens.* Oxford: Clarendon, 1912.

Anderson, Warren D. *Music and Musicians in Ancient Greece.* Ithaca: Cornell University Press, 1994.

Burgess, J. S. *The Tradition of the Trojan War in Homer and the Epic Cycle.* Baltimore: Johns Hopkins University Press, 2001.

Davies, M. *The Epic Cycle.* Bristol: Bristol Classical Press, 1989.

Frazer, R. M., Jr. *The Trojan War: The Chronicles of Dictys of Crete and Dares the Phrygian.* Bloomington: Indiana University Press, 1966.

Hesiod, The Homeric Hymns and Homerica. Translated by Hugh G. Evelyn-White. Loeb Classical Library. Cambridge, Mass.: Harvard University Press, 1936.

Landels, John G. *Music in Ancient Greece and Rome.* New York: Routledge, 1999.

Nagy, Gregory. *Poetry as Performance: Homer and Beyond.* Cambridge: Cambridge University Press, 1996.

West, M. L. *Ancient Greek Music.* New York: Oxford University Press, 1992.

RITUAL PRACTICES

Aitken, Ellen Bradshaw. "The Cult of Achilles in Philostratus's *Heroikos*: A Study in the Relation of Canon and Ritual." Pages 127–35 in *Between Magic and Religion: Interdisciplinary Studies in Ancient Mediterranean Religion and Society.* Edited by Sulochana Asirvatham, Corinne Pache, and John Watrous. Lanham, Md.: Rowman & Littlefield, 2001.

Alexiou, Margaret. *Religion and Ritual Lament in the Greek Tradition.* 2d ed. Lanham, Md.: Rowman & Littlefield, 2002.

Burkert, Walter. *Greek Religion.* Cambridge, Mass.: Harvard University Press, 1985.

———. "Greek Tragedy and Sacrificial Ritual." *GRBS* 7 (1966): 87–121.

———. *Homo Necans: The Anthropology of Ancient Greek Sacrificial Ritual and Myth.* Berkeley: University of California Press, 1983.

———. "Jason, Hypsipyle, and New Fire at Lemnos: A Study in Myth and Ritual." *CQ* n.s. 20 (1970): 1–16.

Clark, Elizabeth A. *Reading Renunciation: Asceticism and Scripture in Early Christianity.* Princeton: Princeton University Press, 1999.

Dillon, Matthew. *Pilgrims and Pilgrimage in Ancient Greece.* New York: Routledge, 1997.

Faraone, Christopher A. and Dirk Obbink, eds. *Magika Hiera: Ancient Greek Magic and Religion.* New York: Oxford University Press, 1991.

Frank, Georgia. *The Memory of the Eyes: Pilgrims to Living Saints in Christian Late Antiquity.* Berkeley: University of California Press, 2000.

Harrison, Jane Ellen. *Prolegomena to the Study of Greek Religion.* 3d ed. Cambridge: Cambridge University Press, 1922. Repr., New York: Meridian, 1955.

Kiley, Mark, ed. *Prayer From Alexander to Constantine. A Critical Anthology.* New York: Routledge, 1997.

MacMullen, Ramsay. *Paganism in the Roman Empire*. New Haven: Yale University Press, 1981.

Parker, Robert. *Miasma: Pollution and Purification in Early Greek Religion*. New York: Clarendon, 1983.

Price, Simon. *Religions of the Ancient Greeks*. New York: Cambridge University Press, 1999.

Valantasis, Richard, ed. *Religions of Late Antiquity in Practice*. Princeton: Princeton University Press, 2000.

Vermeule, Emily. *Aspects of Death in Early Greek Art and Poetry*. Berkeley: University of California Press, 1979.

Wimbush, Vincent L. and Richard Valantasis, eds. *Asceticism*. New York: Oxford University Press, 1995.

Zaidman, Louise Bruit and Pauline Schmitt Pantel. *Religion in the Ancient Greek City*. New York: Cambridge University Press, 1992.

SANCTUARIES AND STATUES

Alcock, Susan E. and Robin Osborne. *Placing the Gods: Sanctuaries and Sacred Space in Ancient Greece*. New York: Oxford University Press, 1994.

Faraone, Christopher A. *Talismans and Trojan Horses: Guardian Statues in Ancient Greek Myth and Ritual*. New York: Oxford University Press, 1992.

Marinatos, Nanno and Robin Hägg, eds. *Greek Sanctuaries. New Approaches*. New York: Routledge, 1993.

Rutkowski, Bogdan. *The Cult Places of the Aegean*. New Haven: Yale University Press, 1986.

SECOND SOPHISTIC AND ITS LITERARY TECHNIQUES (SEE ALSO CULTURAL IDENTITY IN THE ROMAN WORLD)

Alcock, Susan E., John F. Cherry, and Jas Elsner, eds. *Pausanias: Travel and Memory in Roman Greece*. New York: Oxford University Press, 2001.

Anderson, Graham. *The Second Sophistic: A Cultural Phenomenon in the Roman Empire*. London: Routledge, 1993.

Barton, Tamsyn S. *Power and Knowledge: Astrology, Physiognomics, and Medicine under the Roman Empire*. Ann Arbor: University of Michigan Press, 1994.

Bowersock, Glen Warren, ed. *Approaches to the Second Sophistic*. University Park, Penn.: American Philological Association, 1974.

————. *Greek Sophists in the Roman Empire*. Oxford: Clarendon, 1969.

Evans, Elizabeth C. *Physiognomics in the Ancient World*. Philadelphia: American Philosophical Society, 1969.

Fowler, Don. "Narrate and Describe: The Problem of Ekphrasis." *JRS* 81 (1991): 25–35. Repr. as ch. 3 in *Roman Constructions: Readings in Postmodern Latin*. Oxford: Oxford University Press, 2000.

Gleason, Maud W. *Making Men: Sophists and Self-Presentation in Ancient Rome*. Princeton: Princeton University Press, 1995.

Hirzel, Rudolf. *Der Dialog: Ein literarhistorischer Versuch*. 2 vols. Leipzig: Hirzel, 1895.

Webb, Ruth Helen. "*Ekphrasis* Ancient and Modern: The Invention of a Genre." *Word and Image* 15 (1999): 7–18.

SEXUALITY AND DESIRE

Goldhill, Simon. *Foucault's Virginity: Ancient Erotic Fiction and the History of Sexuality*. New York: Cambridge University Press, 1995.

Hallett, Judith P. and Marilyn B. Skinner, eds. *Roman Sexualities*. Princeton: Princeton University Press, 1997.

Richlin, Amy, ed. *Pornography and Representation in Greece and Rome*. New York: Oxford University Press, 1992.

Rousselle, Aline. *Porneia: On Desire and the Body in Antiquity*. New York: Basil Blackwell, 1988.

Winkler, John J. *The Constraints of Desire: The Anthropology of Sex and Gender in Ancient Greece*. New York: Routledge, 1990.

WOMEN AND GENDER IN THE ANCIENT WORLD

Blok, Josine H. *The Early Amazons: Modern and Ancient Perspectives on a Persistent Myth*. Religions in the Greco-Roman World 120. Leiden: Brill, 1995.

Cantarella, Eva. *Pandora's Daughters: The Role and Status of Women in Greek and Roman Antiquity*. Baltimore: Johns Hopkins University Press, 1987.

Dowden, Ken. *Death and the Maiden: Girls' Initiation Rites in Greek Mythology*. London: Routledge, 1989.

Fantham, Elaine et al. *Women in the Classical World: Image and Text*. New York: Oxford University Press, 1994.

Gardner, Jane F. *Women in Roman Law & Society*. Bloomington: Indiana University Press, 1986.

Hawley, Richard and Barbara Levick, eds. *Women in Antiquity: New Assessments*. New York: Routledge, 1995.

Joshel, Sandra P. and Sheila Murnaghan. *Women and Slaves in Greco-Roman Culture: Differential Equations*. London: Routledge, 1998.

Kraemer, Ross Shepard. *Her Share of the Blessings: Women's Religions Among Pagans, Jews, and Christians in the Greco-Roman World*. New York: Oxford University Press, 1992.

Larson, Jennifer. *Greek Heroine Cults*. Wisconsin Studies in Classics. Madison: University of Wisconsin Press, 1995.

Pomeroy, Sarah B. *Goddesses, Whores, Wives, and Slaves: Women in Classical Antiquity*. New York: Schocken, 1975.

Turton, Godfrey. *The Syrian Princesses: The Women Who Ruled Rome, AD 193–235*. London: Cassell, 1974.

Index of Ancient Writings

(Odyssey) 12.37–54   143
  12.39–54   56
  12.85–110   142
  12.153–200   143
  12.154–200   13
  12.245–259   142
  12.268   97
  12.273   97
  13.117–119   38
  14.288–289   2
  17.261–263   137
  18.202–205   xxxi
  18.359   17
  18.603–605   xxxi
  19.518–523   7
  20.57–90   xxxi
  20.357   50
  21.54–57   xxxi
  21.356–358   xxxi
  22.331–356   137
  24.35–95   xxxiv
  24.67–68   xxxii
  24.73–77   xxxi
  24.85–86   xxxii

Homeric Hymn to Aphrodite
  101, 111, 148

Homeric Hymn to Apollo
  251   112
  291   112

Homeric Hymn to Demeter
  108

Hyginus
  Fabulae
  95.2   49, 132
  103   124
  103–104   lv
  104   124
  105   53
  110   74, 139
  117   132

257   144

IG
  12.5.56   100
  12.8.27   li

Isocrates
  Helen
  64–66   115

Julian
  Letters
  19   26

Juvenal
  Satires
  6.296   1

Little Iliad   lxiii, 25, 98, 131,
  137
  4   98

Lucian   xlviii
  Charon   xlix
  7   li
  Dialogues of the Dead
  23   140
  27   34
  27.1   19
  28   lii, liv
  *Menippus, or the Descent into
    Hades*   lxxi
  Parliament of the Gods
  12   liv, 110
  The Dream, or The Cock   xviii
  17   li

Lycophron
  frg. 433, 144

Lycurgus
  Against Leocrates
  102   xxiv

Mimnermus   xxvii

(Heroikos)   1.2   lxxvi, lxxxii
  1.5   li
  1.5–2.5   lxiii
  2.3–4   li
  2.6   lix
  2.6–5.5   xliii
  2.7–11   xviii
  2.8   xxviii
  2.9   xxv, xxvi, xxviii
  2.9–11   xxviii
  2.10   xxv
  2.10–11   lvii
  2.11   xxv, xxvi
  3.1   xxvi, lxxv
  3.2   xxvii, xxviii
  3.2–5   xxvi
  3.3   xxvi
  3.5   xxvii
  3.9–10   lx
  3.13–20   88
  3.21–22   88
  4.1   lxiv
  4.2   lvii, lviii, lxxvii
  4.4–10   xlix
  4.7   xxix
  4.8   lx
  4.9–10   lix
  4.10   xxix
  4.10–11   lix
  5.17   89
  6.3   xxv, lxii
  6.3–6   xliii
  6.4   xxix
  6.7–8.18   xliii
  7.3   xix, xxix, xliv, li, lix,
     lxi, lxxxii
  7.4   xxix, lix, lxii
  7.5   xxix, lxiv
  7.5–6   xxix
  7.6   lxiv
  7.7   xlix
  7.8   lx
  7.9   lxxv
  8.3–13   lxi

8.5–6   lxvii
8.9   lix
8.11   xxix
8.14   100
8.16   lxii
9.1–3   xxxviii, li, liv
9.1–17.6   xliv
9.1–23.30   xxxix
9.5   lv, lviii
9.5–6   liv
9.5–7   lvii
9.6   liv
9.7   xxvii
10.2   xxvii
10.2–4   xxvii
10.3–5   liv
11.1   lvii
11.2   xxvii, lxii
11.3   xxvii
11.4–6   lxxxi
11.7   xxvi
11.8   xxvi
12.1–4   lii
12.3   xxiv, lvi, lvii
13.3   lxxiv
13.3–4   lvii
14.1–2   xix
14.2   xliv
14.4   xxix
14.4–15.10   lx
15.5   xxix
15.8–10   lxxii
16.3–4   lviii
16.5   liii, lvii
16.6   lxxv
18.1   lxxv
18.1–2   lx
18.1–23.1   xliv
18.2–3   xxviii
18.3–19.7   lx
18.4   xxix
19.5–9   xxviii
20.3   lxxix

Subject Index

Note: For a complete index of Greek words that appear in *On Heroes*, consult the full edition of our translation (Jennifer K. Berenson Maclean and Ellen Bradshaw Aitken, trans., *Flavius Philostratus: Heroikos* [SBLWGRW 1; Atlanta: Society of Biblical Literature, 2001]).

44, 65, 66, 83, 97, 103, 114–
16, 119, 122, 123, 127, 129,
130, 131, 135, 136, 137, 140,
142, 144, 146, 148
Troy, 148 and *passim*
truth, xv, xviii, xx, xlv, l, lix–lx, lxi,
lxiii, lxix–lxx, lxxi, lxxiv–
lxxvi, lxxxiii, 6, 10, 12, 30,
39, 44, 54, 57, 58, 59, 65, 66,
69, 81
Tydeus, 42, 53, 109, 132, 148
Tyre, xlvii, lxxviii, 1, 104, 148

vegetation, xxvi, xxvii, xxix,
xxxviii, xliii, xlix, li, liv, lix,
lxxxi, 2–5, 7, 8, 13, 15, 17,
18, 24, 28–29, 37, 53, 59, 68,
81, 84, 87, 88, 102, 103, 109,
119, 127, 130
Vesuvius, 14, 149
voice, *see* physical description of
heroes

vow, 15, 50

wisdom, *see* character traits
wrestling, *see* athletic contests
writing, xviii, xx, xxi, lxii, 31, 45,
49–51, 53, 119, 132, 138, 141

Xanthos, 74, 80, 105, 142
Xeinis the Chersonesian, lviii,
lxxvii, lxxviii, lxxix, 6, 149
Xerxes, lv, 10, 15, 79, 95, 127, 149

Zeus, xxxiii, 10, 14, 15, 35, 36, 39,
49, 50, 58, 62, 64, 73, 75, 81,
84, 88, 96, 97, 99, 100, 101,
102, 103, 104, 108, 109, 111,
112, 114, 115, 117, 118, 120,
122, 123, 124, 125, 127, 128,
129, 130, 133, 140, 142, 143,
145, 147, 149